Joint SIGHUM Workshop on Computational Linguistics for Cultural Heritage, Social Sciences, Humanities and Literature 2017

Held at ACL 2017

Vancouver, Canada
4 August 2017

ISBN: 978-1-5108-4572-5

ACL 2017

**Joint SIGHUM Workshop on
Computational Linguistics for Cultural Heritage,
Social Sciences, Humanities and Literature**

Proceedings of the Workshop

August 4, 2017
Vancouver, Canada

Introduction

LaTeCH-CLfL 2017 continues the tradition of two separate yet not dissimilar events. It is both the 11th Workshop on Language Technology for Cultural Heritage, Social Sciences and Humanities, and the 6th Workshop on Computational Linguistics for Literature—held jointly for the first time, with beneficial effects. We have been able to cast the net more widely. We received more, and more varied, submissions. Nine long papers, five short papers and a position paper will appear at the workshop, a 58% acceptance rate. We also had the advantage of two program committees from past years helping us select the best papers. We are ever so grateful to all those attentive, thorough and helpful reviewers. Sure enough, we thank all authors for the hard work they invested in their submissions.

Our distinguished invited speaker, Andrew Piper, is a perfect match for our joint workshop: he applies tools and techniques of data science to literature as well as to culture. He will introduce new work on the process of characterization: how writers construct animate entities on the page. This contributes to a better understanding of the specific nature of literary characters as linguistic entities.

The papers accepted this year cover an intriguing variety of topics. First off, we have a few papers which deal with poetry, each tackling a very different problem. Vaibhav Kesarwani, Diana Inkpen, Stan Szpakowicz and Chris Tanasescu identify a specific type of literary metaphor in poems. They rely on a combination of statistical analysis and rules. Pablo Ruiz Fabo, Clara Martínez Cantón, Thierry Poibeau and Elena González-Blanco seek to discover enjambment: places in a poem where a syntactic unit is split across two lines. They apply their method to a diachronic corpus of Spanish sonnets, and analyze the results across four centuries. Christopher Hench works on medieval German poetry. He uses syllabification to analyze soundscapes and thus to shed light on how those primarily oral poems may have sounded.

A lot of interesting work revolves around the computational analysis of prose. We have papers which present tools for scholars in Digital Humanities, and more specific studies of certain phenomena or of particular novels. Andre Blessing, Nora Echelmeyer, Markus John and Nils Reiter present an end-to-end environment intended to help analyze relations between entities in a document in a principled way. Evgeny Kim, Sebastian Padó and Roman Klinger adopt lexicon-based methods to the study of the emotional trajectory of novels, and compare their findings across five genres. Stefania Degaetano-Ortlieb and Elke Teich outline a generic data-driven method of tracking intra-textual variation, showing how information-theoretic measures allow the detection of both topical and stylistic patterns of variation.

Liviu Dinu and Ana Sabina Uban verify if characters of a given novel are believable, using methods established in the authorship attribution community. They present the preliminary results for the novel Les Liaisons Dangereuses. Conor Kelleher and Mark Keane describe an experiment in distant reading applied to a post-modern novel with non-linear structure, Wittgenstein's Mistress by David Markson. The paper contrasts the analysis which arises from the distant read with David Foster Wallace's "manual" analysis.

A good portion of our workshop is devoted to historical, low-resource or non-standard languages. Amrith Krishna, Pavankumar Satuluri and Pawan Goyal write about challenges of working with Sanskrit manuscripts. They release a dataset for the segmentation of Sanskrit words. Nina Seemann, Marie-Luis Merten, Michaela Geierhos, Doris Tophinke and Eyke Hüllermeier share the experience of annotating texts in Middle Low German. It turns out that the process is fraught with uncertainties; the Authors discuss them and describe lessons learned.

Next, we have a paper by Maria Sukhareva, Francesco Fuscagni, Johannes Daxenberger, Susanne Görke, Doris Prechel and Iryna Gurevych. In their experiments, they apply distant supervision to the building of a part-of-speech tagger for Hittite. Unsurprisingly, no annotated corpora exist for this ancient language.

Émilie Pagé-Perron, Maria Sukhareva (yes!), Ilya Khait and Christian Chiarcos are no less ambitious. They describe experiments in machine translation of Sumerian texts of an administrative or legal nature. The aim is to make those texts available to a wider audience. Géraldine Walther and Benoît Sagot talk about a productive synergy between fully manual and semi-automatic process when building a corpus of Romansh Tuatschin, a dialect of one of the official languages in southwestern Switzerland.

Two more papers complete this palette of topics. Maria Pia di Buono proposes an ontology-based method of extracting nominal compounds in the domain of cultural heritage. Maciej Ogrodniczuk and Mateusz Kopeć explore modern political discourse in the context of Twitter. They present a series of experiments in on-the-fly analysis of the lexical, topical and visual aspects of political tweets.

There you have it. Welcome to our workshop, and by all means have fun.

Beatrice, Stefania, Anna, Anna, Nils and Stan

Invited Talk

Title: Characterization

Speaker: Andrew Piper

Abstract

Characters are some of the most important, and most beloved, elements of literature. From Ishmael to Mrs. Dalloway to Gregor Samsa, literary characters are woven into the fabric of culture. And yet until recently, little work has been done to understand the specific nature of characters as linguistic entities. This talk will introduce new work by our lab that aims to address this process of characterization – of how writers construct animate entities on the page. It will present a new character feature tool designed to allow researchers to study a variety of qualities surrounding the construction of character as well as a new study where it has been implemented.

About the speaker

Andrew Piper is Professor and William Dawson Scholar in the Department of Languages, Literatures, and Cultures at McGill University. His work explores the application of computational approaches to the study of literature and culture. He is the director of .txtLAB,[1] a digital humanities laboratory at McGill, as well as leader of the international partnership grant, "NovelTM: Text Mining the Novel",[2] which brings together 21 partners across North America to undertake the first large-scale quantitative and cross-cultural study of the novel. He is the author most recently of *Book Was There: Reading in Electronic Times* (Chicago 2012) and is currently completing a new book entitled *Enumerations: The Quantities of Literature*.

---

[1] http://txtlab.org/
[2] http://novel-tm.ca/

Caroline Sporleder, Goettingen University, Germany
Jannik Strötgen, Max-Planck-Institut für Informatik, Germany
Reid Swanson, University of California, Santa Cruz, United States
Elke Teich, Saarland University, Germany
Mariët Theune, University of Twente, Netherlands
Sara Tonelli, FBK, Trento, Italy
Thorsten Trippel, University of Tübingen, Germany
Menno van Zaanen, Tilburg University, Netherlands
Heike Zinsmeister, University of Hamburg, Germany

Invited Speaker:

Andrew Piper, McGill University, Canada

Organizers:

Beatrice Alex, School of Informatics, University of Edinburgh
Stefania Degaetano-Ortlieb, Department of Language Science and Technology, Universität des Saarlandes
Anna Feldman, Department of Linguistics & Department of Computer Science, Montclair State University
Anna Kazantseva, National Research Council of Canada
Nils Reiter, Institute for Natural Language Processing (IMS), Stuttgart University
Stan Szpakowicz, School of Electrical Engineering and Computer Science, University of Ottawa

Table of Contents

Conference Program

August 4th, 2017

09:00–10:00　Session 1

09:00–09:30　*Metaphor Detection in a Poetry Corpus*
Vaibhav Kesarwani, Diana Inkpen, Stan Szpakowicz and Chris Tanasescu

09:30–10:00　*Machine Translation and Automated Analysis of the Sumerian Language*
Émilie Pagé-Perron, Maria Sukhareva, Ilya Khait and Christian Chiarcos

10:00–10:30　Poster Teaser Talks

11:00–12:30　Session 2

11:00–11:30　*Investigating the Relationship between Literary Genres and Emotional Plot Development*
Evgeny Kim, Sebastian Padó and Roman Klinger

11:30–12:00　*Enjambment Detection in a Large Diachronic Corpus of Spanish Sonnets*
Pablo Ruiz, Clara Martínez Cantón, Thierry Poibeau and Elena González-Blanco

12:00–12:30　*Plotting Markson's "Mistress"*
Conor Kelleher and Mark Keane

13:30–14:00   SIGHUM Business Meeting

14:00–15:00   Invited Talk

14:00–15:00   *Characterization*
Andrew Piper

15:00–16:00   Poster Session

15:00–16:00   *Annotation Challenges for Reconstructing the Structural Elaboration of Middle Low German*
Nina Seemann, Marie-Luis Merten, Michaela Geierhos, Doris Tophinke and Eyke Hüllermeier

15:00–16:00   *Phonological Soundscapes in Medieval Poetry*
Christopher Hench

15:00–16:00   *An End-to-end Environment for Research Question-Driven Entity Extraction and Network Analysis*
Andre Blessing, Nora Echelmeyer, Markus John and Nils Reiter

15:00–16:00   *Modeling intra-textual variation with entropy and surprisal: topical vs. stylistic patterns*
Stefania Degaetano-Ortlieb and Elke Teich

15:00–16:00   *Finding a Character's Voice: Stylome Classification on Literary Characters*
Liviu P. Dinu and Ana Sabina Uban

15:00–16:00   *An Ontology-Based Method for Extracting and Classifying Domain-Specific Compositional Nominal Compounds*
Maria Pia di Buono

15:00–16:00   *Speeding up corpus development for linguistic research: language documentation and acquisition in Romansh Tuatschin*
Géraldine Walther and Benoît Sagot

16:00–17:30   Session 4

Metaphor Detection in a Poetry Corpus

Vaibhav Kesarwani, Diana Inkpen,
Stan Szpakowicz, Chris Tanasescu (Margento)
School of Electrical Engineering and Computer Science
University of Ottawa
Ottawa, Ontario, Canada
`vkesa079@uottawa.ca, diana.inkpen@uottawa.ca,`
`szpak@eecs.uottawa.ca, margento.official@gmail.com`

Abstract

Metaphor is indispensable in poetry. It showcases the poet's creativity, and contributes to the overall emotional pertinence of the poem while honing its specific rhetorical impact. Previous work on metaphor detection relies on either rule-based or statistical models, none of them applied to poetry. Our method focuses on metaphor detection in a poetry corpus. It combines rule-based and statistical models (word embeddings) to develop a new classification system. Our system has achieved a precision of 0.759 and a recall of 0.804 in identifying one type of metaphor in poetry.

1 Introduction

Metaphor is crucial in the understanding of any literary text. A metaphor deviates from the normal linguistic usage. It intends to create a strong statement that no literal text can accomplish. Metaphor differs from idioms, because one can understand a metaphor even with no prior knowledge. Here are examples of metaphor in poetry:

- The hackles on my neck are fear (Wright, 1958)

- My eyes are caves, chunks of etched rock (Lorde, 2000)

Literary metaphor operates not only in the local context where it appears. It also functions in the broader context of the whole work or even an author's oeuvre, and in the context of the cultural paradigms associated with a specific metaphor field (Ritchie, 2013). Contrary to the standard view, literary metaphor sometimes also maps not only in one direction (from "vehicle" to "tenor") but in two. It thus helps reshape both concepts involved (Ritchie, 2013, p. 189). In other cases, a metaphor interconnects two concepts and so only develops each of them into independent sources of introspective and emotional stimulation (Ritchie, 2013, p. 193).

Literary metaphor is generally thought to be more stylistically colourful. It is placed somewhere at one extremity of a spectrum that has common-speech metaphor at the other end (Ritchie, 2013). In poetry sometimes the opposite is also true. The most unadorned and literal language can be strongly metaphorical by means of the symbolic import of whole passages or even entire poems: a poem or a longer passage figuratively alludes to an implicit concept. Such is the case, for instance, of Robert Frost's "The Road Not Taken" (Frost, 1962). The poem speaks in its entirety of a consequential choice made in life, without apparently deploying any actual metaphor. Needless to say, it is a type of metaphor possibly even more difficult to process automatically.

A genre-based comparison of metaphor in literature would involve a wide-ranging theoretical and historical comparative analysis of literary genres and tropes. Such analysis is beyond the scope of this paper, and outside the focus of our current research, which concerns itself only with poetry and selects its data accordingly.

We used a few rule-based methods for metaphor detection as a baseline for our experiments. Tur-

1

Joint SIGHUM Workshop on Computational Linguistics for Cultural Heritage, Social Sciences, Humanities and Literature.
Proceedings, pages 1–9, Vancouver, BC, August 4, 2017. ©2017 Association for Computational Linguistics

ney et al. (2011) proposed the Concrete-Abstract rule: a concrete concept, when used to describe an abstract one, represents a metaphor. A phrase like "Sweet Dreams" is one such example. We use the Abstract-Concrete rule as one of the many features in our model. In experiments, it has in fact proved to be quite useful in the case of poetry as well.

Neuman et al. (2013) propose to categorize metaphor by part-of-speech (POS) tag sequences such as Noun-Verb-Noun, Adjective-Noun, and so on. We follow the same methodology to extract the set of sentences that can be metaphorical in nature. Our method differs because we use word embeddings pre-trained on the Gigaword corpus (Pennington et al., 2014) to get word vector representations (vector difference and cosine similarity) of possible metaphorical word pairs. Another difference is the addition of two more types of POS sequences, which we have found to be metaphorical in our Poetry Foundation poetry corpus.[1] We explain the types in section 2.1.

Neuman et al. (2013) describe a statistical model based on Mutual Information and selectional preferences. They suggest using a large-scale corpus to find the concrete nouns which most frequently occur with a specific word. Any word outside this small set denotes a metaphor. Our experiments do not involve finding selectional preference sets directly. Instead, we use word embeddings. We have found the selectional preference sets too limiting. The word span is to be set before the experiments. Some sentences exceed that limit, so the contextual meaning is lost.

Shutova et al. (2016) introduce a statistical model which detects metaphor. So does our method, but their work is more verb-centered, in that verbs are a seed set for training data. Our work looks more into the possible applications for poetry, not generically. We also concentrate on nouns, because our initial experiments concerned Type I metaphor: a copular verb plays only an auxiliary role, so the focus is on the two nouns.

Our current work belongs in the same category as the "GraphPoem" project (MARGENTO, 2012; Lou et al., 2015; Tanasescu et al., 2016). The milieu is the computational analysis of poetry, and the goal is the development of tools that can contribute to the academic study of poetry.

<hr>

[1] We will abbreviate "Poetry Foundation" to "PoFo" throughout the paper.

2 The Method

2.1 Building the Corpus

We have built our own corpus, because there is no publicly available poetry corpus annotated for metaphor. Annotating poetry line by line can be laborious. We have observed empirically that negative samples are too numerous. To ease this task, we applied Neuman's (2013) approach: consider POS tag sequences to extract potential metaphor. We extracted all sentences from the 12,830 PoFo poems that match these tag sequences.

Type I metaphor has a POS tag sequence of Noun-Verb-Noun where the verb is a copula (Neuman et al., 2013). We have extended this to include the tag sequence Noun-Verb-Det-Noun, since we have found that many instances were skipped due to the presence of a determiner. Type II has a tag sequence of Noun-Verb-Noun with a regular, not copula, verb (Neuman et al., 2013). Type III has a tag sequence of Adjective-Noun (Neuman et al., 2013). We also propose two more metaphor types that we noticed in our poetry data: Type IV with a tag sequence of Noun-Verb, and Type V with a tag sequence of Verb-Verb. Here are examples:

- As if the *world were* a *taxi*, you enter it [Type 1] (Koch, 1962)

- I counted the *echoes assembling*, *thumbing* the *midnight* on the piers. [Type 2] (Crane, 2006)

- The moving waters at their *priestlike task* [Type 3] (Keats, 2009)

- The yellow *smoke slipped* by the terrace, made a sudden leap [Type 4] (Eliot, 1915)

- *To die – to sleep* [Type 5] (Shakespeare, 1904)

In this paper, we focus on Type I metaphor. We will work on the remaining four types in the near future. Currently, we are also working on a method independent of POS tag sequences. It employs a dependency parser (de Marneffe et al., 2006) to give all associations in a sentence. We will use associations such as *nsubj*, *dobj* and so on to filter down to get word pairs that need to be checked for metaphor occurrence. Other irrelevant associations will be discarded. We take this generic approach because we feel that POS sequences may be a little restrictive. Some instances

2

that do not follow the specific POS sequence could be missed.

Identifying head words in a sentence is in itself a challenging task. It is like compressing a phrase to a word pair that may or may not be a metaphor. The POS tag sequence does not always provide an understandable word pair. Sometimes we lose critical words that may be of value. When the nouns highlighted by the POS tagger are not enough to identify the head of a sentence (or a phrase), we use the Stanford Parser (de Marneffe et al., 2006) for identification. As an additional step, we extract all *nsubj* associations from these sentences. If the head word is different from the earlier identified head (suggested by the POS tagger), then the head word is updated.

Here is an example (Schwartz, 1989):

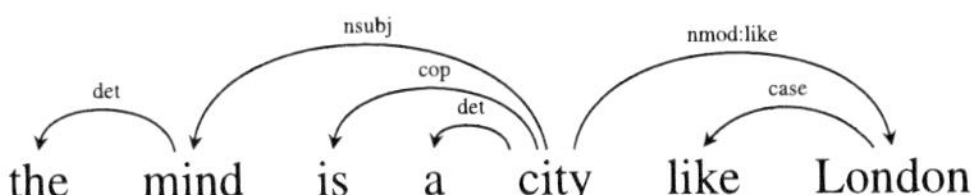

2.2 Annotating the Corpus

We extracted around 1500 sentences with the type I metaphor tag sequence, and annotated the first 720. We employed majority voting. First, two independent annotators annotate the 720 sentences without any communication. Then the value of kappa was calculated. Its value came to 0.39, and agreement to 66.79%. Next, we involved a third annotator who cast a majority vote in case of disagreement. If one of the two annotators agreed to the other's justification, then the disagreement was resolved without the intervention of the third annotator. After this, kappa increased to 0.46 and agreement to 72.94%.

While annotating, we found several highly ambiguous sentences which required a wider context for assessment. In those rare cases, the annotators were allowed to go back to the poem and judge the metaphor candidate by looking at the context in which it appeared. This was done to avoid discarding a legitimate example for lack of sufficient information. In most cases, however, the sentence alone provided enough information.

All sentences given to the annotators were marked to indicate the head of the sentence. The point was to avoid confusion whenever there was more than one noun phrase. For example:

my eyes are caves , chunks of etched rock @2@ (Lorde, 2000)

The number 2 denotes that the word at location 2, "eyes", is a head word. Therefore the second head would be "caves", because this is a sentence with a Type I metaphor tag sequence. Since this is obviously a metaphorical word pair, the annotator would write "y" at the end of the sentence.

The annotators were also allowed to skip a sentence if they could not make up their mind. All in all, a sentence can be labeled as "y" for metaphor, "n" for non-metaphor and "s" for a skipped sentence.

Annotating metaphor is not a trivial task. Borderline cases occur, and there is ambiguity. We have encountered many such situations while annotating. For example:

to me the children of my youth are lords , @7@s (Crabbe, 1950)

It was annotated "s" because full poetic context was lacking. Here the first head word is "youth" and the second head is "lords".

Sometimes we cannot ignore words that are not in the POS tag sequence. For example:

for there christ is the king 's attorney , @3@y (Ralegh, 1895)

Here "christ" is the first head word. If we consider the POS tag sequence, then "king" ought to be the second head, but it does not complete the phrase. Therefore, the whole phrase "king's attorney" is considered while annotating.

And another borderline example, in which the fragment "tree were a tree" can be either metaphorical or literal, depending on the context:

that is , if tree were a tree . @5@n (Baker, 1994)

Cases like these were very difficult to annotate. Most of them had to be forwarded to the third annotator for a final vote. Such cases were responsible for the rather low value of kappa, the inter-annotator agreement.

When the annotation process was concluded, we checked for the distribution of classes. Metaphor turned out to be present in 49.8% instances. Non-metaphor accounted for 44.8%, and 5.4% examples were skipped. We had an almost balanced dataset, so we did not need to apply any re-sampling in our classification. The sentences with skipped annotation were removed from our data. The final dataset contained 680 sentences.[2]

---

[2] The data can be found at `http://www.eecs.uottawa.ca/~diana/resources/metaphor`.

2.3 Rule-based Metaphor Detection

Firstly, we applied rule-based methods to our poetry dataset. We used the Abstract-Concrete (Turney et al., 2011) and Concrete Category Overlap rules (Assaf et al., 2013). The Abstract-Concrete rule needs the hypernym class of each noun; we find that in WordNet (Miller, 1995). We got all hypernyms of head nouns and checked for each parent till we reached the hypernym "abstract entity" or "physical entity".

Apart from the above rules, we used a feature based on ConceptNet (Speer and Havasi, 2012). For each noun in our sentence, we extracted the corresponding SurfaceText from ConceptNet. A SurfaceText contains some associations between the specific word and real-world knowledge. For example, "car" gives the following associations:

- "drive" is related to "car"

- You are likely to find "a car" in "the city"

and so on.

The entities are already highlighted in the SurfaceTexts. We parsed these associations and extracted all the entities. There can be action associations as well:

- "a car" can "crash"

- "a car" can "slow down"

and so on.

These entities and actions were used to establish an overlap in the head nouns of the sentences in the poems. We call this method ConceptNet Overlap. We assigned *true* if there was an overlap and *false* otherwise. This was used as one of the features in our rule-based model.

2.4 Statistical-based Metaphor Detection

To capture the distortion of the context that a metaphor causes to a sentence, we computed the vector difference between the vectors for the head words. The underlying idea is this: the smaller the difference, the more connected the words would be. Conversely, a significant difference implies disconnected words and hence very likely a metaphor. We rendered this difference by means of a 100-dimensional vector representation, and we set it as our first statistical feature. Later we tested with 200 dimensions as well, to observe the effect on our task.

To get the word vectors of head words, we used the GloVe vectors pre-trained on the English Gigaword corpus (Pennington et al., 2014). Earlier, we had used a custom-trained model based on the British National Corpus (Clear, 1993) but we switched to GloVe to test on a larger corpus. Another reason why we tested on two different corpora was to remove any bias that may be perpetuated due to the presence of common-speech metaphor in the corpus. We did not use the available pre-trained word2vec vectors (Mikolov et al., 2013a), because the GloVe vectors had been shown to work better for many lexical-semantic tasks (Pennington et al., 2014).

We did not train word embeddings on the PoFo poems, because the corpus was not large enough for training. Moreover, we needed a corpus that had as few metaphor occurrences as possible, and poetry was obviously not an ideal choice. Training on a poetry corpus would generate word embeddings suited to poems in general, and might miss metaphor instances commonly occurring in poetry. In this task, we were more concerned with the detection of all types of metaphor, not just poetic metaphor. In effect, distinguishing between common-speech and poetic metaphor has been left for our future work.

We computed the cosine similarity for all word vector pairs, and made it another feature of our model. We also added a feature based on Pointwise Mutual Information in order to measure if a word pair is a collocation:

$$ln\frac{C(x,y).N}{C(x)C(y)}$$

N is the size of the corpus, C(x,y) is the frequency of x and y together, C(x) and C(y) are the frequencies of x and y in corpus, respectively.

3 The Results

We applied our method to the sentences extracted from the 12,830 PoFo poems and annotated manually (see section 2.2). For training data, we used a combination of the datasets such as TroFi (Birke and Sarkar, 2006) and Shutova (Mohammad et al., 2016) with our own poetry dataset. We included other datasets annotated for metaphor, in addition to poetry, in order to increase the training set and thus get better classification predictions. We report all results explicitly for the test set throughout this paper.

Table 1 shows the results for the class

Experiments	Train	Test	Precision	Recall	F-score
Rules (CA+CCO+CN)	340 PoFo	340 PoFo	0.615	0.507	0.555
PoFo poetry data	340 PoFo	340 PoFo	0.662	0.675	0.669
TroFi data	1771 Tr	1771 Tr	0.797	0.860	0.827
Shutova data	323 Sh	323 Sh	0.747	0.814	0.779
PoFo + TroFi + Shutova	4383 All	487 PoFo	0.759	0.804	0.781

Table 1: Results for the class metaphor

	"metaphor"			"literal"		
Classifier	Precision	Recall	F-score	Precision	Recall	F-score
ZeroR	0.565	1.000	0.722	0.000	0.000	0.000
Random Forest	0.741	**0.822**	0.779	**0.731**	0.627	0.675
JRip	0.635	0.745	0.686	0.573	0.443	0.500
J48	0.71	0.615	0.659	0.574	0.675	0.620
KNN	**0.782**	0.756	0.769	0.697	**0.726**	**0.711**
SVM (linear poly.)	0.656	0.742	0.696	0.597	0.495	0.541
SVM (norm. poly.)	0.657	0.767	0.708	0.614	0.481	0.540
SVM (Puk)	0.759	0.804	**0.781**	0.724	0.670	0.696
Naive Bayes	0.663	0.665	0.664	0.564	0.561	0.563
Bayes Net	0.695	0.662	0.678	0.587	0.623	0.604
Adaboost (RF)	0.760	0.713	0.735	0.655	0.708	0.680
Multilayer Perceptron	0.772	0.713	0.741	0.661	0.726	0.692

Table 2: Results for classifiers trained on PoFo+TroFi+Shutova data, and tested on the 487 poetry sentences

metaphor. For rule-based experiments, we included Concrete-Abstract, Concrete-Class-Overlap and ConceptNet features (CA, CCO and CN). Training was done on 340 PoFo poem sentences, and testing on the remaining 340 sentences. For PoFo data, training and testing were the same, but with the word vector feature set instead of rules. For the TroFi data, training and testing was done on 1771 instances, each with the same feature set as PoFo. For Shutova's data, training was done on 323 instances and testing on the other 323. Lastly, all the above datasets were aggregated as training data, in order to build a model and to test it on 487 PoFo sentences. Training for this aggregated set was done on 3543 TroFi instances, 647 Shutova instances, and the remaining 193 PoFo instances.

When analyzing the results, one can observe that the TroFi data give the best values overall. Still, a comparison of the PoFo results with the aggregate results shows that the values of all three metrics have drastically increased when the training data volume grew. The precision on isolated PoFo data is 0.662, whereas on aggregate data it is 0.759. This also establishes that in detecting metaphor in poetry non-poetry data are as helpful as poetry data.

It can be argued that the recall which we report is not the recall of metaphor throughout the whole poem. Instead, it is the recall of the specific POS tag sequence extracted by our algorithm. There can indeed be sentences that are metaphorical in nature, but are missed due to a different POS tag sequence. We agree with this argument, and are therefore working on a type-independent metaphor identification algorithm to handle such missing cases.

For data preprocessing, we have performed attribute selection by various algorithms, including Pearson's, Infogain and Gain ratio (Yang and Pedersen, 1997). We report the results for the highest accuracy among these algorithms. For classification, we have used the following classifiers: Random Forest, JRip, J48, K-Nearest Neighbor,

5

Experiments	Train	Test	Precision	Recall	F-score
Rules (CA+CCO+CN)	340 PoFo	340 PoFo	0.462	0.408	0.433
PoFo poetry data	340 PoFo	340 PoFo	0.585	0.570	0.577
TroFi data	1771 Tr	1771 Tr	0.782	0.697	0.737
Shutova data	323 Sh	323 Sh	0.810	0.743	0.775
PoFo + TroFi + Shutova	4383 All	487 PoFo	0.724	0.670	0.696

Table 3: Results for the class *non-metaphor*

Experiments	Method	Precision	Recall	F-score
TroFi (our method)	Rule+Stat	0.797	0.860	**0.827**
TroFi (Birke and Sarkar, 2006)	Active Learning	N/A	N/A	0.649
Shutova (our method)	Rule+Stat	0.747	0.814	**0.779**
Shutova (Shutova et al., 2016)	MIXLATE	0.650	0.870	0.750

Table 4: Results of the direct comparison with related work (Rule+Stat = rule-based and statistical)

SVM (Linear Polynomial Kernel), SVM (Normalized Polynomial Kernel), SVM (Pearson Universal Kernel), Naïve Bayes, Bayes Net and Multilayer Perceptron. We have experimented with almost all classifiers available in the Weka software suite (Hall et al., 2009); we report the 10 best results.

Table 2 shows a comparison of the results for all classifiers that we tested on the PoFo+TroFi+Shutova data, keeping the training and test set exactly the same. The results are reported on the 487 poetry test data points, as noted before. In the case of ZeroR, the classifier just keeps all the instances in the metaphor class, because it is the larger class with 56% of the instances.

For the results in Tables 1 and 3, the SVM classifier (with PUK kernel) was used because it gave the best F-score for the metaphor class (as compared to other classifiers and to SVM with other types of kernels). For attribute selection, we used the Gain ratio evaluator.

Metaphor detection is our prime task, but we cannot ignore the *non-metaphor* class. We need to have an acceptable F-score for that as well, so as to maintain the credibility of our classification. Table 3 shows the results for the class *non-metaphor*. The precision values of the *metaphor* and *non-metaphor* classes are almost equal. On the other hand, the recall of the *non-metaphor* class is lower at 0.670 than for the class *metaphor* at 0.804. Error analysis (see section 4) showed that these "skipped" cases were mostly archaic words or poetic terms that do not have word vector representations. Still, we observe that the statistical method scored better than the rule-based method for all metrics.

Table 4 shows a direct comparison between our method – rule-based and statistical – and the methods of Shutova (2016) and Birke (2006) on their test data (not poetry). Our method performed better than the best-performing method MIXLATE (Shutova et al., 2016) on Mohammad et al.'s metaphor data (Mohammad et al., 2016). Our method also performed better than the Active Learning method of Birke and Sarkar (2006) on the TroFi dataset.

We also tested on 200-dimensional word vectors in order to investigate the effect of increasing the number of dimensions from 100 to 200 on accuracy metrics. Results showed that the accuracy dropped by 1%, along with a slight decline in the values of other metrics.

4 Error Analysis

Table 5 shows selected PoFo sentences that were predicted incorrectly by the classifier. We did error analysis on the PoFo test set to find the cause of these errors. The major cause was the absence of word vectors for certain poetic words: *blossomer*, *fadere*, *hell-drivn*, and so on. Another significant cause was the presence of multi-word expressions not identified correctly by the parser, for example *household word* (#11).

#	PoFo sentence	Original class	Predicted class
1	my father 's **farm** is an apple **blossomer** .	L	M
2	what is the answer ? the **answer** is the **world** .	L	M
3	long ago , this **desert** was an inland **sea** . in the mountains	L	M
4	so utterly absorbed that **love** is a **distraction** ; even	L	M
5	the **interviewer** was a **poet** . mann offered him no coffee , and	L	M
6	the body and the material things of the **world** are the **key** to any	L	M
7	though **beauty** be the **mark** of praise ,	L	M
8	strephon , who found the **room** was **void** ,	L	M
9	where **people** were **days** becoming months and years .	M	L
10	the **law** was **move** or die . lively from tigers	M	L
11	my **name** is a household **word** , writes the hid teacher	M	L
12	that the hot **wind** is **friend** , lifter of stones , trembler of heavy	M	L
13	**brilliance** is a **carcass**	M	L
14	to thee , whose **temple** is all **space** ,	M	L
15	**age** is **naught** but sorrow .	M	L

Table 5: A selection of incorrectly predicted PoFo sentences (L = literal, M = metaphorical)

Multiple word senses were also responsible for some of the errors, such as *key* in #6. There were also borderline cases which even human annotators found difficult to annotate (e.g., #2). Finally, quite a few errors were caused by the absence of compositionality while choosing word pairs. For example, *temple* and *space* in #14 are not enough to express a metaphor. There should be a composition of *all* and *space* as well, to capture the holistic meaning of the phrase. We aim to handle errors of those types in our future work in order to improve our classification.

5 Conclusions and Future Work

To the best of our knowledge, this is the first paper on the computational analysis of poetic metaphor. The preliminary results with Type I metaphor encourage us to continue, and to apply more methods. We are already working on type-independent metaphor identification to increase the recall of our analysis. When it comes to rule-based methods, we could work on context overlap in order to remove the ambiguity between various senses that a word may have. This may increase classification accuracy.

There are many statistical methods to look into. To begin with, we will analyze phrase compositionality (Mikolov et al., 2013b) in order to handle multi-word expressions and phrases better. Since we are identifying metaphor in word pairs rather than in the whole sentence, the accuracy of the vector representation for those words is crucial. If a word pair extracted by the algorithm does not represent the whole phrasal meaning, then the classification that follows may obviously prove inaccurate. We are considering deep-learning classifiers such as CNN as well, so as to improve precision further.

Next, we plan to distinguish between poetic and common-speech metaphor, a rather major undertaking. Finally, we plan to explore ways of quantifying commonalities and hierarchies between metaphor occurrences and thus develop metrics for metaphor quantification. Eventually such a metric will be used in the graph rendering, in visualization and in the analysis of poetry corpora.

The recent advances in natural language processing invite new and more consistent automatic approaches to the study of poetry. We intend to establish that poetry is amenable to computational methods. We also want to demonstrate that the statistical features which this research examines can indeed contribute significantly to the field of digital literary studies, and to academic poetry criticism and poetics in general. A case in point is our observation that non-poetry data are as helpful as poetry data in the task of metaphor detection in poetry.

So far, we have built on types of metaphor already defined by NLP scholars, and added two types we identified. Those types are based on parts of speech and syntactic structure. Our future work will study a generic concept, trying to track down metaphor based on vector disparity between words and phrases, irrespective of the POS or syntax involved. In a perspective more explicitly informed by Digital Humanities, we will also explore the applicability of both established and unconventional approaches to metaphor in the humanities. It will therefore be interesting, for example, to look into the computability of metaphor as strictly POS-based (nominal, verbal etc.) as a general framework, alongside marginal but intriguing concepts such as that of prepositional metaphor (Lakoff and Johnson, 2003). The latter has a not insignificant following in contemporary linguistics and stylistics (Goatly, 2011).

Acknowledgements

Support for this work has come from the Social Sciences and Humanities Research Council of Canada and the Natural Sciences and Engineering Research Council of Canada.

References

Dan Assaf, Yair Neuman, Yohai Cohen, Shlomo Argamon, Newton Howard, Mark Last, Ophir Frieder, and Moshe Koppel. 2013. Why "dark thoughts" aren't really dark: A novel algorithm for metaphor identification. In *Computational Intelligence, Cognitive Algorithms, Mind, and Brain (CCMB), 2013 IEEE Symposium on*, pages 60–65. IEEE.

David Baker. 1994. Murder. In *After the Reunion*. University of Arkansas Press.

Julia Birke and Anoop Sarkar. 2006. A Clustering Approach for Nearly Unsupervised Recognition of Nonliteral Language. In *Proc. EACL*, pages 329–336.

Jeremy H. Clear. 1993. The British National Corpus. In *The digital word*, pages 163–187. MIT Press.

George Crabbe. 1950. *The village*. University Tutorial Press.

Hart Crane. 2006. *Complete Poems and Selected Letters*. Library of America.

Marie-Catherine de Marneffe, Bill MacCartney, and Christopher D. Manning. 2006. Generating Typed Dependency Parses from Phrase Structure Parses. In *Proc. LREC*, pages 449–454.

Thomas Stearns Eliot. 1915. The Love Song of J. Alfred Prufrock. *Poetry*, 6(3):130–135.

Robert Frost. 1962. The Road Not Taken. In *The Poetry of Robert Frost*. Holt, Rinehart & Winston.

Andrew Goatly. 2011. *The Language of Metaphors*. Routledge.

Mark Hall, Eibe Frank, Geoffrey Holmes, Bernhard Pfahringer, Peter Reutemann, and Ian H. Witten. 2009. The WEKA data mining software: an update. *ACM SIGKDD Explorations Newsletter*, 11(1):10–18.

John Keats. 2009. *Bright Star: Love Letters and Poems of John Keats to Fanny Brawne*. Penguin.

Kenneth Koch. 1962. *Thank You, and other Poems*. Grove Press.

George Lakoff and Mark Johnson. 2003. *Metaphors we live by*. University of Chicago Press.

Audre Lorde. 2000. *The collected poems of Audre Lorde*. WW Norton & Company.

Andrés Lou, Diana Inkpen, and Chris Tanasescu. 2015. Multilabel Subject-Based Classification of Poetry. In *Proc. FLAIRS*, pages 187–192.

MARGENTO. 2012. *NOMADOSOPHY*. Max Blecher Press.

Tomas Mikolov, Kai Chen, Greg Corrado, and Jeffrey Dean. 2013a. Efficient Estimation of Word Representations in Vector Space. *arXiv preprint arXiv:1301.3781*.

Tomas Mikolov, Ilya Sutskever, Kai Chen, Greg S. Corrado, and Jeff Dean. 2013b. Distributed Representations of Words and Phrases and their Compositionality. In *Advances in neural information processing systems*, pages 3111–3119.

George A. Miller. 1995. WordNet: a lexical database for English. *Communications of the ACM*, 38(11):39–41.

Saif M. Mohammad, Ekaterina Shutova, and Peter D. Turney. 2016. Metaphor as a Medium for Emotion: An Empirical Study. In *Proc. *SEM*, pages 23–33.

Yair Neuman, Dan Assaf, Yohai Cohen, Mark Last, Shlomo Argamon, Newton Howard, and Ophir Frieder. 2013. Metaphor Identification in Large Texts Corpora. *PLOS ONE*, 8(4):1–9.

Jeffrey Pennington, Richard Socher, and Christopher D. Manning. 2014. Glove: Global Vectors for Word Representation. In *Proc. EMNLP*, volume 14, pages 1532–1543.

Sir Walter Ralegh. 1895. The Passionate Man's Pilgrimage. In Felix E. Schelling, editor, *A Book of Elizabethan Lyrics*, pages 129–131. Ginn and Company.

L. David Ritchie. 2013. *Metaphor (Key Topics in Semantics and Pragmatics)*. Cambridge University Press.

Delmore Schwartz. 1989. *Last & Lost Poems*, volume 673. New Directions Publishing.

William Shakespeare. 1904. *The Tragedy of Hamlet*. Cambridge University Press.

Ekaterina Shutova, Douwe Kiela, and Jean Maillard. 2016. Black Holes and White Rabbits: Metaphor Identification with Visual Features. In *Proc. 2016 NAACL: HLT*, pages 160–170.

Robert Speer and Catherine Havasi. 2012. Representing General Relational Knowledge in ConceptNet 5. In *Proc. LREC*, pages 3679–3686.

Chris Tanasescu, Bryan Paget, and Diana Inkpen. 2016. Automatic Classification of Poetry by Meter and Rhyme. In *The Twenty-Ninth International Flairs Conference*.

Peter D. Turney, Yair Neuman, Dan Assaf, and Yohai Cohen. 2011. Literal and Metaphorical Sense Identification through Concrete and Abstract Context. In *Proc. EMNLP*, pages 680–690. Association for Computational Linguistics.

James Wright. 1958. At the Executed Murderer's Grave. *Poetry*, pages 277–279.

Yiming Yang and Jan O. Pedersen. 1997. A Comparative Study on Feature Selection in Text Categorization. In *Proc. ICML*, volume 97, pages 412–420.

Machine Translation and Automated Analysis
of the Sumerian Language

Émilie Pagé-Perron[†], Maria Sukhareva[‡], Ilya Khait[¶], Christian Chiarcos[‡],

[†] University of Toronto
e.page.perron@mail.utoronto.ca

[‡] University of Frankfurt
sukhareva@em.uni-frankfurt.de
chiarcos@em.uni-frankfurt.de

[¶] University of Leipzig
ges12bry@studserv.uni-leipzig.de

Abstract

This paper presents a newly funded international project for machine translation and automated analysis of ancient cuneiform[1] languages where NLP specialists and Assyriologists collaborate to create an information retrieval system for Sumerian.[2]

This research is conceived in response to the need to translate large numbers of administrative texts that are only available in transcription, in order to make them accessible to a wider audience. The methodology includes creation of a specialized NLP pipeline and also the use of linguistic linked open data to increase access to the results.

1 Context

The project Machine Translation and Automated Analysis of Cuneiform Languages (MTAAC)[3] focuses on the application of NLP methods to Sumerian, a Mesopotamian language spoken in the 3rd millennium B.C. Assyriology, the study of ancient Mesopotamia, has benefited from early developments in NLP in the form of projects which digitally compile large amounts of transcriptions and metadata, using basic rule- and dictionary-based methodologies.[4] However, the orthographic, morphological and syntactic complexities of the Mesopotamian cuneiform languages have hindered further development of automated treatment of the texts. Additionally, digital projects do not necessarily use the same standards and encoding schemes across the board, and this, coupled with closed or partial access to some projects' data, limits larger scale investigation of machine-assisted text processing.

The history and society of ancient Mesopotamia are mostly known to the general public through works that draw on myths and royal inscriptions as primary sources, texts which are mostly translated and readily available. Among these works the Sumerian texts and their translations form a perfect testbed for distantly supervised NLP methods such as annotation projection and cross-lingual tool adaptation. However, the aforementioned translated texts make up only around 10% of the total amount of transcribed Sumerian data. The majority of the Sumerian texts are administrative

---

[1]The Cuneiform script was invented in Ancient Iraq more than 5000 years ago. Signs were drawn, and later impressed, onto a tablet-shaped fresh lump of clay using a reed stylus. This script was in use for 4000 years to record texts in different languages such as Sumerian, Akkadian and Elamite. See figure 1 in section 1b for an example.

[2]We would like to thank the reviewers, and Robert K. Englund and Heather D. Baker, for their insightful comments and suggestions.

[3]The project is generously funded by the Deutsche Forschungsgemeinschaft, the Social Sciences and Humanities Research Council, and the National Endowment for the Humanities through the T-AP Digging into Data Challenge. See the project website at https://cdli-gh.github.io/mtaac.

[4]Among others, the Cuneiform Digital Library initiative (CDLI) http://cdli.ucla.edu/ and the Open Richly Annotated Cuneiform Corpus (ORACC) http://oracc.museum.upenn.edu/ are two examples of such endeavors.

Joint SIGHUM Workshop on Computational Linguistics for Cultural Heritage, Social Sciences, Humanities and Literature.
Proceedings, pages 10–16, Vancouver, BC, August 4, 2017. ©2017 Association for Computational Linguistics

and legal in nature. The manual annotation and translation of these texts is hardly possible, owing to the large volume of the data and the need for an extremely rare expertise in Mesopotamian languages. However, having a parallel corpus, the solution to automatic processing of these texts lies in using machine translation (MT) techniques: Sumerian texts can be automatically translated and information extraction methods can be applied to the resulting translations.

In this paper we present a newly funded international project that will apply state-of-the-art NLP methods to Sumerian texts. We seek to create a pipeline for cuneiform languages with three major components: NLP processing, machine translation, and information extraction. The NLP tools for Sumerian created in the framework of the project will also be applicable to other cuneiform languages. The resource interoperability will be achieved through linking the annotation with linguistic linked open data ontologies (LLOD).

2 Data

The data for this project takes the form of unannotated raw transliterations of almost 68,000 Sumerian texts of the Ur III period (21st century B.C.) comprising 1.5 million transliteration lines. Around 1600 of these texts have also been translated. Each text entry is augmented with a set of metadata which describes the medium of the text, its context, and some elements of internal analysis. These texts are restricted in style and topic, and include a large proportion of numero-metrological elements. They are also repetitive, brief, and formulaic. As the inscribed medium comes in varied sizes and shapes, structural elements in the transliterations indicate on which surface of the artifact the text appears. Figure 1 shows an example of an ASCII transliteration and translation of a cuneiform text, accompanied with a picture of the obverse and reverse of the artifact. [5]

3 NLP Pipeline for Sumerian

State-of-the-art statistical NLP widely uses supervised classifiers to produce automatic linguistic annotation. Although some Sumerian and Akkadian corpora have been annotated through the ORACC platform in the form of various sub-projects,[6] manual annotation of large enough training sets to train a supervised classifier is not possible as it demands a rare expertise and is time-consuming. We thus propose a pipeline that uses distantly supervised methods (e.g. annotation projection) to create automatic linguistic annotation of Sumerian. Figure 2 shows the workflow of the NLP module. The majority of the data at hand comprises untranslated Sumerian texts. The distantly supervised methods will be applied to Sumerian texts and their English translations. The core of the pipeline is the annotation projection module that will produce morphosyntactically and syntactically annotated training data for supervised NLP tools. This section will further discuss in detail each module of the NLP pipeline.

3.1 Data Preprocessing

After verifying the uniformity in the standardization of the texts, we will convert the data to a machine readable format and sign readings will be verified against our digital syllabary. Transliterations and translation of our gold standard will be tokenized, lemmatized, and morphologically analyzed. The error rate of the corpus transliterations will be calculated against the curated gold standard.

3.2 Morphological analysis

Our morphological analyzer will be partly based on existing tools such as Tablan et al. (2006)'s rule-based morphology and Liu et al. (2015)'s algorithm to identify named entities. We will design a custom parser for numero-metrological content for the occasion. Since Sumerian affixes are ambiguous, we will build on previous work on the disambiguation of morphologically rich languages, such as Sak et al. (2007)'s neural methods for Turkish and Rios and Mamani (2014)'s conditional random fields used to disambiguate Quechua morphology. Morphological tags assigned following rule-based algorithms will be reranked using different machine learning (ML) approaches. The disambiguated morphology will be used for syntactic parsing, MT, and information extraction. We plan to develop a lemmatizer that will exploit a high-coverage dictionary. The available off-the-shelf lemmatizer for Sumerian[7] was

---

[5] Cuneiform text of the Ur III period from the settlement of Garshana, Mesopotamia (Owen, 2011, no. 851) and its transliteration as stored in the Cuneiform Digital Library Initiative (CDLI) database http://cdli.ucla.edu/P322539 (picture reproduced here with the kind permission of David I. Owen)

[6] http://oracc.museum.upenn.edu/

[7] http://oracc.museum.upenn.edu/doc/help/languages/ sumerian/sumerianprimer/

(1) P322539 = CUSAS 03, 0851.

tablet.

obverse.

   1.   `1(disz) kusz udu niga`
       1 hide, grain-fed sheep;

   2.   `1(disz) kusz masz2 niga`
       1 hide, grain-fed goat;

   3.   `kusz udu sa2-du11`
       sheep hides, regular offerings,

   4.   `ki {d}iszkur-illat-ta`
       from Adda-illat,

reverse.

   1.   `a-na-ah-i3-li2`
       Anah-ili;

   2.   `szu ba-an-ti`
       did receive.

   3.   `iti ezem-an-na`
       Month: An-festival,

   4.   `mu na-ru2-a-mah mu-ne-du3`
       Year: He erected the great stele for them.

(a) ASCII transliteration and English translation   (b) Example of a Sumerian source text

Figure 1: Artifact and its digitization

applied to our corpus during the preparation of this project and it was revealed that its coverage and accuracy are not sufficient for our needs since headwords are assigned to tokens without taking into account the textual context, although part of this software might be reused.

3.3 POS tagging

An important part of the NLP pipeline is the distantly supervised POS Tagging. As the corpus is currently unannotated, a supervised approach to POS tagging would not be applicable as it demands annotated training data. The creation of such training data through manual POS annotation of the data would demand an extremely rare expertise and is a time-consuming process. Therefore, we have to turn our attention to distantly supervised methods.

As we are in possession of parallel English translations of Sumerian texts, an annotation projection (Tiedemann, 2014) approach would be a most suitable distantly supervised method. English texts can be tokenized, stemmed, lemmatized, POS tagged and parsed by off-the-shelf freely available NLP tools. Using an off-the-shelf word-alignment tool Giza++ (Och and Ney, 2003), we can produce word alignment between English and the Sumerian texts. After we automatically tag English parallel texts, the assigned POS will be projected onto the aligned Sumerian words. The general assumption behind the annotation projection based on the word alignment is that translated words are likely to have the same POS as the source words. It is quite clear that this is a very bold assumption and there are a number of exceptions. Thus, both manual and automatic POS correction will be needed. However, the distantly supervised solution is temporary as there are parallel efforts to annotate the texts manually to produce training data for a supervised classifier.

3.4 Syntactic parsing

In order to facilitate MT and information extraction from our source texts, we will syntactically parse the corpus. In a similar manner to POS tags, dependency labels can be projected into Sumerian texts. Annotation projections of both POS tags and dependency labels need to be manually corrected. Using an adapted scheme for Sumerian, we will annotate a gold standard composed of a total of 10,000 sentences with dependencies and POS tags to train a supervised dependency parser and POS tagger. The rest of the data will be tagged and parsed automatically. The quality of the dependency parses will be estimated by labeled and unlabeled attachment score (UAS and LAS), and different parsing toolkits will be evaluated (Chen and Manning 2014, Nivre 2003, etc.).

4 Machine Translation

As MT for cuneiform languages is a novel task and there is no prior research, we will have to experiment with several approaches in order to establish the one most suitable for these languages. The standard phrase-based translation will form a good baseline.

Currently, there are over 1600 parallel Sumerian and English texts which are aligned sentence-wise. The baseline will be created by the Moses SMT toolkit (Koehn et al., 2007). It will be trained on these parallel texts and applied to the rest of the data to create automatic translations.

Nevertheless, due to the spelling variations and morphological richness of the language, data sparsity is inevitable. Thus, the baseline will be compared with a character-based MT system based on Phrasal ITG Aligner (Pialign) (Neubig et al., 2012) but tailored towards cuneiform data. Pialign uses synchronous context-free grammars and substring prior probabilities to produce many-to-many character alignment; it can thus efficiently capture mid-distance dependencies, as required for dealing with rich morphology and ideosyllabic writing systems without explicit word separators (e.g., Japanese).

In addition to this state-of-the-art SMT system, we will also apply innovative neural techniques to the translation of Sumerian cuneiform text. Neural Machine Translation (NMT) (Bahdanau et al., 2014) has been applied to various language pairs in the past few years, with successful applications for translating structurally different languages: Eriguchi et al. (2016) applied an attention-based neural network on Japanese and English that we will take as our point of departure, as the writing system of Japanese is structurally similar to cuneiform (using both ideographic and syllabic components), and they demonstrated that their approach is capable of generalizing over smaller amounts of training data than normally required by NMT systems. Following their syntax-

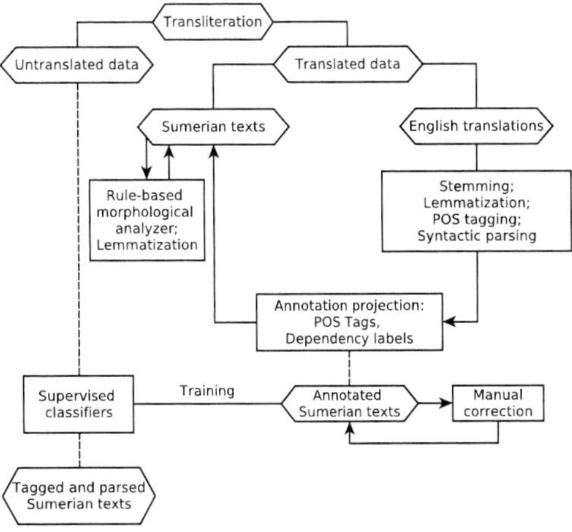

Figure 2: NLP pipeline for Sumerian

based extension of the traditional sequence-based encoder-decoder approach, we will integrate syntactic dependency annotation.

5 Information Extraction

In this project, we intend to go beyond automatic (morpho)syntactic annotation and collocation analysis to create an information extraction system for the Sumerian language. This system will aim to identify concepts and relations in the text, and the results will be available in human-readable format to integrate into the interface, alongside their labels and definitions.

The main objective of this step is to prepare data for prosopographical[8] research into the Ur III historical period. The Sumerian texts have an abundance of individuals' names but tracing them throughout various texts is not a trivial task. For example, the proper name ^{d}iškur-illat can be found 1212 times in 1092 texts. Additionnaly, it can be used as a toponym, a road name, or as a personal name that occurs in at least five different cities. Thus, it is impossible to tell at first sight whether these occurrences represent a single individual or five or more different people. In order to mitigate this problem, we will apply automatic collocation-based classification of proper names into specific entity categories (people, places, gods, etc.). A prosopographical study of extracted names will include a profiling of the individuals, which will entail identifying an individual's activities, titles,

---

[8]Prosopography is the study of past individuals and their relationships through sparse sources that give clues concerning their activities as groups.

properties and other pertinent information. We will then build a graph representation of the social connections of an individual. These structured features will be used for the disambiguation of individuals' profiles.

5.1 Research in Social History

Until now, prosopographical studies in Sumerian have focused on specific private or institutional archives (e.g. Dahl 2007) or have been based on a specific topic of inquiry but restricted to a region and period: their scope has always been limited. This selective nature of prosopographical study in Sumerian is largely due to the fact that the creation of the individuals' profiles involves a significant amount of manual work. The automatic translations and annotations produced by our NLP pipeline will enable us to automatically extract descriptions of individuals which will in turn enable us to perform large-scale social inquiries using a full prosopographical network based on the corpus at hand.

The main question that will be researched in this context is looking at is the dynamics of social mobility in the Ur III period. Administrative texts of the Ur III period are often dated with a ruler name, year name and month, sometimes days. This makes it possible to trace individuals through time when they appear in the archives. With our social network graph in place, it will be possible to identify clues to social mobility such as displacement, change in role, responsibility level, ego network variations, changes in property status, name and title. We will also take into account the influence of political and environmental changes through time. Such unprecedented large-scale prosopographical study can reveal important social and political trends that will shed light on the processes that enable or limit social mobility at that period.

6 Direct Applications

6.1 Linked Open Data

As an integral part to the project, all the manual and automatic linguistic annotations will be mapped to the *Ontologies of Linguistic Annotation* (Chiarcos, 2008), a reference terminology of Linguistic Linked Open Data (LLOD) which will ensure the interoperability of our annotation scheme and greatly increase the reusability of our data. As part of our prosopographical project, we will map our results onto the Standards for Networking Ancient Prosopographies (SNAP:DRGN)[9] that we will augment with a custom extension if needed. Pleiades[10] and Periodo[11] will be considered for mapping places and periods respectively. A machine readable interface will be developed to share all these prepared linked data.

6.2 Interface

One way of interfacing with the data generated will be through a new web facade designed with known audiences in mind, but also applying principles of universal design in order to increase the accessibility of the data and interface to a wider public of knowledge drawn from cuneiform sources. Translations will be easily retrievable and researchers will benefit from an advanced search engine. Concepts and entities present in the texts and metadata will be interlinked to permit navigation through the texts. Other visualization tools will be available, from dependency visualization to automated plotting of network analysis graphs, as well as traditional graphs to display statistics concerning a chosen group of texts. Data will also be available for download in full and in part, in different open formats.

6.3 Future Applications

Following this project, we expect to extend the scope of our pipeline to process other genres and periods of Sumerian texts and then work with the Akkadian language and other cuneiform languages. We expect that parts of our work can serve as test cases for other languages such as Basque and Turkish that share agglutinative and split-ergative characteristics and also logo-syllabic languages such as Japanese.

Having these tools available will foster future research into Ur III texts since they will be more accessible, including to machines. There is already a renewed interest in the study of Ur III texts because Assyriologists are starting to employ statistical methods to study larger groups of texts, so our project will also open doors for these interested scholars.

Because we will be using LLOD, new studies across languages, including Sumerian, will become possible. This will enrich the pool of varia-

---

tions of language morphology, especially because Sumerian is an isolate.

7 Challenges and Risks

The automatic processing of Sumerian texts is not a trivial task. Among others, we will face most of the traditional challenges of historical corpora. First of all, data sparsity will be inevitable. Sumerian is an agglutinative language with productive affixation which leads to an extremely high number of word forms, but we will significantly reduce data sparsity by means of lemmatization as explained in section 3.2. Regional variations can also increase the data sparsity: words can have different meanings, different readings, and different spellings depending on contextual factors such as the type of text, the period, the archive, and the region. Code-switching and foreign words pose an additional challenge for the morphological analyzer, but the texts have been marked with a structural language switch for ease of processing since Sumerian texts can be sprinkled with Akkadian words, for example verbs and personal names.

Other difficulties arise in the annotation projection and machine translation from the fact that the Sumerian language does not have any modern descendants. This is particularly important for the annotation projection, as previous studies have shown that diachronic relatedness is an important factor that affects the quality of annotation projection (Sukhareva and Chiarcos, 2014). Thus, we plan to conduct our pilot experiments on modern languages such as Turkish and Basque that are grammatically similar to Sumerian (agglutinative, split-ergative) to guarantee the scalability of our implementation, but more importantly to be able to conduct experiments in parallel with the morphological and syntactic annotation of the Sumerian texts.

8 Conclusion

Even though some basic NLP methods are already being employed in cuneiform studies, the use of modern computer science methods is still in its infancy and such powerful methods as ML and statistics are yet to be properly introduced into the field. Our MT and information extraction project, based on a practical research need in the Humanities, will contribute a methodology, its implementation, and a body of translated and analyzed texts. It will also assist in the processing of a host of related datasets, as well as setting an example for ML and MT in the Humanities. Moreover, it will facilitate studies of grammar and semantics of a language that is still not fully understood. The project will provide a unified access to a highly representative corpus of early writing, and will foster an unprecedented scholarly cooperation among researchers in a variety of disciplines. We think this is a unique opportunity to make a leap forward in natural language processing for ancient languages that will at the same time open up to a networked public the heritage of ancient civilizations.

References

Dzmitry Bahdanau, Kyunghyun Cho, and Yoshua Bengio. 2014. Neural machine translation by jointly learning to align and translate. *CoRR* abs/1409.0473. http://arxiv.org/abs/1409.0473.

Danqi Chen and Christopher D Manning. 2014. A fast and accurate dependency parser using neural networks. In *EMNLP*. pages 740–750.

Christian Chiarcos. 2008. An ontology of linguistic annotations. *LDV Forum* 23(1):1–16.

Jacob L Dahl. 2007. *The ruling family of Ur III Umma: a prosopographical analysis of an elite family in Southern Iraq 4000 years ago*. Nederlands Instituut voor het Nabije Oosten.

Akiko Eriguchi, Kazuma Hashimoto, and Yoshimasa Tsuruoka. 2016. Tree-to-sequence attentional neural machine translation. *CoRR* abs/1603.06075. http://arxiv.org/abs/1603.06075.

Philipp Koehn, Hieu Hoang, Alexandra Birch, Chris Callison-Burch, Marcello Federico, Nicola Bertoldi, Brooke Cowan, Wade Shen, Christine Moran, Richard Zens, Chris Dyer, Ondřej Bojar, Alexandra Constantin, and Evan Herbst. 2007. Moses: Open source toolkit for statistical machine translation. In *Proceedings of the 45th Annual Meeting of the ACL on Interactive Poster and Demonstration Sessions*. Association for Computational Linguistics, Stroudsburg, PA, USA, ACL '07, pages 177–180. http://dl.acm.org/citation.cfm?id=1557769.1557821.

Yudong Liu, Clinton Burkhart, James Hearne, and Liang Luo. 2015. Enhancing sumerian lemmatization by unsupervised named-entity recognition. In *The 2015 Conference of the North American Chapter of the Association for Computational Linguistics-Human Language Technologies (NAACL HLT 2015)*.

Graham Neubig, Taro Watanabe, Shinsuke Mori, and Tatsuya Kawahara. 2012. Machine translation without words through substring alignment. In *Proceedings of the 50th Annual Meeting of the Association for Computational Linguistics: Long Papers - Volume 1*. Association for Computational Linguistics, Stroudsburg, PA, USA, ACL '12, pages 165–174. http://dl.acm.org/citation.cfm?id=2390524.2390548.

Joakim Nivre. 2003. An efficient algorithm for projective dependency parsing. In *Proceedings of the 8th International Workshop on Parsing Technologies (IWPT)*. pages 149–160.

Franz Josef Och and Hermann Ney. 2003. A systematic comparison of various statistical alignment models. *Computational Linguistics* 29(1):19–51.

David I. Owen. 2011. *Garsana studies*. CDL Press.

Annette Rios and Richard Castro Mamani. 2014. Morphological disambiguation and text normalization for southern quechua varieties. *COLING 2014* page 39.

Haşim Sak, Tunga Güngör, and Murat Saraçlar. 2007. Morphological disambiguation of turkish text with perceptron algorithm. In *International Conference on Intelligent Text Processing and Computational Linguistics*. Springer Berlin Heidelberg, pages 107–118.

Maria Sukhareva and Christian Chiarcos. 2014. Diachronic proximity vs. data sparsity in cross-lingual parser projection. a case study on germanic. In *Proceedings of the First Workshop on Applying NLP Tools to Similar Languages, Varieties and Dialects*. Association for Computational Linguistics and Dublin City University, Dublin, Ireland, pages 11–20. http://www.aclweb.org/anthology/W14-5302.

Valentin Tablan, Wim Peters, Diana Maynard, Hamish Cunningham, and K Bontcheva. 2006. Creating tools for morphological analysis of sumerian. In *5th Language Resources and Evaluation Conference (LREC), Genoa, Italy*.

Jörg Tiedemann. 2014. Rediscovering annotation projection for cross-lingual parser induction. In *Proceedings of COLING 2014, the 25th International Conference on Computational Linguistics: Technical Papers*. Dublin City University and Association for Computational Linguistics, Dublin, Ireland, pages 1854–1864. http://www.aclweb.org/anthology/C14-1175.

Investigating the Relationship between
Literary Genres and Emotional Plot Development

Evgeny Kim, Sebastian Padó and Roman Klinger
Institut für Maschinelle Sprachverarbeitung
University of Stuttgart
Pfaffenwaldring 5b, 70569 Stuttgart, Germany
`{evgeny.kim,sebastian.pado,roman.klinger}@ims.uni-stuttgart.de`

Abstract

Literary genres are commonly viewed as
being defined in terms of content and style.
In this paper, we focus on one particular
type of content feature, namely lexical expressions of *emotion*, and investigate the
hypothesis that emotion-related information correlates with particular genres. Using genre classification as a testbed, we
compare a model that computes *lexicon-
based emotion scores* globally for complete
stories with a model that tracks *emotion
arcs* through stories on a subset of Project
Gutenberg with five genres.

Our main findings are: (a), the global emotion model is competitive with a large-
vocabulary bag-of-words genre classifier
$(80\% F_1)$; (b), the emotion arc model
shows a lower performance $(59\% F_1)$ but
shows complementary behavior to the
global model, as indicated by a very good
performance of an oracle model $(94\% F_1)$
and an improved performance of an ensemble model $(84\% F_1)$; (c), genres differ in
the extent to which stories follow the same
emotional arcs, with particularly uniform
behavior for anger (mystery) and fear (ad-
ventures, romance, humor, science fiction).

1   Introduction and Motivation

Narratives are inseparable from emotional content
of the plots (Hogan, 2011). Recently, Reagan et al.
(2016) presented an analysis of fictional texts in
which they found that there is a relatively small
number of universal plot structures that are tied
to the development of the emotion *happiness* over
time ("emotional arcs"). They called the arcs "Rags
to riches" (rise), "Tragedy" (fall), "Man in a hole"
(fall-rise), "Icarus" (rise-fall), "Cinderella" (rise-
fall-rise), and "Oedipus" (fall-rise-fall). They also
clustered fictional texts from Project Gutenberg[1]
by similarity to emotion arc types, suggesting that
their arc types could be useful for categorizing literary texts. At the same time, their analysis suf-
fered from some limitations: it was mostly qualitative and limited to the single emotion of happiness.
Crucially, they did not investigate the relationship
between emotions and established literary classification schemes more concretely.

The goal of our study is to investigate exactly this
relationship, extending the focus beyond one single emotion, and complementing qualitative with
quantitative insights. In this, we build on previous
work which has shown that stories from different
literary genres tend to have different flows of emotions (Mohammad, 2011). The role of emotion has
been investigated in different domains, including
social media (Pool and Nissim, 2016; Dodds et al.,
2011; Kouloumpis et al., 2011; Gill et al., 2008),
chats (Brooks et al., 2013), and fairy tales (Alm
et al., 2005).

As the basis for our quantitative analysis, we
adopt the task of genre classification, which makes
it possible for us to investigate different formula-
tions of emotion features in a predictive setting.
Genres represent one of the best-established classifications for fictional texts, and are typically defined to follow specific communicative purposes
or functional traits of a text (Kessler et al., 1997),
although we note that literary studies take care to
emphasize the role of artistic and aesthetic properties in genre definition (Cuddon, 2012, p. 405),
and take a cautious stance towards genre definition (Allison et al., 2011; Underwood et al., 2013;
Underwood, 2016).

Traditionally, computational studies of genre
classification use either *style-based* or *content-*

---

[1]`https://www.gutenberg.org`

17

Joint SIGHUM Workshop on Computational Linguistics for Cultural Heritage, Social Sciences, Humanities and Literature.
Proceedings, pages 17–26, Vancouver, BC, August 4, 2017. ©2017 Association for Computational Linguistics

based features. Stylistic approaches measure, for instance, frequencies of non-content words, of punctuation, part-of-speech tags and character n-grams (Karlgren and Cutting, 1994; Kessler et al., 1997; Stamatatos et al., 2000; Feldman et al., 2009; Sharoff et al., 2010). Content-aware characteristics take into account lexical information in bag-of-words models or build on top of topic models (Karlgren and Cutting, 1994; Hettinger et al., 2015, 2016). A precursor study to ours is Samothrakis and Fasli (2015), who assess emotion sequence features in a classification setting. We extend their approach by carrying out a more extensive analysis.

In sum, our contributions are:

1. We perform genre classification on a corpus sampled from Project Gutenberg with the genres *science fiction, adventure, humor, romantic fiction, detective and mystery stories.*

2. We define two emotion-based models for genre classification based on the eight fundamental emotions defined by Plutchik (2001) – *fear, anger, joy, trust, surprise, sadness, disgust,* and *anticipation.* The first one is an *emotion lexicon model* based on the NRC dictionary (Mohammad and Turney, 2013). The second one is an *emotion arc model* that models the emotional development over the course of a story. We avoid the assumption of Reagan et al. (2016) that absence of happiness indicates fear or sadness.

3. We analyze the performance of the various models quantitatively and qualitatively. Specifically, we investigate how *uniform* genres are with respect to emotion developments and discuss differences in the importance of lexical units.

2 Experimental Setup

To analyze the relationships between emotions expressed in literature and genres, we formulate a genre classification task based on different emotion feature sets. We start with a description of our data set in the following Section 2.1. The features are explained in Section 2.2 and then how they are used in various classification models (in Section 2.3).

2.1 Corpus

We collect books from Project Gutenberg that match certain tags, namely those which correspond

Genre	Count
adventure	569
humor	202
mystery	379
romance	327
science fiction	542
$\sum$	2019

Table 1: Statistics for our Gutenberg genre corpus.

to the five literary genres found in the Brown corpus (Francis and Kucera, 1979): adventure (Gutenberg tag: "Adventure stories"), romance ("Love stories" and "Romantic fiction"), mystery ("Detective and mystery stories"), science fiction ("Science fiction"), and humor ("Humor"). All books must additionally have the tag "Fiction". We exclude books which contain one of the following tags: "Short stories", "Complete works", "Volume", "Chapter", "Part", "Collection". This leads to a corpus of 2113 stories. Out of these, 94 books (4.4 %) have more than one genre label. For simplicity, we discard these texts, which leads to the corpus of 2019 stories with the relatively balanced genre distribution as shown in Table 1.

2.2 Feature Sets

We consider three different feature sets: bag-of-words features (as a strong baseline), lexical emotion features, and emotion arc features.

Bag-of-words features. An established strong feature set for genre classification, and text classification generally, consists of bag-of-words features. For genre classification, the generally adopted strategy is to use the n most frequent words in the corpus, whose distribution is supposed to carry more genre-specific rather than content- or domain-specific information. The choice of n varies across stylometric studies, from, *e.g.*, 1,000 (Sharoff et al., 2010) to 10,000 (Underwood, 2016). We set $n = 5,000$ here. We refer to this feature set as BoW.

Lexical emotion features. Our second feature set, EMOLEX, is a filtered version of BoW, capturing lexically expressed emotion information. It consists of all words in the intersection between the corpus vocabulary and the NRC dictionary (Mohammad and Turney, 2013) which contains 4,463 words associated with 8 emotions. Thus, it incor-

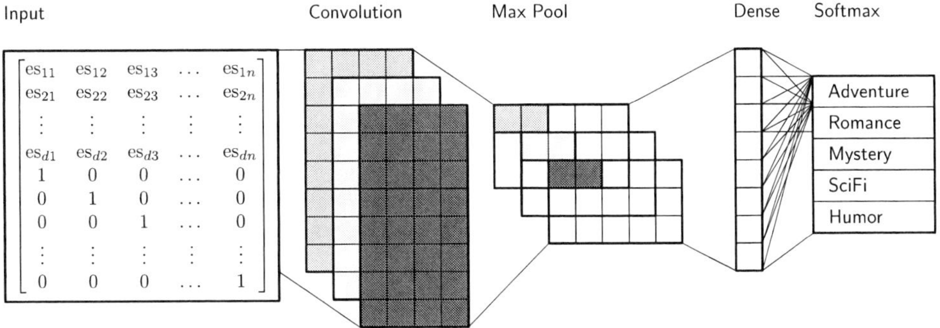

Figure 1: Architecture of CNN model

porates the assumption that words associated with emotions reflect the actual emotional content (Bestgen, 1994). We do not take into account words from "positive"/"negative" categories or those that are not associated with any emotions. This model takes into account neither emotion labels nor position of an emotion expression in the text.

Emotion arc features. The final feature set, EMOARC, in contrast to the lexical emotion features, takes into account both emotion labels and position of an emotion expression. It represents an emotion arc in the spirit of Reagan et al. (2016), but considers all of Plutchik's eight fundamental emotion classes. We split each input text into k equal-sized, contiguous segments S corresponding to spans of tokens $S = \langle t_n, \ldots, t_m \rangle$. We treat k as a hyper-parameter to be optimized (*cf.* Section 2.4).

We define a score $\text{es}(e, S)$ for the pairs of all segments S and each emotion e as

$$\text{es}(e, S) = \frac{c}{|D_e| \cdot |S|} \sum_{t_i \in S} \mathbf{1}_{t_i \in D_e} \, ,$$

where D_e is the NRC dictionary associating words with emotions, c is a constant set for convenience to the maximum token length of all texts in the corpus C ($c = \max_{S \in C} |S|$), and $\mathbf{1}_{t_i \in D_e}$ is 1 if $t_i \in D_e$ and 0 otherwise. This score, which makes the same assumption as the lexical emotion features, represents the number of words associated with emotion e per segment, normalized in order to account for differences in vocabulary size and book length.

The resulting features form an $8 \times k$ "emotion-segment" matrix for each document that reflects the development of each of the eight emotions throughout the timecourse of the narrative (*cf.* Section 2.3).

2.3 Models for Genre Classification

In the following, we discuss the use of the feature sets defined in Section 2.2 with classification methods to yield concrete models.

We use the two lexical feature sets, BOW and EMOLEX, with a random forest classifier (RF, Breiman (2001)) and multi-layer perceptron (MLP, Hinton (1989)). RF often performs well independent of chosen meta parameters (Criminisi et al., 2012), while MLP provides a tighter control for overfitting and copes well with non-linear problems (Collobert and Bengio, 2004).

The emotion arc feature set (EMOARC) is used for classification in a random forest, multi-layer perceptron, and a convolutional neural network (CNN). For the first two classification methods, we flatten the emotion-segment matrix into an input vector. From these representations, the classifiers can learn which emotion matters for which segment, like, *e.g.*, "high value at position 2", "low value at position 4" and combinations of these characteristics. However, they are challenged by a need to capture interactions such as "position 2 has a higher value than position 3", or similar relationships at different positions, like "highest value at position around the middle of the book".

To address this shortcoming, we also experiment with a convolution neural network, visualized in Figure 1. The upper part of the input matrix corresponds to the emotion-segment matrix from Section 2.2. Below, we add k one-hot row vectors each of which encodes the position of one segment. This representation enables the CNN with EMOARC features to capture the development of different emotions between absolute segment positions – it can compare the "intensity" of different emotions over time steps. By considering all emotions through time steps in a text, the CNN can model patterns

		adventure	humor	mystery	romance	sci-fi	Micro-Av.		
Model	Features	P R F_1	P R F_1	P R F_1	P R F_1	P R F_1	P	R	F_1
RF	BoW	75 89 81✔O	83 51 63✔O	82 78 80✔O	73 74 74✔O	88 87 87✔O	80✔O	80✔O	80✔O
MLP	BoW	73 75 74	69 58 63	70 70 70	66 71 68	85 84 85	74	74	74
RF	EmoLex	69 88 78	91 39 54	81 74 78	75 73 74	83 84 84	77	77	77
MLP	EmoLex	80 79 80✔✗✱	78 78 78✔✗	80 79 79✔✗✱	71 76 73✔✗✱	91 89 90✔✗✱	81✔✗✱	81✔✗✱	81✔✗✱
RF	EmoArc	51 72 59	70 27 39	55 33 41	59 63 61	70 73 71	58	58	58
MLP	EmoArc	55 60 57	56 36 44	49 47 48	57 71 63	72 65 68	58	58	58
CNN	EmoArc	56 60 58O✗	56 43 48O✗	49 46 48O✗	57 70 63O✗	74 68 71O✗	59O✗	59O✗	59O✗
SVM	Ensemble	80 86 83✱	80 78 79	87 79 83✱	79 78 78✱	90 91 91✱	84✱	84✱	84✱

Table 2: Results for genre classification on the Gutenberg corpus (percentages). We use bootstrap resampling (Efron, 1979) to test for significance of differences ($\alpha = 0.05$) (a), pairwise among the best models for each feature set (RF BoW, MLP EmoLex, CNN EmoArc) and (b), between the best individual model (MLP EmoLex) and the SVM Ensemble model. Legend: ✔ MLP EmoLex vs. RF BoW, ✗ CNN EmoArc vs. MLP EmoLex, O CNN EmoArc vs. RF BoW, ✱ Ensemble SVM vs. MLP EmoLex.

outside the expressivity of the simpler classifiers.

Formally, the CNN consists of an input layer, one convolutional layer, one max pooling layer, one dense layer, and an output layer. The convolutional layer consists of 32 filters of size $(8 + k) \times 4$. The max pooling layer takes into account regions of size 1×2 of the convolutional layer and feeds the resulting matrices to the fully connected dense layer with 128 neurons.

2.4 Meta-Parameter Setting

We choose the following meta-parameters: For RF, we set the number of trees to 250 in BoW and EmoLex and to 430 in EmoArc. In MLP, we use two hidden layers with 256 neurons each, with an initial learning rate of 0.01 that is divided by 5 if the validation score does not increase after two consecutive epochs by at least 0.001. Each genre class is represented by one output neuron. For the number of segments in the text, we choose $k = 6$.

3 Genre Classification Results

Table 2 shows the main results in a 10-fold cross-validation setting. The BoW baseline model shows a very strong performance of 80 % F_1. Limiting the words to those 4,463 which are associated with emotions in EmoLex significantly improves the classification of humorous and science fiction books, which leads to a significant improvement of the micro-average precision, recall, and F_1 by 1 percentage point. This result shows that emotion-associated words predict genre as well as BoW

model even though fewer words, and particularly less content-related words are considered. This aspect is further discussed in the model analysis in Section 4.3 and Table 7. We test for significance of differences ($\alpha = 0.05$) using bootstrap resampling (Efron, 1979), see the caption of Table 2 for details.

Among the EmoArc models, we find the best performance (59 % F_1) for the CNN architecture underlining the importance of the model to capture emotional *developments* rather than just high or low emotion values. The EmoArc models significantly underperform the lexical approaches. At the same time, their results are still substantially better than, *e.g.*, a most frequent class baseline (which results in 12 % F_1). Thus, this result shows the general promise of using emotion arcs for genre classification, even though the non-lexicalized emotion arcs represent an impoverished signal compared to the lexicalized BoW and EmoLex models.

This raises the question of whether a model combination could potentially improve the overall result. Table 3 quantifies the complementarity of the models: Its diagonal shows true positive counts for each model. The other cells are true positive hits for the column models which were *not* correctly classified by the row model. Therefore, the additional contribution, *e.g.*, by MLP EmoArc over MLP EmoLex consists in 123 additional correctly classified texts. Conversely, 586 texts are correctly classified by MLP EmoLex, but not by MLP EmoArc.

Model	Features	RF BoW	MLP BoW	RF EmoLex	MLP EmoLex	RF EmoArc	MLP EmoArc	CNN EmoArc
RF	BoW	**1616**	110	38	184	73	98	103
MLP	BoW	228	**1498**	215	298	172	182	176
RF	EmoLex	99	158	**1555**	240	72	111	114
MLP	EmoLex	161	157	156	**1639**	133	123	131
RF	EmoArc	503	484	441	586	**1186**	194	197
MLP	EmoArc	536	502	488	584	202	**1178**	100
CNN	EmoArc	520	475	470	571	184	79	**1199**

Table 3: Model comparison. Numbers on the diagonal show the numbers of overall true positives for the respective model. Numbers in other cells denote the number of instances correctly classified by the column model, but not by the row model.

These numbers indicate that our models and feature sets are complementary enough to warrant an ensemble approach. This is bolstered by an experiment with an oracle ensemble. This oracle ensemble takes a set of classifiers and considers a classification prediction to be correct if at least one classifier makes a correct prediction. It measures the upper bound of performance that could be achieved by a perfect combination strategy. Taking into account predictions from all the models in Table 2 yields a promising result of 94 % F_1 (precision=recall=94 %), an improvement of 14 percentage points in F_1 over the previous best model.

Following this idea of a combination strategy, we implement an ensemble model that is an L1-regularized L2-loss support vector classification model that takes predictions for each book from all the models as input and performs the classification via a 10-fold cross-validation. The results for this experiment are given in Table 2 in the last row. Overall, we observe a significant improvement over the best single model, the MLP EMOLEX model.

As the results show, the outcome of our ensemble experiment is still far from the upper bound achieved by the oracle ensemble. At the same time, even the small, but significant, improvement over the best single model provides a convincing evidence that further improvement of the classification is possible. However, finding a more effective practical combination strategy presents a multiaspect problem with vast solution space which we leave for future work. We now proceed to obtaining a better understanding of the relationship between emotion development and genres.

Emotion	Genre				
	Adv.	Humor	Myst.	Rom.	Sci-fi
Anger	0.21	0.20	**0.25**	0.28	0.18
Anticipation	0.12	0.10	0.17	0.15	0.16
Disgust	0.17	0.22	0.14	0.21	0.14
Fear	**0.28**	**0.22**	0.19	**0.32**	**0.19**
Joy	0.15	0.09	0.14	0.19	0.16
Sadness	0.21	0.18	0.12	0.25	0.15
Surprise	0.17	0.16	0.19	0.23	0.17
Trust	0.16	0.17	0.07	0.07	0.13

Table 4: Average uniformity of emotion-genre pairs measured by Spearman correlation. Highest uniformity per genre marked in bold.

4 Model and Data Analysis

4.1 Uniformity of Prototypical Arcs

The results presented in the previous section constitute a mixed bag: even though overall results for the use of emotion-related features are encouraging, the specific EMOARC model was not competitive. We now investigate possible reasons.

Our first focus is the fundamental assumption underlying the EMOARC model, namely that *all works of one genre develop relatively uniformly with respect to the presence of individual emotions over the course of the plot*. We further concretize this notion of *uniformity* as correlation with the *prototypical emotion development for a genre* which we compute as the average vector of all emotion scores (*cf.* Section 2.2) for the genre in question.

We formalize the *uniformity* of a emotion arc of a text with scores $\langle \mathrm{es}_1, \ldots, \mathrm{es}_k \rangle$ as the Spearman rank correlation coefficient with the prototypical vector $\langle \overline{\mathrm{es}}_1, \ldots, \overline{\mathrm{es}}_k \rangle$. Spearman coefficients range between -1 and 1, with -1 indicating a perfect inverse correlation, 0 no correlation, and 1 perfect correlation. In contrast to, *e.g.*, a Euclidean distance, this measures the emotion arc in a similar manner to the CNN.

Figure 2 shows the results in an emotion-genre matrix. Each cell presents the emotion scores for the six segments, shown as vertical dotted lines. The thick black line is the prototypical development, and the grey band around it a 95% confidence interval. We see the three most correlated (*i.e.*, most prototypical) books in blue, and the curves for the three least correlated (*i.e.*, most idiosyncratic) books in dashed red.

The figure shows that there are considerable differences between emotions-genre pairs: some of them have narrow confidence bands (*i.e.*, more uni-

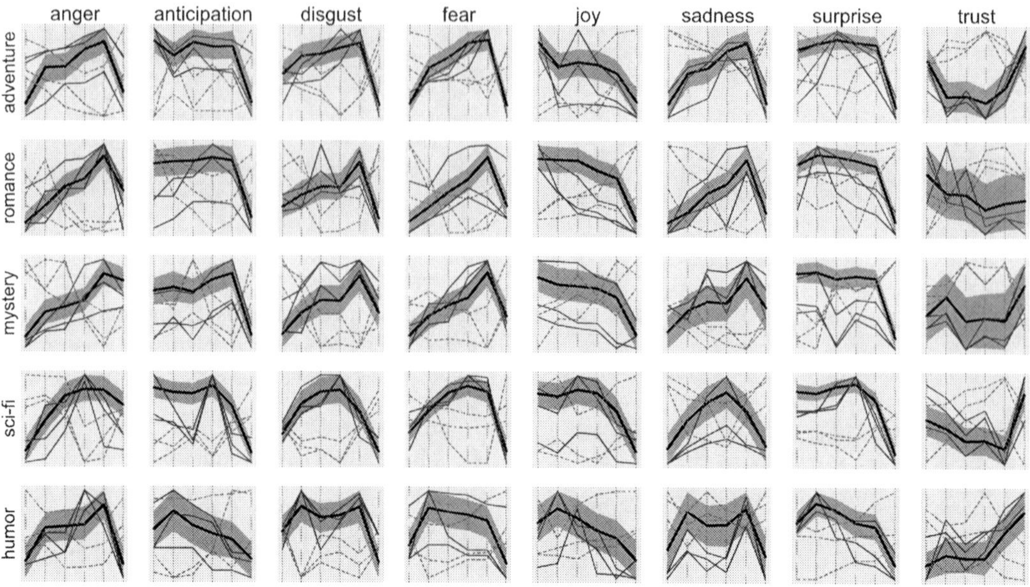

Figure 2: Emotion developments per genre. Thick black line: prototypical development. Grey band: 95% confidence interval. Blue lines: 3 most correlated books within each emotion-genre pair. Red dashed lines: 3 least correlated books within each emotion-genre pair.

form behavior), such as *fear*, while others have broad confidence bands (*i.e.*, less uniform behavior), such as *trust* and *anticipation*. Table 4, which lists the average uniformity (Spearman correlation) for each genre-emotion pair, confirms this visual impression: the emotions that behave most consistently within genres are *fear* (most uniform for four genres) and *anger* (most uniform for *mystery*). In contrast, the emotions *anticipation* and *trust* behave nonuniformly, showing hardly any correlation with prototypical development.

These findings appear plausible: *fear* and *anger* are arguably more salient plot devices in fiction than *anticipation* and *trust*. More surprisingly, *happiness/joy* is not among the most uniform emotions either. In this respect, our findings do not match the results of Reagan et al. (2016): according to our results, *joy* is not a particularly good emotion to base a genre classification on. We discuss reasons for this discrepancy below in Section 5.

At the level of individual books, Figure 2 indicates that we find "outlier" books (shown in dashed red) with a development that is almost completely inverse compared to the prototype for essentially *all* emotion-genre pairs, even the most uniform ones. This finding can have two interpretations: either it indicates unwarranted variance in our analysis method (*i.e.*, the assignment of emotions to text segments is more noisy than we would like it to be), or it indicates that the correlation between the emotional plot development and the genre is weaker than we initially hypothesized.

As a starting point for a close reading investigation of these hypotheses, Table 5 lists the three most and least prototypical books for each genre, where we averaged the books' prototypicality across emotions. We cannot provide a detailed discussion here, but we note that the list of least prototypical books contains some well-known titles, such as *La dame aux Camilias*, while the top list contains lesser known titles. A cursory examination of the emotion arcs for these works indicates that the arcs make sense. Thus, we do not find support for noise in the emotion assignment; rather, it seems that more outstanding literary works literally "stand out" in terms of their emotional developments: their authors seem to write more creatively with respect to the expectations of the respective genres.

4.2 Emotion Arcs and Genre Classification

Above, we have established that arcs for some emotions are more uniform than others, and that there are outlier texts for every emotion and genre. But does the degree of uniformity matter for classification? To assess this question, we analyze the average prototypicality among books that were classi-

Genre	Most prototypical	Least prototypical
adventure	*Bert Wilson in the Rockies*, Duffield, J. W. *The Outdoor Girls of Deepdale; Or, camping and tramping for fun and health*, Hope, L. *Blown to Bits; or, The Lonely Man of Rakata*, Ballantyne, R. M.	*Chasing the Sun*, Ballantyne, R. M. *The Bronze Bell*, Vance, L.J. *Chester Rand; or, The New Path to Fortune*, Alger, H.
romance	*The Girl in the Mirror*, Jordan, Elizabeth Garver *The Unspeakable Perk*, Adams, Samuel Hopkins *The Maid of Maiden Lane*, Barr, Amelia	*La Dame aux Camilias*, Dumas, A. *Through stained glass*, Chamberlain, George *Daddy-Long-Legs*, Webster, Jean
mystery	*The Woman from Outside [On Swan River]*, Footner, H. *The Old Stone House and Other Stories*, Green, A.K. *In Friendship's Guise*, Graydon, W.M.	*The Grell Mystery*, Froest, F. *My Strangest Case*, Boothby, G. *The Treasure-Train*, Reeve, A. B.
scifi	*The Great Drought*, Meek, S. P. *The Finding of Haldgren*, Diffin, Charles *The Tree of Life*, Moore, C. L.	*Looking Backward, 2000 to 1887*, Bellamy, E. *Let 'Em Breathe Space!*, Del Rey, L. *The Second Deluge*, Serviss, Garrett P.
humor	*Captains All and Others*, Jacobs, W. *The Rubáiyát of a Bachelor*, Rowland, H. *The Temptation of Samuel Burge (Captains All, Book 8)*, Jacobs, W. W.	*Just William*, Crompton, Richmal *Baby Mine*, Mayo, Margaret *Torchy and Vee* , Ford, Sewell

Table 5: Most and least prototypical books regarding overall emotional development in each genre

Model Family	Classification	Avg. Spearman on +	Avg. Spearman on −	Δ between + and −
BOW	RF	0.185	0.164	0.021
	MLP	0.184	0.170	0.014
EMOLEX	RF	0.182	0.176	0.006
	MLP	0.181	0.179	0.002
EMOARC	RF	0.193	0.162	0.031
	MLP	0.206	0.144	0.062
	CNN	0.205	0.145	0.060

Table 6: Average prototypicality (measured as correlation with prototypical emotion arc) for books that are correctly (+) and incorrectly (−) predicted by each model. Positive Δ means higher prototypicality for correct classifications.

fied correctly and incorrectly for each classification model from Section 2.3.

The results in Table 6 show that the average prototypicality is always higher for correctly than for incorrectly classified books. That being said, there appears to be a relationship between the feature set used and the size of this effect, Δ. This size is smallest for the BOW models and not much larger for the EMOLEX models. It is considerably larger for the EMOARC models and particularly higher for the MLP EMOARC model.

We draw three conclusions from this analysis:

(1), EMOARC features and models based on them are meaningful for the task of literary genre classification, as evidenced by higher correlation coefficients in the correctly predicted instances. (2), since emotion arcs are exactly the type of information that the CNN EMOARC model bases its classification decision on, emotional uniformity is indeed a prerequisite for successful classification by EMOARC, and its lack for some genres and emotions explains why EMOARC does not do as well as the more robust BOW and EMOLEX models. (3), the difference in correlation ranks between correct and incorrect predictions validates the idea of an ensemble classification scheme and may serve as a starting point for deeper investigation of differences between models in future work.

4.3 Feature Analysis of Lexical Models

After having considered EMOARC in detail, we now complete our analysis in this paper by a more in-depth look at the feature level. We focus on features that are most strongly associated with the genres, using a standard association measure, pointwise mutual information (PMI), which is considered to be a sensible approximation of the most influential features within a model.

Table 7 shows that most strongly associated features with each genre differ in their linguistic status between BOW and EMOLEX. For example, for the genre *romance*, most BOW features are infrequent words like specific character names which do not generalize to unseen data (*e.g., Gerard, Molly*).

BoW					EmoLex				
Adv.	Humor	Mystery	Romance	SciFi	Adv.	Humor	Mystery	Romance	SciFi
tarzan	ses	coroner	gerard	planet	hermit	wot	murderer	sally	projectile
damon	iv	kennedy	molly	solar	hut	wan	jury	mamma	rocket
canoes	sponge	detective	willoughby	planets	fort	comrade	attorney	marry	beam
blacks	ay	inspector	fanny	projectile	lion	rat	robbery	tenderness	scientist
indians	says	detectives	clara	mars	tribe	bye	police	loving	blast
ned	wot	trent	maggie	rocket	spear	beer	crime	charity	bomb
savages	wan	scotland	eleanor	rip	jungle	idiot	criminal	love	emergency
spain	mole	murderer	cynthia	jason	swim	jest	murder	marriage	system
whale	ha	rick	yo	phone	rifle	school	suicide	passionate	center
eric	ma	scotty	jill	globe	don	mule	clue	holiday	pilot

Table 7: Top ten EmoLex and BoW features by pointwise mutual information values with each genre.

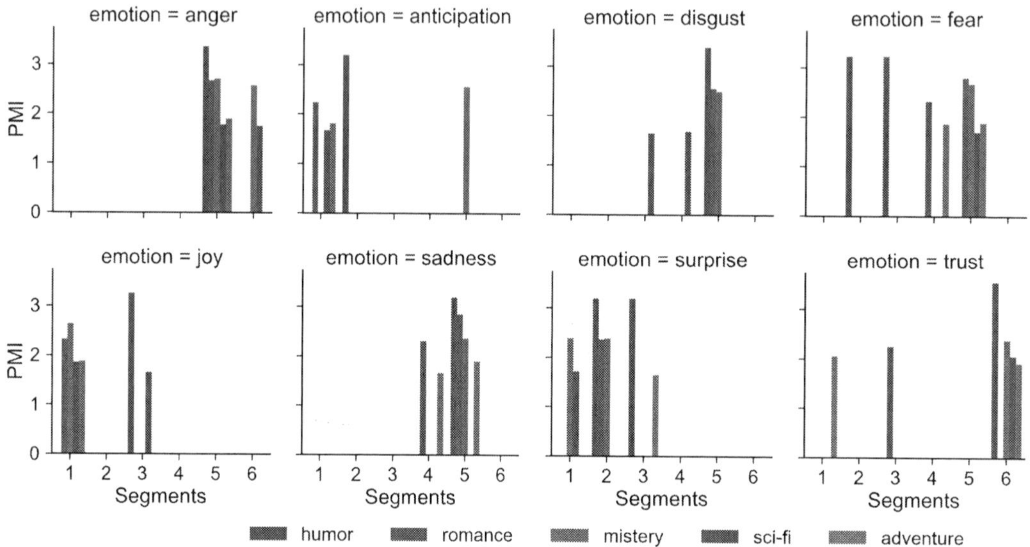

Figure 3: Top EmoArc features for each genre ranked according to their PMI values.

The EmoLex features consist of words related to emotions (*e.g., mamma, marry, loving*). In *mystery*, the most important BoW features express typical protagonists of crime stories (*e.g., coroner, detective, inspector, Scotland*). For EmoLex, we see similar results with a stronger focus on affect-related roles (*e.g., murderer, jury, attorney, robbery, police, crime*). In sum, we observe that the feature sets pick up similar information, but from different perspectives: the BoW set focusing more on the objective ("what") and the EmoLex set more on the subjective ("how") level.

As a combination of the analysis in Section 4.2 with the PMI approach, Figure 3 visualizes the EmoArc features as "peak" features that fire when an emotion is maximal in one specific segment (*cf.* Section 3). The results correspond well to the prominent maxima of emotion arcs shown in Figure 2. For the genre of adventure, *e.g., trust* and *anticipation* peak at the beginning. *Sadness, anger,* and *fear* peak towards the end, however, the very end sees a kind of "resolution" with trust becoming the dominating emotion again. At the same time, *anger* and *sadness* seem to be dominating all genres towards the end, and *joy* plays an important role in the first half of the books for most genres.

5 Discussion and Conclusion

In this paper, we analyzed the relationship between emotion information and genre categorization. We considered three feature sets corresponding to three levels of abstraction (lexical, lexical limited to emotion-bearing words, emotion arc) and found interesting results: classification based on emotion-words performs *on par* with traditional genre feature sets that are based on rich, open-vocabulary lexical information. Our first conclusion is therefore that emotions carry information that is highly relevant for distinguishing genres.

A further aggregation of emotion information into emotion arcs currently underperforms compared to the lexical methods, indicating that relevant information gets lost in our current representation. We need to perform further research regarding this representation as well as the combination of different feature sets, since these appear to contribute complementary aspects to the analysis of genres, as the excellent performance of an oracle shows. Our ensemble approach significantly outperforms the best single model but still outperforms the oracle result.

Our subsequent, more qualitative analysis of the uniformity of emotion arcs within genres indicated that some, but not all, emotions develop moderately uniformly over the course of books within genres: *Fear* is most uniform in all genres except mystery stories, where *anger* is more stable. Unexpectedly, *joy* is only of mediocre stability. At the same time, our study of outliers indicates that this conforming to the prototypical emotion development of a given genre appears to be a *sufficient, but not necessary* condition for membership in a genre: we found books with idiosyncratic emotional arcs that were still unequivocally instances of the respective genres. As with many stylistic properties, expectations about emotional development can evidently be overridden by a literary vision.

This raises the question of what concept of genre it is that our models are capturing. Compared to more theoretically grounded concepts of genre in theoretical literary studies, our corpus-based grounding of genres is shaped by the books we sampled from Project Gutenberg. Many of these are arguably relatively unremarkable works that exploit the expectations of the genres rather than seminal works trying to redefine them. The influence of corpus choice on our analysis take may also explain the apparent contradictions between our by-emotion results and the ones reported by Reagan et al. (2016), who identified *happiness/joy* as the most important emotion, while this emotion came out as relatively uninteresting in our analysis. Our observations about the influence of individual artistic decisions have, however, made us generally somewhat hesitant regarding Reagan et al.'s claim about "universally applicable plot structures".

In future work, we want to pursue (a) the close reading direction and analyse a relatively small number of classical works for each genre with respect to their prototypicality in more detail, as well as (b) the distance reading direction, investigating the potential for a better combination of the different classification schemes into an ensemble model.

References

Sarah Danielle Allison, Ryan Heuser, Matthew Lee Jockers, Franco Moretti, and Michael Witmore. 2011. *Quantitative formalism: an experiment*. Stanford Literary Lab.

Cecilia Ovesdotter Alm, Dan Roth, and Richard Sproat. 2005. Emotions from text: machine learning for text-based emotion prediction. In *Proceedings of the Conference on Human Language Technology and Empirical Methods in Natural Language Processing*. Vancouver, BC, pages 579–586.

Yves Bestgen. 1994. Can emotional valence in stories be determined from words? *Cognition & Emotion* 8(1):21–36.

Leo Breiman. 2001. Random forests. *Machine learning* 45(1):5–32.

Michael Brooks, Katie Kuksenok, Megan K Torkildson, Daniel Perry, John J Robinson, Taylor J Scott, Ona Anicello, Ariana Zukowski, Paul Harris, and Cecilia R Aragon. 2013. Statistical affect detection in collaborative chat. In *Proceedings of the Conference on Computer-Supported Cooperative Work*. pages 317–328.

Ronan Collobert and Samy Bengio. 2004. Links between perceptrons, MLPs and SVMs. In *Proceedings of the Twenty-first International Conference on Machine Learning*. New York, NY, USA, ICML.

Antonio Criminisi, Jamie Shotton, and Ender Konukoglu. 2012. Decision forests: A unified framework for classification, regression, density estimation, manifold learning and semi-supervised learning. *Foundations and Trends® in Computer Graphics and Vision* 7(2–3):81–227.

John Anthony Cuddon. 2012. *Dictionary of literary terms and literary theory*. John Wiley & Sons.

Peter Sheridan Dodds, Kameron Decker Harris, Isabel M. Kloumann, Catherine A. Bliss, and Christopher M. Danforth. 2011. Temporal patterns of happiness and information in a global social network: Hedonometrics and twitter. *PloS one* 6(12):e26752.

Bradley Efron. 1979. Bootstrap methods: another look at the jackknife. *The annals of Statistics* 7(1):1–26.

Sergey Feldman, Marius Marin, Julie Medero, and Mari Ostendorf. 2009. Classifying factored genres with part-of-speech histograms. In *Proceedings of*

Human Language Technologies: The 2009 Annual Conference of the North American Chapter of the Association for Computational Linguistics, Companion Volume: Short Papers. Boulder, Colorado, pages 173–176.

W. Nelson Francis and Henry Kucera. 1979. Brown corpus manual. Online: http://clu.uni.no/icame/brown/bcm.html.

Alastair J. Gill, Robert M. French, Darren Gergle, and Jon Oberlander. 2008. Identifying emotional characteristics from short blog texts. In *Proceedings of the 30th Annual Conference of the Cognitive Science Society*. pages 2237–2242.

Lena Hettinger, Martin Becker, Isabella Reger, Fotis Jannidis, and Andreas Hotho. 2015. Genre classification on german novels. In *Proceedings of the 26th International Workshop on Database and Expert Systems Applications*. pages 249–253.

Lena Hettinger, Fotis Jannidis, Isabella Reger, and Andreas Hotho. 2016. Classification of literary subgenres. In *Proceedings of DHd 2016*. Leipzig, Germany.

Geoffrey E Hinton. 1989. Connectionist learning procedures. *Artificial intelligence* 40(1):185–234.

Patrick Colm Hogan. 2011. *What literature teaches us about emotion*. Cambridge University Press.

Jussi Karlgren and Douglass Cutting. 1994. Recognizing text genres with simple metrics using discriminant analysis. In *Proceedings of the 15th International Conference on Computational Linguistics*. Kyoto, Japan, pages 1071–1075.

Brett Kessler, Geoffrey Nunberg, and Hinrich Schütze. 1997. Automatic detection of text genre. In *Proceedings of the 35th Annual Meeting of the Association for Computational Linguistics*. Madrid, Spain, pages 32–38.

Efthymios Kouloumpis, Theresa Wilson, and Johanna Moore. 2011. Twitter sentiment analysis: The good the bad and the OMG! In *International AAAI Conference on Web and Social Media*. Barcelona, Spain, pages 538–541.

Saif Mohammad. 2011. From once upon a time to happily ever after: Tracking emotions in novels and fairy tales. In *Proceedings of the 5th ACL-HLT Workshop on Language Technology for Cultural Heritage, Social Sciences, and Humanities*. pages 105–114.

Saif M Mohammad and Peter D Turney. 2013. Crowdsourcing a word–emotion association lexicon. *Computational Intelligence* 29(3):436–465.

Robert Plutchik. 2001. The nature of emotions human emotions have deep evolutionary roots, a fact that may explain their complexity and provide tools for clinical practice. *American Scientist* 89(4):344–350.

Chris Pool and Malvina Nissim. 2016. Distant supervision for emotion detection using Facebook reactions. *arXiv preprint arXiv:1611.02988* .

Andrew J. Reagan, Lewis Mitchell, Dilan Kiley, Christopher M. Danforth, and Peter Sheridan Dodds. 2016. The emotional arcs of stories are dominated by six basic shapes. *EPJ Data Science* 5(1):31.

Spyridon Samothrakis and Maria Fasli. 2015. Emotional sentence annotation helps predict fiction genre. *PloS one* 10(11):e0141922.

Serge Sharoff, Zhili Wu, and Katja Markert. 2010. The web library of babel: evaluating genre collections. In *Proceedings of the Seventh conference on International Language Resources and Evaluation (LREC'10)*. European Language Resources Association (ELRA), Valletta, Malta.

Efstathios Stamatatos, Nikos Fakotakis, and George Kokkinakis. 2000. Automatic text categorization in terms of genre and author. *Computational Linguistics* 26(4):471–495.

Ted Underwood. 2016. The life cycles of genres. *Cultural Analytics* 1. https://doi.org/doi:10.7910/DVN/XKQOQM.

Ted Underwood, Michael L Black, Loretta Auvil, and Boris Capitanu. 2013. Mapping mutable genres in structurally complex volumes. In *Proceedings of the IEEE International Conference on Big Data*. pages 95–103.

Enjambment Detection in a Large Diachronic Corpus of Spanish Sonnets

Pablo Ruiz Fabo[1,3], **Clara I. Martínez Cantón**[2,3], **Thierry Poibeau**[1] and
Elena González-Blanco[2,3]

[1]Laboratoire LATTICE. CNRS, ENS, U Paris 3, PSL Research U, USPC
92120 Montrouge, France
{pablo.ruiz.fabo,thierry.poibeau@ens.fr}

[2]Department of Spanish Literature and Literary Theory. UNED
28040 Madrid, Spain

[3]LINHD: Digital Humanities Innovation Lab. UNED
28040 Madrid, Spain
{cimartinez,egonzalezblanco@flog.uned.es}

Abstract

Enjambment takes place when a syntactic unit is broken up across two lines of poetry, giving rise to different stylistic effects. In Spanish literary studies, there are unclear points about the types of stylistic effects that can arise, and under which linguistic conditions. To systematically gather evidence about this, we developed a system to automatically identify enjambment (and its type) in Spanish. For evaluation, we manually annotated a reference corpus covering different periods. As a scholarly corpus to apply the tool, from public HTML sources we created a diachronic corpus covering four centuries of sonnets (3750 poems), and we analyzed the occurrence of enjambment across stanzaic boundaries in different periods. Besides, we found examples that highlight limitations in current definitions of enjambment.

1 Introduction

Enjambment takes place when a syntactic unit is broken up across two lines of poetry (Domínguez Caparrós, 1988, 103), giving rise to different stylistic effects (e.g. increased emphasis on elements of the broken-up phrase, or contrast between those elements), or creating double interpretations for the enjambed lines (García-Page Sánchez, 1991).

The literature shows a debate on the stylistic effects emerging from a mismatch between syntactic and metrical units (Martínez Cantón, 2011). The types of effects possible and the syntactic units where the effects can be said to be attested are a matter of current research. Quilis (1964) characterized enjambment as occurring in a series of very specific syntactic contexts. The definition is still considered current, however, some aspects in it have been questioned: Are these the only syntactic configurations where such effects are observed? Are syntactic criteria enough to predict when these effects arise?

Given these unclear points, it is relevant to systematically collect large amounts of enjambment examples, according to current definitions of the phenomenon. This can provide helpful evidence to assess scholars' claims. To this end, we developed a system to automatically detect enjambment in Spanish, applying it to a corpus of ca. 3750 sonnets by 1000 authors (15th to 19th century).

We are not aware of a systematic large-sample study of enjambment across periods, literary movements, or versification types in Spanish, or other languages. Automatic detection can help answer interesting questions in verse theory, which would benefit from a quantitative approach, complementing small-sample analyses, e.g.: "To what an extent is enjambment used differently in free verse vs. traditional versification?" or "Does the use of enjambment increase in movements that seek distance from traditional forms?"

Finally, our study complements automatic metrical analyses of Spanish Golden Age sonnets by

Joint SIGHUM Workshop on Computational Linguistics for Cultural Heritage, Social Sciences, Humanities and Literature.
Proceedings, pages 27–32, Vancouver, BC, August 4, 2017. ©2017 Association for Computational Linguistics

Navarro-Colorado (2016; 2017), by focusing on enjambment and covering a wider period.

The paper is structured thus: First we provide the definition of enjambment adopted. Then, our corpus and system are described, followed by an evaluation of the system's outputs. Finally, findings on enjambment in our diachronic sonnet corpus are discussed. Our project website provides details omitted here for space reasons.[1]

2   Enjambment in Spanish

Syntactic and metrical units often match in poetry. However, this trend has been broken since antiquity for various reasons (Parry (1929) on Homer, or Flores Gómez (1988) on early classical poetry).

Enjambment is considered to take place when a pause suggested by poetic form (e.g. at the end of a line or across hemistichs) occurs between strongly connected lexical or syntactic units, triggering an unnatural cut between those units.

Quilis (1964) carried out reading experiments, proposing that several strongly connected elements give rise to enjambment, should a poetic-form pause break them up:

1. **Lexical enjambment**: Breaking up a word.
2. **Phrase-bounded enjambment**: Within a phrase, breaking up sequences like *noun + adjective, noun + prepositional phrase complementing it, verb + adverb, auxiliary verb + main verb*, among others.
   For instance, the italicized words in the following lines by Matthew Arnold would be an enjambment, as a line-boundary intervenes between the noun *roar* and the prepositional phrase complementing it (*Of pebbles*): "Listen! you hear the grating *roar // Of pebbles* which the waves draw back, and fling, // At their return, up the high strand".
3. **Cross-clause enjambment**: Between a noun antecedent and the pronoun heading a defining relative clause that complements the antecedent (e.g. "*people // who* persevere may succeed").

Besides the enjambment types above, Spang (1983) noted that if a subject or direct object and their related verbs occur in two different lines of poetry, this can also feel unusual for a reader, even if the effect is less remarkable than in the environments identified by Quilis. To differentiate these cases from enjambment proper, Spang calls these cases *enlace*, translated here as ***expansion***.

The procedure in Quilis (1964, 55ff.) for assessing the strength of the cohesion within syntactic elements was as follows: Around 50 participants were asked to read literary prose excerpts. Syntactic units within which it was rare for participants to produce a pause were considered to be strongly cohesive (see the list above). The unnaturalness of producing a pause within these units was seen as contributing to an effect of mismatch between meter and syntax, should the units be interrupted by a metrical pause.

Quilis (1964) was the only author so far to gather reading-based experimental evidence on Spanish enjambment. His typology is still considered current, and was adopted by later authors, although complementary enjambment typologies have been proposed, as Martínez Cantón (2011) reviews. Our system identifies Quilis' types, in addition to Spang's expansion cases.

Above we listed Quilis' three broad types, but there are subtypes for each, equally annotated by our system; a detailed description and examples for each type and subtype is on our site.[2]

3   Diachronic Sonnet Corpus

The corpus is based on two public online collections (García González, 2006a,b). The first one covers 1088 sonnets by 477 authors from the 15th–17th centuries. The second one contains 2673 sonnets by 685 authors from the 19th century. We created scripts to download the poems, remove HTML and extract dates of birth and death for the authors. The corpus covers canonical as well as minor authors, inspired in distant reading approaches (Moretti, 2005, 2013). The distribution of sonnets and authors over periods is given on the project's site.[3]

3.1   System Description

The system has three components: a preprocessing module to format input poems uniformly, an NLP pipeline, and the enjambment-detection module itself.

We used the IXA Pipes library as the NLP pipeline (Agerri et al., 2014), obtaining part-of-speech tags, syntactic constituents and syntactic dependencies with it.

In the absence of data annotated for enjambment, that may allow applying a machine learning approach, we created a rule and dictionary-based system that exploits the information provided by the NLP pipeline. A total of ca. 30 rules identify enjambed lines, assigning them a type among a list of 11 types, based on the typology in section 2. Some of the rules are very shallow, only taking the part-of-speech sequences around a line boundary into account. Some other rules additionally exploit constituency information. Dependency parsing results are used to detect among other cases *subject/object/verb* relations, relevant for the *expansion* cases defined by Spang (see section 2). For any type of rule, custom dictionaries can restrict rule application to a set of terms. E.g. certain verbs govern arguments introduced by one specific preposition; we itemized these verbs and their prepositions in a dictionary, to complement information provided by the NLP pipeline or to correct parsing errors. The lists of verbs and prepositions were obtained from online resources on the descriptive grammar of Spanish.[4]

An example of a rule would be the following: If line n contains a verb v, and line $n + 1$ has a prepositional argument pa governed by v, and v is listed in the custom dictionary as accepting arguments introduced by pa's preposition, assign enjambment type *verb_cprep* to line-pair $\langle n, n + 1 \rangle$.

It is possible, but rare in or corpus, for more than one enjambment type to be applicable to a line-pair. At the moment, the system annotates only one type per line, following a fixed rule order. In the future, criteria to output and evaluate multiple types per line could be developed.

The rules are currently implemented as Python functions. Future work that could benefit non-programmer users would be to make the rules configurable rather than written directly in code.

Enjambment annotations are output in a stand-off format; the project's site provides details.[5]

[4]http://www.wikilengua.org/index.php/
Lista_de_complementos_de_régimen_A
[5]https://sites.google.
com/site/spanishenjambment/
annotation-and-result-format

4 Evaluation and Result Discussion

We describe the evaluation method (the reference sets, the task and metrics), and present the results along with a brief discussion of error sources. Comments about the relevance of the results for literary studies are provided in section 5.

4.1 Test Corpora

To evaluate the system, we created two reference-sets (*SonnetEvol* and *Cantos20th*), which were manually annotated for enjambment by a metrics professor and a linguist.

1. *SonnetEvol*: 100 sonnets (1400 lines) from our diachronic sonnet corpus of ca. 3750 sonnets. This test-set contains 260 pairs of enjambed lines.
2. *Cantos20th*: 1000 lines of 20th century poetry (Colinas, 1983), showing natural contemporary syntax. We identified 277 pairs of enjambed lines.

The SonnetEvol diachronic test-set covers all centuries, with ca. 70% of sonnets from the 15th–17th centuries and 30% from the 19th. The test-sets cover all enjambment types, but some types are infrequent in them, as in Spanish poetry overall.

We annotated the Cantos20th corpus in order to assess the system's performance on contemporary Spanish with natural diction, compared to its behaviour with the SonnetEvol corpus, which includes some archaic constructions and often shows an elevated register.

The distribution of enjambment types in both test-corpora is shown on Table 1. The enjambment types are described in detail, with examples, on our site[2]. The type labels generally stand for the constituents that take part in an enjambment, e.g. *noun_prep* and *adj_prep* mean, respectively, a noun or an adjective and the prepositional phrase complementing them.

To have an indication of the reliability of the annotation scheme, 50 sonnets of the SonnetEvol corpus were each tagged by two annotators. The ratio of matching labels across both annotators was 91.7%. Besides, a set of 120 sonnets (not from the test-sets) annotated by our students were later corrected by the professor; the ratio of matching labels was 89.7%. Getting several annotators' input on more sonnets, and obtaining inter-annotator agreement metrics (e.g. Artstein and Poesio (2008)) is part of our planned future work.

Corpus	SonnetEvol		Cantos20th	
Type	**Count**	**%**	**Count**	**%**
Phrase-Bounded	104	40.00	175	63.18
adj_adv	2	0.77	1	0.36
adj_noun	29	11.15	54	19.49
adj_prep	14	5.38	11	3.97
adv_prep	0	0	3	1.08
noun_prep	39	15.00	85	30.69
relword	1	0.38	2	0.72
verb_adv	5	1.92	7	2.53
verb_cprep	9	3.46	2	0.72
verb_chain	5	1.92	10	3.61
Cross-Clause	23	8.85	31	11.19
Expansions	133	51.15	71	25.63
dobj_verb	65	25.00	39	14.08
subj_verb	68	26.15	32	11.55
Total	260	100	277	100

Table 1: Distribution of enjambment types in both test corpora (the diachronic *SonnetEvol* and the contemporary *Cantos20th* corpus): Number and percentage of items.

Corpus	Match	N	P	R	F1
SonnetEvol	untyped	260	74.18	87.64	80.35
	typed		61.24	72.31	66.31
Cantos20th	untyped	277	84.01	89.17	86.51
	typed		78.04	83.39	80.63

Table 2: Overall enjambment detection results. Number of test-items (N), Precision, Recall, F1 in our two test-corpora, for the untyped and typed-match tasks.

4.2 Enjambment-detection Tasks Evaluated

We defined two enjambment-detection tasks: *untyped match* and *typed match*. In **untyped match**, the positions of enjambed lines proposed by the system must match the positions in the reference corpus for a correct result to be counted. In **typed match**, for a correct result, both the positions and the enjambment type assigned by the system to those positions must match the reference.

The untyped match task can be seen as an enjambment *recognition* task, and typed match corresponds to an enjambment *classification* task.

4.3 System Results and Discussion

Precision, recall and F1 were obtained. Table 2 provides overall results for both corpora. Table 3 provides the per-type results on the diachronic

Type	N	P	R	F1
Phrase-Bounded	104	66.19	88.46	75.72
adj_adv	2	100	50.00	66.67
adj_noun	29	54.55	82.76	65.75
adj_prep	14	58.82	71.43	64.52
noun_prep	39	55.36	79.49	65.26
relword	1	100	100	100
verb_adv	5	50.00	100	66.67
verb_cprep	9	83.33	55.56	66.67
verb_chain	5	100	80.00	88.89
Cross-Clause	23	76.00	82.61	79.17
Expansions	133	61.54	66.17	63.77
dobj_verb	65	60.00	69.23	64.29
subj_verb	68	63.24	63.24	63.24

Table 3: Enjambment detection results per type on the *SonnetEvol* corpus. Number of items per type (N), Precision, Recall, F1 on the *typed match* task.

test-corpus (SonnetEvol). The project's site shows more detailed results.[6] Lexical enjambment is not listed on the tables above, as no occurrences were found in the test corpora.

For untyped match, F1 reaches 80 points in the SonnetEvol corpus, whereas F1 for typed match is 66.31. For the contemporary Spanish corpus (Cantos20th), F1 is higher: 80.63 typed match, and 86.51 untyped match. This reflects additional difficulties posed by archaic language and historical varieties for the NLP system whose outputs our enjambment detection relies on.

A common source of error was hyperbaton: the displacement of phrases triggers constituency and dependency parsing errors. Prepositional phrase (PP) attachment also posed challenges: Verbal adjuncts get mistaken for PPs complementing nouns or adjectives.[7] Creating a reparsing module to manage hyperbaton and improve PP attachment results may be fruitful future work.

Further interesting future work would be a detailed analysis of error sources. This would help determine the extent to which errors are due to the enjambment detection rules in themselves or to the NLP pipeline. In the second case, it would be useful to know the extent to which POS-tagging

---

[6] `https://sites.google.com/site/ spanishenjambment/evaluation`

[7] PP attachment is a difficulty even in current languages (e.g. Agirre et al. (2008) for English). For historical varieties, Stein's (2016) results for verbal adjuncts and prepositional complements in Old French also suggest this difficulty.

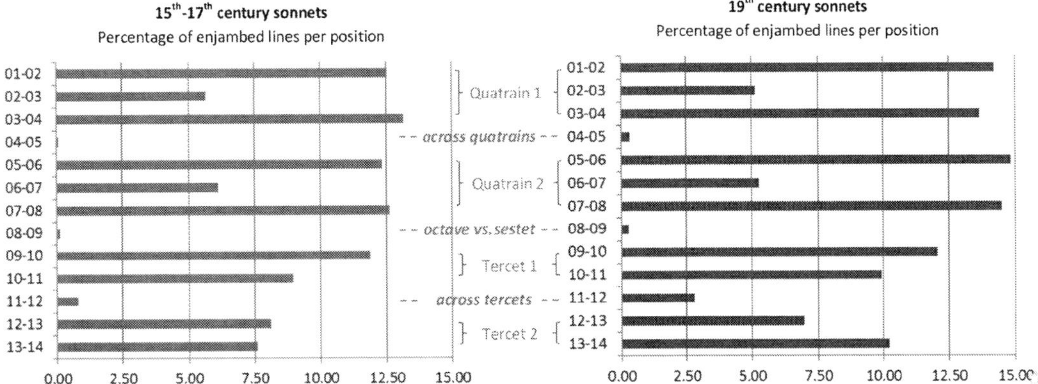

Figure 1: Percentage of enjambments per position in the 15th–17th centuries vs. the 19th. The y-axis represents line-positions; the x-axis is the percentage of enjambed line-pairs for a position over all enjambed line-pairs in the period. Enjambment across quatrains and across the octave-sestet divide is very rare, with a small increase in the 19th century. The division between the tercets blurs in the 19th century, in the sense that enjambment across them is clearly higher than in the previous period.

or parsing errors are due to archaic features and complex diction in some of the earlier sonnets in the corpus. The earlier varieties of Spanish covered in the corpus have a large lexical and syntactic overlap with contemporary Spanish, which justified applying NLP models for current Spanish to the entire corpus (besides the fact that we are not aware of NLP tools for 15th–17th century Spanish). However, it would be relevant to quantify error sources per period.

5 Relevance for Literary Studies

The system's goal is detecting enjambment to help literary research on the phenomenon, via providing systematic evidence for its analysis. For instance, in our result validation, we find that the system annotates line-pairs that formally fit the description of an enjambment context (see section 2), but that we'd actually consider unlikely to yield a stylistic effect. Conversely, our annotators are sometimes surprised that line-pairs where they perceive an unnatural mismatch between syntactic and line-boundaries are not captured by our typology and left unannotated by the system.

Regarding the system's potential for quantitative analyses, we consider our untyped detection results helpful, given an F1 of ca. 80 points on the diachronic test-set. As an example application, we examined the distribution of enjambment according to position in the poem, particularly in positions across a verse-boundary (lines 4–5, 8–9 and 11–12). Comparing the results for the 15th-to-

17th centuries vs. the 19th century (Figure 1), we see that enjambment across the tercets increases clearly in the 19th century, with a small increase of enjambment across the quatrains (lines 4–5) and across the octave-sestet divide (lines 8–9). Performing such analyses on a large corpus opens the door for scholars to assess the literary relevance of the findings, and search for the best interpretation.

6 Outlook

With automatic enjambment detection, our goal is to help gather systematic large scale evidence to study the complex phenomenon of enjambment, which poses challenges for metrical and stylistic theory to characterize, and for critical practice to apply. Our metrics students have so far manually annotated enjambment for 400 sonnets; their work will permit computing inter-annotator agreement, and performing new tests of the automatic system. As our manually annotated corpus grows, we will examine the possibility of using supervised machine learning to train a sequence labeling and classification model to complement our current rules. A specific goal is improving enjambment type detection for the typed match task.

Acknowledgments

Pablo Ruiz Fabo was supported by a PhD scholarship from Région Île-de-France. The research was also supported by Starting Grant ERC-2015-STG-679528 POSTDATA. We are grateful to the anonymous reviewers for their valuable comments.

References

Rodrigo Agerri, Josu Bermudez, and German Rigau. 2014. IXA pipeline: Efficient and Ready to Use Multilingual NLP tools. In *Proceedings of LREC 2014, the 9th International Language Resources and Evaluation Conference*. Reykjavik,Iceland, volume 2014, pages 3823–3828. http://www.lrec-conf.org/proceedings/lrec2014/pdf/775_Paper.pdf.

Eneko Agirre, Timothy Baldwin, and David Martinez. 2008. Improving Parsing and PP Attachment Performance with Sense Information. In *Proceedings of ACL 2008, Conference of the Association for Computational Linguistics*. Citeseer, Colombus, Ohio, US, pages 317–325. http://www.anthology.aclweb.org/P/P08/P08-1.pdfpage=361.

Ron Artstein and Massimo Poesio. 2008. Intercoder agreement for computational linguistics. *Computational Linguistics* 34(4):555–596. www.mitpressjournals.org/doi/abs/10.1162/coli.07-034-R2.

Antonio Colinas. 1983. *Noche más allá de la noche. [Night beyond Night]*. Visor, Madrid.

José Domínguez Caparrós. 1988. *Métrica y poética, bases para la fundamentación de la métrica en la teoría literaria moderna. [Metrics and Poetics: Grounding Metrics in Modern Literary Theory]*. Universidad Nacional de Educación a Distancia.

María Esperanza Flores Gómez. 1988. Coincidencia y distorsión (encabalgamiento) de la unidad rítmica verso y las unidades sintácticas. [Coincidence and distortion (enjambment) between the line as a rhythmic unit and syntactic units]. *Estudios clásicos* 30(94):23–42.

Ramón García González, editor. 2006a. *Sonetos del siglo XV al XVII. [Sonnets of the 15th to 17th Centuries]*. Biblioteca Virtual Miguel de Cervantes, Alicante. http://www.cervantesvirtual.com/obra/sonetos-del-siglo-xv-al-xvii–0/.

Ramón García González, editor. 2006b. *Sonetos del siglo XIX. [Sonnets of the 19th Century]*. Biblioteca Virtual Miguel de Cervantes, Alicante. http://www.cervantesvirtual.com/obra/sonetos-del-siglo-xix–0/.

Mario García-Page Sánchez. 1991. En torno al encabalgamiento: Pausa virtual y duplicidad de lecturas. [About enjambment: Virtual pause and multiple readings]. *Revista de literatura* 53(106):595–618.

Clara Isabel Martínez Cantón. 2011. *Métrica y poética de Antonio Colinas. [Metrics and Poetics of Antonio Colinas]*. Padilla Libros Editores & Libreros, Sevilla, Spain.

Franco Moretti. 2005. *Graphs, Maps, Trees: Abstract Models for a Literary History*. Verso.

Franco Moretti. 2013. *Distant Reading*. Verso Books, London & New York.

Borja Navarro-Colorado. 2017. A metrical scansion system for fixed-metre Spanish poetry. *Digital Scholarship in the Humanities* https://doi.org/10.1093/llc/fqx009.

Borja Navarro-Colorado, María Ribes Lafoz, and Noelia Sánchez. 2016. Metrical Annotation of a Large Corpus of Spanish Sonnets: Representation, Scansion and Evaluation. In *Proceedings of the Tenth International Conference on Language Resources and Evaluation, Portoroz, Slovenia*. Portorož, Slovenia, pages 4630–4634. http://www.lrec-conf.org/proceedings/lrec2016/pdf/453_Paper.pdf.

Milman Parry. 1929. The distinctive character of enjambement in Homeric verse. In *Transactions and Proceedings of the American Philological Association*. JSTOR, volume 60, pages 200–220. http://www.jstor.org/stable/282817.

Antonio Quilis. 1964. *Estructura del encabalgamiento en la métrica española. [The Structure of Enjambement in Spanish Metrics]*. Consejo Superior de Investigaciones Científicas, patronato Menéndez y Pelayo, Instituto Miguel de Cervantes.

Kurt Spang. 1983. *Ritmo y versificación: teoría y práctica del análisis métrico y rítmico. [Rhythm and Versification: Theory and Practice of Metrical and Rhythmic Analysis]*. Universidad de Murcia, Murcia.

Achim Stein. 2016. Old French dependency parsing: Results of two parsers analyzed from a linguistic point of view. In *Proceedings of LREC the 11th International Language Resources and Evaluation Conference*. Portorož, Slovenia, pages 707–713. http://www.lrec-conf.org/proceedings/lrec2016/pdf/829_Paper.pdf.

Plotting Markson's "Mistress"

Conor Kelleher
School of Computer Science
University College Dublin
Dublin, Ireland
conor.kelleher.1@ucdconnect.ie

Mark T. Keane
Insight Data Analytics Centre
University College Dublin
Dublin, Ireland
mark.keane@ucd.ie

Abstract

The post-modern novel "Wittgenstein's Mistress" by David Markson (1988) presents the reader with a very challenging non-linear narrative, that itself appears to one of the novel's themes. We present a distant reading of this work designed to complement a close reading of it by David Foster Wallace (1990). Using a combination of text analysis, entity recognition and networks, we plot repetitive structures in the novel's narrative relating them to its critical analysis.

1 Introduction

Certain novels not only cry out for critical interpretations but actually try to direct them.
(Wallace, 1990, p. 244)

In recent years, a considerable body of research has contrasted the close reading of traditional literary criticism with distant readings based on text and network analytics (e.g., Jänicke et al., 2015; Moretti, 2005, 2013; Serlen, 2010). In this paper, we take the ecumenical position that distant readings can surface unappreciated patterns in a literary work to support close readings (c.f., Coles et al., 2014; Jänicke et al., 2015). For instance, a number of distant readings have supported close readings by providing abstractions showing the social networks of characters involved in a literary work (Agarwal et al., 2012; Grayson et al., 2016; Elson et al., 2010). The present work has, in part, been inspired by these distant readings, thought it explores phrase repetition and association networks. Specifically, we analyse the structure of repetitions in the post-modern novel "Wittgenstein's Mistress" (1988) by the American author, David Markson to support a close reading of the novel by David Foster Wallace (1990).

1.1 Close Reading "Wittgenstein's Mistress"

David Markson's (1988) novel "Wittgenstein's Mistress" (WM) is renowned for it use of an experimental, non-linear narrative structure. The novel deals with the thoughts of a woman – simply known as Kate – who appears to be the last living person on earth. The narrative captures the streamed consciousness of her thoughts about art, her travels though her empty world, and her reflections on the imprecision of language. The novel has no chapters but consists of almost 4,000 short paragraphs many of which are single sentences, exemplified by following excerpt:

> *Gaetano Donizetti being still another person whom I otherwise might have mixed up with Vincenzo Bellini. Or with Gentile Bellini, who was also Andrea Mantegna's brother-in-law, being Giovanni Bellini's brother.*
>
> *Well I did mix him up. With Luigi Cherubini.*
>
> *Music is not my trade.*
>
> *Although Maria Callas singing in that particular scene has always sent shivers up and down my spine.*
>
> *When Van Gogh was mad, he actually once tried to eat his pigments.*
>
> *Well, and Maupassant, eating something much more dreadful than that, poor soul.*
>
> *The list becomes distressingly longer.*

(Markson, 1988, p. 111)

One major feature of the narrative is Kate's repetitive turn of thought. Regularly, phrases and paragraphs are repeated throughout the novel, or the same entities, people and places are mentioned over and over again. To the reader the narrative often seems like a long piece of classical music where various motifs and themes are repeated and returned to at definite intervals; but, this structure is almost impossible to grasp because the "musical phrases" are "word phrases", repetitions of named people (e.g., Maupassant), places (e.g., Rome) and turns-of-phrase (e.g., 'so

Joint SIGHUM Workshop on Computational Linguistics for Cultural Heritage, Social Sciences, Humanities and Literature.
Proceedings, pages 33–39, Vancouver, BC, August 4, 2017. ©2017 Association for Computational Linguistics

to speak'). Understanding this repetitive stream of consciousness and its significance is perhaps one of the main critical challenges of the novel. In his critical commentary, David Foster Wallace (1990) says:

> *You could call this technique 'deep nonsense', meaning I guess a linguistic flow of strings, strands, loops and quiffs that through the very manner of its formal construction flouts the ordinary cingula of 'sense' and through its defiance of sense's limits manages somehow to 'show' what cannot ordinarily be 'expressed'.*
>
> (Wallace, 1990, p. 248)

One way to think about the current distant reading is that it is an attempt to surface the "formal construction" of WM, to better understand its message.

A second major feature of the novel is it concern with language itself, or rather many of the concerns raised by Wittgenstein in his early and late philosophy of language. Wallace argues that the book could be viewed as "a weird cerebral *roman a clef*" that attempts to dramatise "the very bleak mathematical world (of) Wittgenstein's *Tractus*"; that it tries to show what it would like "if somebody really had to live in a *Tractatus*ized world" (Wallace p. 246). In particular, Wallace points to the atomistic, independence of words and what they refer to, in this world, quoting Wittgenstein:

> *The world is everything that is the case; the world is nothing but a huge mass of data, of logically discrete facts that have no* intrinsic *connection to one another. Cf the* Tractus *1.2: 'The world falls apart into facts...' 1.2.1"* 'Any one fact can be either the case, or not the case, and everything else remains the same'.
>
> (Wallace, 1990, p. 254)

Faced with this world where there is no connection between 'facts', Wallace points out "that Kate's textual obsession is simply to find connections between things, any strands to bind the historical facts & empirical data that are all her world comprises" (pp. 254-255).

It is clear that a close reading of WM presents real challenges for anyone attempting to understand its structure. Hence, in this paper, have attempted a distant reading using text analytic techniques to surface the novel's repetition-structures to support Wallace's critical analysis.

2 Analysing Markson's Mistress

We believed that the key to the narrative structure of *Wittgenstein's Mistress* lies in surfacing the repetitive aspects of the narrative, taking the novel's short paragraphs as a sort of "fundamental unit of analysis". Hence, we progressively analysed the text in four distinct ways to surface these repeating structures, exploring:

* *Repeated Phrases*: generating all n-grams of differential lengths from (2-32) we identified repeating unique, maximal strings of characters in the text (aka repeated phrases)
* *Named Entities*: taking these maximal n-gram strings, we extracted all the entities mentioned in them, as the narrative often relies heavily on repeated references to people, places and things
* *Networks of Association*: we then used these named entities to build associative networks, on basis of how "close" they were to one another in these repeating text-fragments (see our definitions of "close" in later section)
* *Sequences of Repetitions*: finally, we examined whether these networks (clumps of associated entities) occurred in definite sequences; that is, was there a definite tendency for one cluster to follow another in patterned sequences, to determine whether we could sketch the "DNA of the novel"

In the following subsections, we elaborate the specific methods used to perform these different analyses and what we discovered using them.

2.1 Finding Repeated Phrases

Intuitively, reading WM one has a strong sense that certain phases are consistently re-used throughout the text. However, is very hard to get a sense of the scale of this repetition or, indeed, its structure without resorting to text analytic methods. So, to capture the extent of the repetition we performed an analysis of the novel's repeated phrases.

We transformed a PDF of the novel into a plain text file retaining its punctuation and paragraph boundaries. The novel has 3,804 paragraphs, 4,352 sentences and a total of 81,970 words, referring to approximately 3,058 named entities (*people, places, organisations, etc.*) of which 462 are unique, named entities. Treating this text as a long string of words, we used different-sized, n-gram windows and slid them over the text to find repeated phrases (using the NLTK tokenisation packages and our own n-gram program). Using this method all possible n-grams were computed from 2-grams up to 32-grams halting the search when no further repetition was found in the n-gram set. As we looped through n-grams of different window sizes, we retained repeated n-grams and discarded any that only occurred once. Furthermore, across n-gram sets of different sizes we discarded n-grams that had word-sequences that were subsets of longer n-grams, so we ended up with a list of all the unique, maximally-sized n-grams that had been repeated at least two times or more in the novel.

N-gram	N
Was it really some other person I was so anxious to discover when I did all of that looking or was it only my own solitude that I could not abide ?	32
Although doubtless when I say they are half empty I should really be saying they are half filled since presumably they were totally empty before somebody half filled them	29
Still I find it extraordinary that young men died there in a war that long ago and then died in the same place three thousand years after that	28
Even if a part I have always liked is when Orestes finally comes back after so many years and Electra does not recognize her own brother	26
Then again it is not impossible that they were once filled completely becoming half empty only when somebody removed half of the books to the basement	25

Table 1: Top-5 Longest Repeated N-grams

In our n-gram search upto 32-grams, we identified a large number of unique, maximal n-grams; there were 4,503 phrases, different-sized n-grams that were repeated at least twice in the text (see Tables 1 and 2).

Table 1 shows the top-5 n-grams by length found in the text (i.e., number of words they contain), each of which only occurred twice in the novel. Table 2 shows the top-10 most frequently repeating n-grams found in the text. Notably, the most frequent maximal n-grams are typically quite short.

This analysis gives us a first sense of the extent of the repetition in the text, indicating that this repetition is being deployed systematically to achieve some narrative effect. Indeed, of the 3,804 paragraphs in the novel, 3,323 contain at least one or more maximal n-gram with >3 words. In the next sub-section, we get a sense of the systematicity that may lie in this repetition by identifying the named entities involved in these repeated sequences.

N-gram	N
now that I think about it	8
There would appear to be no	7
doubtless I would not have	7
Even if I have no	7
When one comes right down to it	6
But be that as it may	6
As a matter of fact the	6
As a matter of fact what	6
And to tell the truth I	6
God the things men used to do	5

Table 2: Top-10 Frequently Repeated N-grams

2.2 Identifying Named Entities

To further analyse the repeated text fragments found in the n-gram analysis, we used the NLTK's Stanford Named Entity Recogniser (NER) package to find all the named entities mentioned in the set of maximal n-grams; though we needed to manually extend its functionality to remove incorrect identifications and to add missing entities (to deal with problems like "William de Kooning" and "de Kooning" being treated as separate entities). The full text yielded 462 unique entities (from 3,804 paragraphs) and when we searched our maximal n-gram set, we found that 117 of these entities were mentioned in the paragraphs containing repeated phrases (341 paragraphs). We used this set of entities as a basis for examining the repetitions of people, places and things in networks of association.

2.3 Networks of Association

To get a real sense of the structure of the repetition we constructed networks of association between the 314 unique named entities that were mentioned in our n-gram text-fragments. We build two different networks based on different measures of association (for other possibilities see Grayson et al., 2016). First, we build networks for entities that were *associated by virtue of being mentioned in the same paragaph* (see Figures 1-5). Second, we build networks for entities that were *associated by virtue of being mentioned in the same and/or the immediately following paragraph* (see Figure 6). These networks revealed that there are definite and distinct repetitive-structures of association in the novel.

For example, Figure 2 shows one of the smaller networks – which we call the Homeric Network --- showing associations between a variety of Greek-related entities, reflecting references to Homer (e.g., Illiad, Sirens, Odysseus). Note, that the thickness of the link in this network indicates the frequency with which these two entities were repeatedly associated within the paragraphs of the novel. So, for instance, the link between Achilles and Odysseus is thicker because they are mentioned together in paragraphs several times.

Performing this type of analysis we found five disjoint networks of different sizes between other named entities that we have titled after their dominant associations: (i) Paris Network (Figure 1), (ii) Homeric Network (Figure 2), the Rome Network (Figure 3), (ii) the Spanish Network (Figure 4), (iii) the Gallery Network (Figure 5).

These five networks show Kate's swirling, repetitive thoughts about these entities when we define the association very tightly (i.e., same paragraph mentions). They show a considerable amount of local coherence. However, if we widen the definition of "association" to one-paragraph further out, we find that all of these networks become inter-connected. Figure 6 shows the swirling complexity of the associations between all of the named entities as the more local networks get connected together. Note, again, that the width of the links in this network indicates repeated associations.

This wider definition of association shows that that the original in-paragraph networks are reinforced and expanded with new entities; though they still retain their identity as distinct networks. Figure 6 also shows that there are hub-like entities (e.g., Dylan Thomas, Nightwatch, La Mancha) that play a role in cross-connecting the in-paragraph networks; perhaps indicating that these entities are pivotal in Kate's thinking (n.b., Markson claimed Dylan Thomas as a major influence). Such hubs could be further elucidated by a pagerank analysis.

3   What Does it All Mean?

We began this paper by proposing that Wallace's close reading of WM could be complemented by a distant reading of the novel. We have shown that a text analytic and network analysis of the repeated mentions of people, places and things in the novel can reveal some definite structures. But, what does it all mean?

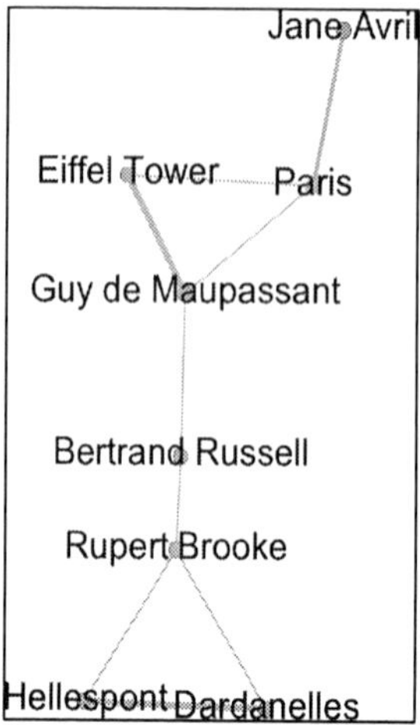

Figure 1: The Paris Network

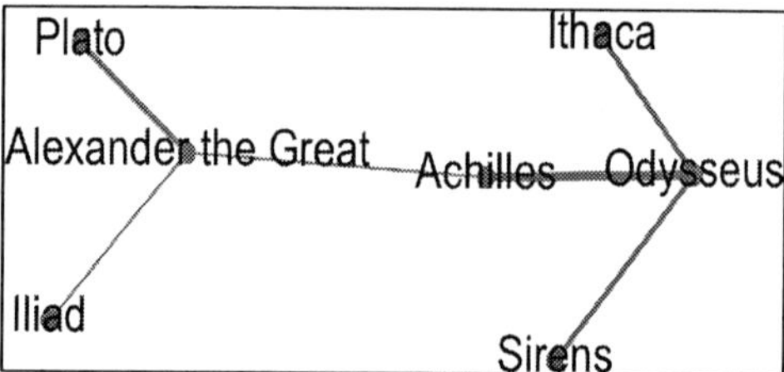

Figure 2: The Homeric Network

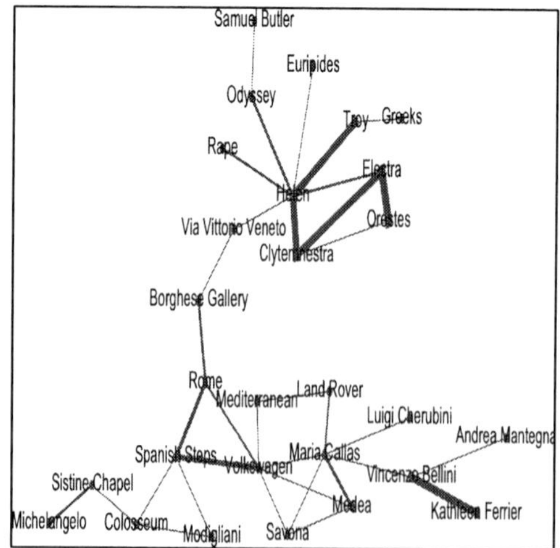

Figure 3: The Rome Network

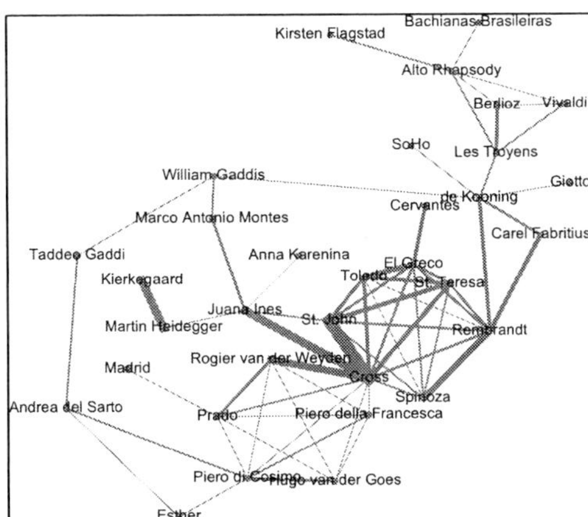

Figure 4: The Spanish Network

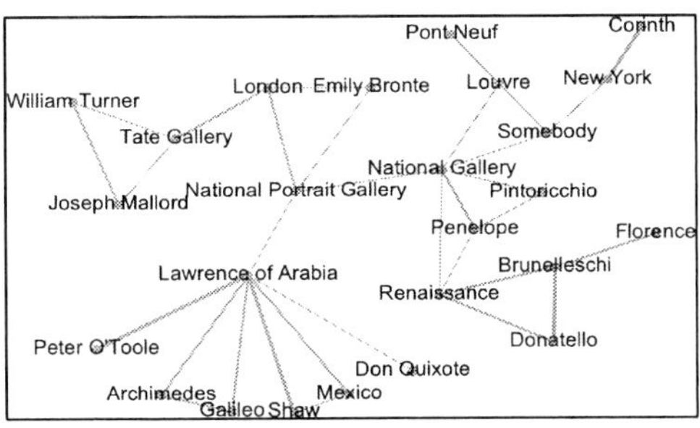

Figure 5: The Gallery Network

Wallace's (1990) contention was that the repetition in WM reflects Kate's response to a *Tractus*ized world; that she is endeavouring to connect things to establish a meaning that is absent. Our distant reading shows the obsessive persistence with which Kate pursues this attempt to connect; she appears to run over the same path of association again and again, hoping it becomes reinforced so that it persists as something "real". This analysis is consistent with one of Wallace's claims about Kate's predicament:

...that Kate's textual obsession is simply to find connections between things, any strands to bind the historical facts & empirical data that are all her world comprises. And always – necessarily – genuine connections elude her. All she can find is an occasional synchronicity: the fact that certain names are similar enough to be richly confusing -- William Gaddis and Taddeo Gaddi – or that certain lives & events happened to overlap in space & time. And these very thin connections turn out not to be 'real', features only of her imagination;

(Wallace, 1990, pp. 254-255)

If one examines the five disjoint networks (Figures 1-5) one notable feature of them is how they are all only *partly-thematic*, as their themes are often upset by outliers. For instance, the Homeric network (Figure 2) has mostly Homeric entities, but then Alexander the Great and Plato are thrown in (people associated by place and race but not part of the Homeric tales). Similarly, the Spanish network (Figure 4) has a lot of Spanish-related nodes (e.g., Madrid, El Greco, Prada) but then it veers into outlier sub-networks involving European philosophers and American writers. These structures confirm Wallace's proposition that Kate's networks of repetition ultimately lack real coherence and meaning, beyond that which she tries to impose by obsessive repetition. In this way, we see this network analysis as providing a highly complementary reading to that of Wallace.

4   The DNA of a Novel

There is one outstanding question that is invited by the current analysis, though we do not have a complete answer to it. Namely, are there definite sequences in the references made to different networks in the novel? That is, is there a tendency for a reference to one network to follow the reference to another, defining a type of higher-level DNA for the novel?

Figure 7 shows the paragraphs of the novel numbered from 1-3804 with each paragraph coloured on the basis of whether it refers to the Homeric (pink, Figure 2) or Rome Networks (blue, Figure 3). It shows a number of interesting properties: (i) these two networks dominate large parts of the novel, even though they are not the largest of the five found, (ii) there are definite sections of the novel where they dominate or fail to be referenced (i.e., the blank, white strips), (iii) references to them form definite banded sequences. To verify the latter point we analysed the frequency of these two networks in sequences of different lengths. Table 3 shows that they tend to commonly follow one another, sometimes in quite long sequences.

Overall, this shows that there are higher levels of repetitive structure that could yield other insights about repetition in WM. Indeed, it may well be that the novel has definite higher-level structure (yet to be found) that could constitute the "DNA of the novel" (see Figure 8).

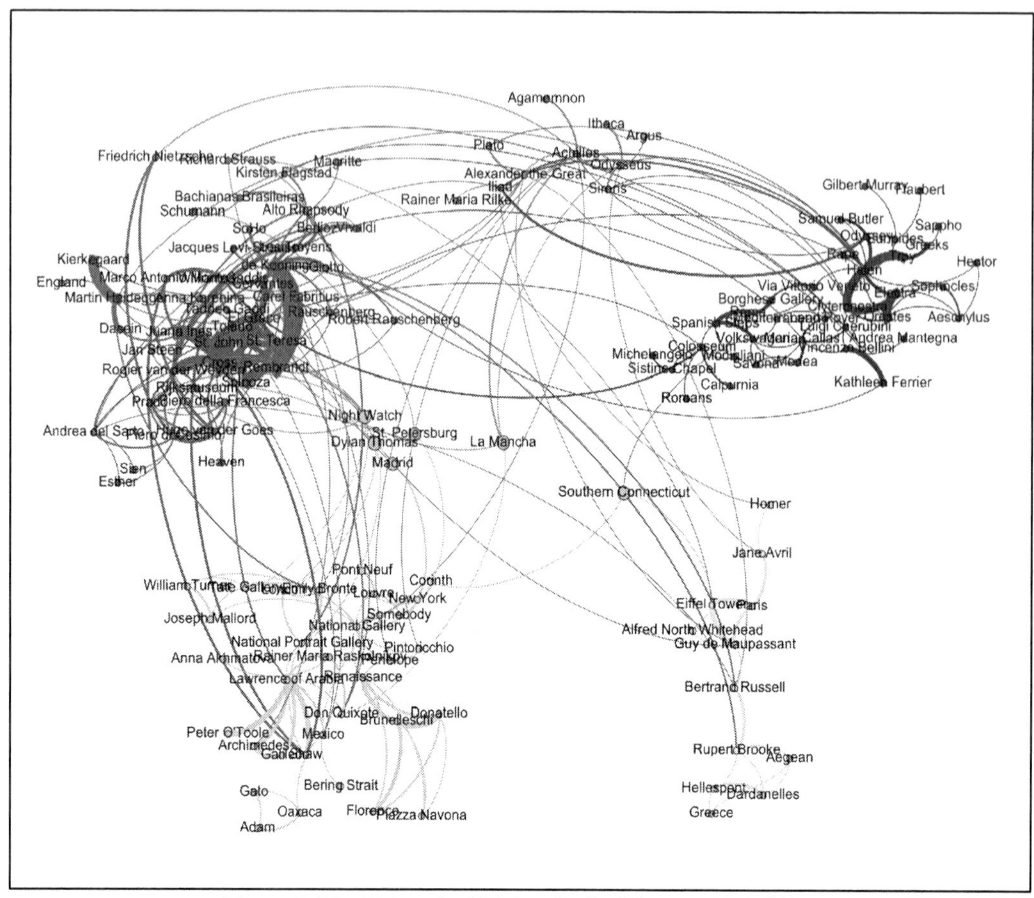

Figure 6. The Network of Networks in *Wittgenstein's Mistress*

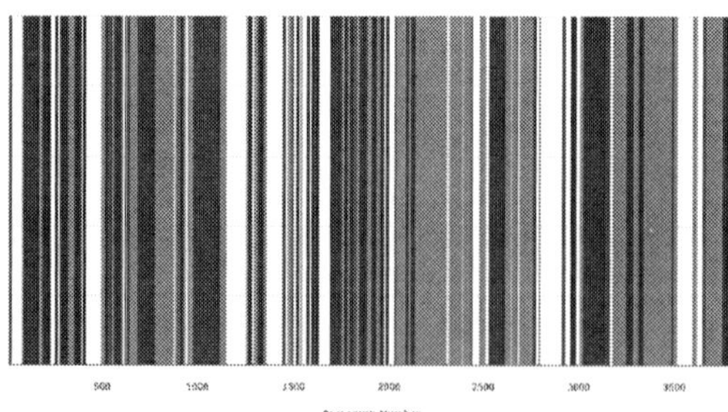

Figure 7: Paragraphs Where the Homeric (pink) and Rome Networks (blue) Are Referenced

5 Conclusion

In this paper, we have considered the use of data analytics techniques to provide a distant reading of David Markson's novel "Wittgenstein's Mistress". We have tried to address the role of repetition in the novel and to pursue evidence for proposals made by David Foster Wallace in his close reading of the text. In the round, specifically supporting patterns have been found in our analysis. Obviously, more could be done, in particular perhaps around the exploration of the repeating references to networks we have found; in this respect we are currently examining techniques in time-series analysis and sequence induction with this question in mind.

This analysis also invites comparative treatments of such associative references in other works that (i) are equally concise at the paragraph-level but which lack explicit repetition (e.g., Hemingway) or (ii) aim for similar stream-of-consciousness effects (e.g., Joyce). Such analyses could reveal new insights into repeated, associative referencing in diverse literary works.

Acknowledgements

This research was an undergraduate final-year project by the first author, supervised by the second author, and was supported by Science Foundation Ireland (SFI) under Grant Number SFI/12/RC/2289.

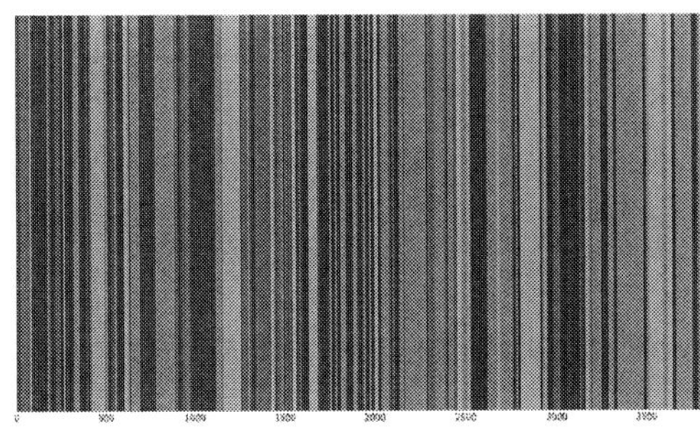

Figure 8: Paragraphs Referencing Networks:
(i) Paris (cyan), (ii) Homeric (pink), (iii) Rome
(blue), (iv) Spanish (red), (v) Gallery (green)

<3,2>	39
<2,3>	35
<2,3,2>	24
<3,2,3>	21
<2,3,2,3>	15
<3,2,3,2>	14
<2,3,2,3,2>	11
<3,2,3,2,3>	10
<2,3,2,3,2,3>	8
<3,2,3,2,3,2>	9
<2,3,2,3,2,3,2>	7
<3,2,3,2,3,2,3>	6
<2,3,2,3,2,3,2,3>	4
<3,2,3,2,3,2,3,2>	5
<2,3,2,3,2,3,2,3,2,3>	2
<3,2,3,2,3,2,3,2,3,2>	2

Table 3: Frequencies of Paragraph Sequences
Referencing Homeric (2) & Rome Networks (3)

Reference

Agarwal Apoorv, Augusto Corvalan, Jacob Jensen, and Owen Rambow. 2012, June. Social network analysis of Alice in Wonderland. In *Workshop on Computational Linguistics for Literature*, pp. 88-96. 2012.

Coles Katharine, Meyer Miriah, Lein Julie Gonnering, McCurdy, Nina. 2014. Empowering Play, Experimenting with Poems: Disciplinary Values and Visualization Development. *Proceedings of the Digital Humanities, 2014.*

Elson David, Nicholas Dames, and Kathleen R. McKeown. 2010, July. Extracting social networks from literary fiction. In *Proceedings of the 48th annual meeting of the association for computational linguistics* (pp. 138-147). Association for Computational Linguistics.

Grayson Siobhan, Wade Karen, Meaney Gerardine. and Greene Derek. 2016. May, The sense and sensibility of different sliding windows in constructing co-occurrence networks from literature. In *Computational History and Data-Driven Humanities: 2nd IFIP WG 12.7 International Workshop, Dublin, Ireland,* (pp. 65-77). Springer International Publishing.

Grayson, Siobhan, Wade, Karen, Meaney Gerardine, Rothwell Jennie, Mulvany Maria, and Greene Derek. 2016, May. Discovering structure in social networks of 19th century fiction. In *8th ACM Conference on Web Science* (pp. 325-326). ACM.

Jänicke, Stefan, Greta Franzini, Muhammad Faisal Cheema, and Gerik Scheuermann. 2015. On close and distant reading in digital humanities: A survey and future challenges. *Proc. of EuroVis—STARs*, pp.83-103.

Markson, David. 1988. *Wittgenstein's mistress.* Dalkey Archive Press. (Reproduced 1995 with afterword containing Wallace, 1990).

Moretti, Franco. 2005. *Graphs, maps, trees: Abstract models for a literary history.* Verso Books.

Moretti, Franco. 2013. *Distant reading.* Verso Books.

Serlen, Rachel. 2010. The distant future? *Literature Compass*, 7(3), pp.214-225.

Wallace David Foster. 1990. The empty plenum: David Markson's "Wittgenstein's Mistress". *Review of Contemporary Fiction, 10*(2), p.219 (Reproduced as an afterword in 1995 printing of Markson, 1988).

Annotation Challenges for Reconstructing the Structural Elaboration of Middle Low German

Nina Seemann
Michaela Geierhos
Paderborn University
Heinz Nixdorf Institute

Marie-Luis Merten
Doris Tophinke
Paderborn University
Department of German Linguistics
and Comparative Literature

Eyke Hüllermeier

Paderborn University
Department of
Computer Science

`seemann@hni.upb.de`   `mlmerten@mail.upb.de`   `eyke@upb.de`
`geierhos@hni.upb.de`   `doris.tophinke@upb.de`

Abstract

In this paper, we present the annotation challenges we have encountered when working on a historical language that was undergoing elaboration processes. We especially focus on syntactic ambiguity and gradience in Middle Low German, which causes uncertainty to some extent. Since current annotation tools consider construction contexts and the dynamics of the grammaticalization only partially, we plan to extend CorA – a web-based annotation tool for historical and other non-standard language data – to capture elaboration phenomena and annotator unsureness. Moreover, we seek to interactively learn morphological as well as syntactic annotations.

1 Tracing Elaboration Processes

Language elaboration is a continuous development. According to Traugott and Trousdale (2013), it involves processes that change existing constructions with respect to formal or semantic aspects *(constructional change)* and processes in which new constructions emerge *(constructionalization)*. To distinguish between these processes and to be able to describe their dynamics, one needs a sophisticated inventory of descriptive categories. Those categories should capture formal and/or semantic micro-changes as well as ambiguity and vagueness. Assuming that constructions are "holistically" determined by interacting formal and semantic/functional characteristics, a single characteristic is always judged by its construction binding, i.e. in cooccurrence with other characteristics. Capturing (diachronic) semantic changes of constructions that are formally (yet) hardly visible or – vice versa – to recognize that formal characteristics have not (yet) the grammatical function that they will acquire in later language stages is only possible in a given context.

1.1 Related Annotation Work and Tools

Over the last years, historical texts gained a lot of interest from both computational and corpus linguistics. Due to the graphematic and grammatical variability, those texts are interesting and analytically challenging (Dipper et al., 2013b; Bollmann et al., 2014). Accordingly, many works emerged that deal with the annotation of historical texts. For German, Dipper et al. (2013a) introduced a tag set for historical language levels (called HiTS). Multiple projects developed different reference corpora for historical language levels that were annotated with or in analogy with HiTS. Recently, a reference corpus Middle Low German/Low Rhenish (1200–1650) was compiled in a collaboration between the German universities of Hamburg and Münster. Additionally, annotation tools ANNIS (Zeldes et al., 2009) and CorA (Bollmann et al., 2014) were introduced. In the context of literature studies, the heureCLÉA project used CATMA (Meister et al., 2017) to annotate their data in correspondence with strict annotation guidelines that cover aspects of uncertainty/ambiguity (Gius and Jacke, 2016).

1.2 Problem Definition

However, current annotation tools consider construction contexts and the dynamics of the grammaticalization only partially. Although these problems are well known (Dipper et al., 2013a; Bollmann et al., 2014), satisfying solutions are

Joint SIGHUM Workshop on Computational Linguistics for Cultural Heritage, Social Sciences, Humanities and Literature.
Proceedings, pages 40–45, Vancouver, BC, August 4, 2017. ©2017 Association for Computational Linguistics

still missing. For our purposes, an annotation tool should provide the following features/labels:

- *Part-of-speech (POS) tag ambiguity*: If a human annotator cannot clearly indicate which POS tag can be assigned on morphological or syntactic level, there must be an option to annotate which one is more likely. However, the annotator should not be forced to disambiguate – several (prioritized) interpretations should be allowed.

- *Syntactic gradience* (Aarts, 2007): Even in case of syntactic constructions, the above-mentioned grammatical indeterminacy will occur for construction tags.

- *Individual annotation order:* Instead of using the common text analysis pipeline with a strict order, where first POS tags and then constructions tags are assigned, our tool supports the cognitive annotation process. In some contexts, it is easier for annotators to start with (local) syntactic segmentation before POS tags can be disambiguated within its corresponding construction borders.

- *Annotator support*: We provide auto-suggestions (i.e. POS and/or construction tags and their corresponding uncertainty values stating a certain annotator unsureness) for unlabeled corpus data based on an interactive machine learning approach.

- *Annotator unsureness*: We need to express if human annotators are (un)sure about their annotation decision. In case of unsureness, we need additional comments which explain their incapability to make a clear decision.

We settled on the aforementioned features within our interdisciplinary group, especially valuing the expertise in Middle Low German from the group's linguists. In order to significantly reconstruct the temporal and spatial dynamics of elaboration processes, it is essential to analyze bigger corpora. Methodologically, it is not possible to do that on the basis of single occurrences. Moreover, on the basis of statistically significant evidence provided by our tool, the difference between the construction change and the emergence of new constructions can be detected much easier. To face the above-mentioned features, we will extend CorA (Bollmann et al., 2014) instead of starting from scratch.

1.3 Scope of Study

Although there are some annotation tools dealing with historical German, they do not perfectly fit our purposes. For one, it is clear that we are dealing with highly ambiguous data (due to the language shift) and this can result in uncertainty. Next, having a large corpus means a lot of manual annotation. As this is very time intensive work, we want to develop a parser that learns over time to suggest possible annotations for each token and even constituents. Finally, as language elaboration involves the change and emergence of constructions, we need syntactic/grammatical annotations for such constructions. None of the features mentioned in Section 1.2 is currently supported by any annotation tool.

The outline of the paper is as follows. In Section 2, we give an overview of our project goals, data, and scope before we show in Section 3 what kind of uncertainties we are facing. Finally, we will draw our conclusions and present some future work in Section 4.

2 Interactive Grammar Analysis

2.1 Project Aims

As already stated above, we investigate the (structural) elaboration of Middle Low German (MLG) from the 13th century to the written language shift (16th/17th century). During this period, MLG lost its dominant position as a supraregional written language accompanied with the growing influence of (written) Early New High German (ENHG). The study makes an important contribution to the reconstruction of grammatical developments in written MLG, which are hitherto examined only to some extent. Our overall aim is to verify the assumption that written ENHG instantiates – despite an ENHG lexis – a MLG syntax/grammar. Particularly, we have four questions that we intend to answer: (1) Which kind of elaboration processes do occur? (2) How far does the elaboration go? (3) How fast does each elaboration process establish itself? (4) Are spatial points of origin identifiable?

2.2 Key Facts about our Corpus

Our empirical base is a corpus that consists of legal texts from the 13th to the 17th century.

2.2.1 Characteristics

There are several reasons why we focus on *urban legal statutes*: We assume that processes of language elaboration can be investigated especially in legal texts. They have to construe complex (legal) issues understandable independently of contextual information, so that elaborated linguistic structures capable of such a construal must be developed. These legal issues specifically occur in the form of *conditional relations*; consequently, we are able to examine changes concerning the linguistic construction of conditionality during the investigation period. Furthermore, legal statutes are locatable and datable, with the result that developmental dynamics of elaboration processes can be spatio-temporally reconstructed.

2.2.2 Distribution and Size

The corpus is divided into two parts: *MLG* consists of Middle Low German texts from 1227 to 1650 and covers about 1.2 million tokens. *ENHG* contains a selection of the first ENHG texts (400,000 tokens) arising in the Low German language area after the written language shift.

2.2.3 Text Sources

Another important aspect of our corpus is the use of primary materials for transcriptions and not editions. We want the transcriptions to be as diplomatic as possible, i.e. we keep text structuring elements like numbering, paragraphs, rubrifications, initials, and similar. In a broader sense, changes in the layout of a written text can be seen as elaboration phenomena (Krämer et al., 2012). It is conceivable that structural elements were introduced to separate or highlight textual and/or grammatical units. Keeping this information enables us to examine whether the language shift was accompanied by grammaticalization of interpunction.

2.3 Human-in-the-Loop Annotation Support

It is common practice for annotation tools to provide annotation suggestions (e.g. Cunningham et al. (2011); Stenetorp et al. (2012); Yimam et al. (2014); Bollmann et al. (2014); Bögel et al. (2015)). We also plan to develop an interactive procedure that combines machine learning and expert feedback (Holzinger, 2016) to solve one of the most central problems of existing annotation tools for historical texts. Due to the historical dynamics of grammar, we cannot use existing parsing and tagging system since those require static (a priori defined) syntactic rules and grammatical categories. We want to discover an evolving, dynamic grammar by using rule-based text

analysis techniques and machine learning methods (Hüllermeier, 2011). This enables us to reconstruct the language elaboration in an evidence-based way, which is a novelty.

3 Annotation Uncertainties

None of the current annotation tools cover the aspect of *uncertainty* as we do. Of course, this aspect is known and projects have strategies to cover it. In the end, it always comes down to the annotators being forced to decide for exactly one annotation. Instead, our tool allows for multiple annotations with an option to state which one is more likely. A similar idea by Jurgens (2013) allowed weighted multiple word sense annotations, and his results show improvements in the task of word sense disambiguation. In the following, we will explain our morphological (3.1) and syntactic (3.2) uncertainty.

3.1 POS Tag Ambiguity

The sentence in example (1) shows an excerpt for a specific state of the language shift process. The function word group *na deme dat* consists formally of a *preposition*$_1$ + *reanalyzed pronoun*$_2$ + *primary subjunction*$_3$ but expresses a functional unit [*complex subjunction*]$_4$. This is an obvious interpretation, as the unit *na deme dat* establishes a (temporal) relation between two entities construed as processes. From a cognitive grammar point of view, this functional characteristic is the crucial subjunctional criterion. Besides that, its further grammaticalization – which can be reconstructed based on our texts – suggests such an analysis as complex secondary subjunction (early state of a so called subjunctionalization). In the following stadium, as part of a formal erosion powered by frequency effects, we can observe the reduction of the primary subjunction *dat* and the univerbation of *na* and *dem(e)* as shown in example (2). Furthermore, as a result of desemantication, a causal relation is encoded. In our tool, users can annotate each member of the function word group of example (1) with its respective POS tag as well as assigning a POS tag to the whole group. Additionally, they can state which analysis is more likely.

When annotating historical texts, one could be uncertain which POS tag to assign due to missing context information or other circumstances. This is quite normal, but we are facing uncertainty due to our goal to analyze a language that is undergo-

(1) *We   sik   erue   g$\overset{u}{o}$des vnderwint   · oder an sprikt · [**na**$_1$ **deme**$_2$ / **dat**$_3$]$_4$ it*
Who himself hereditary goods takes possession of · or   claims   · after this   / that   it
im   vordelet is vor   gherichte · Dat is en vredebrake
him denied   is before court   · This is a   breach of peace
'Who takes possession of hereditary goods or claims them after it was denied through a court order to do so:
This is a breach of peace.'   (Goslar, 1350)

(2) [***Nademe***]$_4$ *yt ein groht / und erschrecklyk Laster / unde S$\overset{e}{u}$nde ys den Nahmen des*
After   it a   great / and terrible   vice / and sin   is the   name   of
Allm$\overset{e}{a}$chtigen Gades tho miszbruken. §.1. So scho+elen vo+erdann dejennigen / de   ...
Almighty   God   to misuse. §.1. So shall   henceforth all those   / who ...
'Thus, it is a great and terrible vice as well as a sin to misuse the name of the Almighty God. Henceforth, all
those who ...'   (Dithmarschen, 1567)

ing a shift. In our case, we will have to face issues where it is hard to tell if a token is still a member of category A or already a member of category B. So we should add a degree of how certain an annotation is and give annotators the possibility to exactly state why the annotation is uncertain in this case. This provides a great level of transparency and may lead to new insights.

3.2 Syntactic Gradience

Our aim is the analysis of constructions in the area of language elaboration (Maas, 2010; Tophinke, 2012; Merten, 2015). Therefore, we focus on constructions that model conditional relations of circumstances or have a conditional interpretation. Additionally, we capture all characteristics that cooccur for each construction given the temporal aspect that proved to be typical for this form. Furthermore, we investigate gradient structures and describe constructional changes in their gradual nature in a detailed way. We are interested in changes concerning form and/or meaning/function with respect to the textual perspective: from texts meant to be read out to texts that were designed for reading for oneself (Tophinke, 2009).

In previous work, we already identified some constructions that proved to be relevant to evidently reconstruct the language shift. These syntactic constructions are of varying complexity that can be either called *phrases* (i.e. nominal phrase, prepositional phrase, ...) or *transphrases* (i.e. complex sentences). An interesting constructionalization is the evolution of subjunctional constructions. In our earliest texts, those have the form "[situational context] [specification of situation]" and differ a lot from (literate) subjunctional constructions as we know them today. Al-

though they are formally marked as subjunctional entities (initial subjunction markers like *of, (so) wanne, weret also dat*[1] + verb final position), they are not integrated into a (supposed) matrix structure. This is illustrated in Example (3) through bracketing. From a syntactic perspective, the relation between the syntagma introduced by the subjunction and the following entity is much more loose than we know it from typical subjunctional constructions of present times. But focusing on semantic-functional aspects, one has to emphasize their specific functionality: They are typical structures of so called *space building* (Merten, 2016) which is highly linked to/functionalized with respect to the reception of these (older) texts. As they were meant to be read out, these orate structures ensured – to a certain extent – an easier access for potential listeners (Szczepaniak, 2015). As a result of the ongoing syntactic elaboration processes, the form turned into "$[[$subjunctional sentence$]$ matrix structure$]$" where the complete sentence is a subordinative conditional construction that exhibits the nowadays common *if-then* structure. We show an excerpt from our texts in Example (4).

4 Conclusion and Future Work

We showed that there are still missing features in current annotation tools and how we plan to provide them. Our CorA-based annotation tool will be able to handle uncertainties and allow syntactic annotations. Additionally, it will have a feature that provides annotation suggestions to support the human annotator in his/her work.

---

[1] All three markers translate to *if*. The literal meaning of *weret also dat* is *were it so that = if*.

(3)   [*So wanne enen manne ein pant gheset wert.*] [*it si erue*   *that eme ane*
      So when a   man a   pawn given was.   it is inheritance that him without
sinen danch   *wert gheset. ofte ein kisten pant. that scal he up beden to theme*
his   knowledge was given. Or a   mobile pawn. This shall he up weigh to the
nagesten thinghe.]
next   thing.

'If a man is offered a pawn and it is - unknowingly to him - an inheritance that was offered or a mobile pawn. This he should upweigh to the next thing.   (Stade, 1279)

(4)   [[*WAnnehr einer syne Sake dorch T$\overset{e}{u}$gen wahr maken und bewysen wil* /] *schal*
      If   one his case through witnesses true make and prove want /   shall

he de T$\overset{e}{u}$gen im Rechten nahmk$\overset{e}{u}$ndig maken]
he the witnesses in law   name   make   (Dithmarschen, 1667)

'If one wants to introduce witnesses to prove his case, he must legally name those witnesses.'

In the future, we plan to also integrate an information retrieval system that allows one to search for certain grammatical/syntactical constructions. As we are interested in temporal-spatial aspects, limiting the search to a specific time span and/or a specific region should be possible. In the long run, it is planned that the tool displays the search results on a (dynamic) map over time.

All tools created in the course of this project will be made available. We will report our progress and news on the project website: `http://www.uni-paderborn.de/forschungsprojekte/intergramm/`

Acknowledgments

The authors thank the reviewers for their helpful comments. Furthermore, we want to express our gratitude to the *ReN project* for providing us with data and *Marcel Bollmann* for his transfer of CorA. All authors are financially supported by the German Research Foundation (DFG).

References

Bas Aarts. 2007. *Syntactic Gradience. The Nature of Grammatical Indeterminacy.* Oxford University Press, New York.

Tomas Bögel, Michael Gertz, Evelyn Gius, Janina Jacke, Jan Christoph Meister, Marco Petris, and Jannik Strötgen. 2015. Collaborative Text Annotation meets Machine Learning: heureCLÉA, a Digital Heuristic Narrative. *DHCommons Journal* 1. http://dhcommons.org/journal/issue-1/collaborative-text-annotation-meets-machine-learning-heureclé-digital-heuristic.

Marcel Bollmann, Florian Petran, Stefanie Dipper, and Julia Krasselt. 2014. CorA: A web-based annotation tool for historical and other non-standard language data. In *Proceedings of the 8th Workshop on Language Technology for Cultural Heritage, Social Sciences, and Humanities (LaTeCH).* pages 86–90.

Hamish Cunningham, Diana Maynard, Kalina Botcheva, Valentin Tablan, Niraj Aswani, Ian Roberts, Genevieve Gorrel, Adam Funk, Angus Roberts, Danica Damljanovic, Thomas Heitz, Mark A. Greenwood, Horacio Saggion, Johann Petrak, Yaoyong Li, and Wim Peters. 2011. *Text Processing with GATE (version 6).* University of Sheffield Department for Computer Science.

Stefanie Dipper, Karin Donhauser, Thomas Klein, Sonja Linde, Stefan Müller, and Klaus-Peter Wegera. 2013a. HiTS: ein Tagset für historische Sprachstufen des Deutschen. *Journal for Language Technology and Computational Linguistics* 28:85–137.

Stefanie Dipper, Anke Lüdeling, and Marc Reznicek. 2013b. NoSta-D: A Corpus of German Non-Standard Varieties. In Marcos Zampieri and Sascha Diwersy, editors, *Non-standard Data Sources in Corpus-based Research*, Shaker Verlag, Aachen, pages 69–76.

Landrecht Dithmarschen. 1667. Print from 1667. `https://books.google.de/books?id=t88pAAAAYAAJ&pg=PR6&source=gbs_selected_pages&cad=2#v=onepage&q&f=false`. Online; accessed March 24, 2017.

Evelyn Gius and Janina Jacke. 2016. Zur Annotation narratologischer Kategorien der Zeit. Guidelines zur Nutzung des CATMA-Tagsets. `http://heureclea.de/wp-content/uploads/2016/11/guidelinesV2.pdf`.

Andreas Holzinger. 2016. Interactive Machine Learning (iML). *Informatik-Spektrum* 39(1):64–68.

Eyke Hüllermeier. 2011. Fuzzy machine learning and data mining. *Wiley Interdisciplinary Reviews: Data Mining and Knowledge Discovery* 1(4):269–283.

David Jurgens. 2013. Embracing ambiguity: A comparison of annotation methodologies for crowdsourcing word sense labels. In *Human Language Technologies: Conference of the North American Chapter of the Association of Computational Linguistics*. Association for Computational Linguistics, pages 556–562.

Gustav Korlén. 1950. Das Stader Stadtrecht vom Jahre 1279. In Erik Rooth, editor, *Lunder Germanistische Forschungen*, Håkan Ohlssons Boktryckery, Lund, volume 22, pages 23–117.

Sybille Krämer, Eva Cancik-Kirschbaum, and Rainer Totzke. 2012. *Schriftbildlichkeit*. de Gruyter, Berlin.

Maik Lehmberg. 2013. *Der Goslaer Ratskodex - Das Stadtrecht um 1350: Edition, Übersetzung und begleitende Beiträge*. Verlag für Regionalgeschichte, Bielefeld.

Utz Maas. 2010. Einleitung / Literat und orat. Grundbegriffe der Analyse geschriebener und gesprochener Sprache. In *Grazer linguistische Studien*, Institut für Sprachwissenschaft, Universität Graz, volume 73, pages 5–150.

Jan Christoph Meister, Evelyn Gius, Janina Jacke, Marco Petris, and Malte Meister. 2017. CATMA 5.0. http://catma.de/. Tool homepage; accessed June 07, 2017.

Marie-Luis Merten. 2015. Sprachausbau im Kontext rechtssprachlicher Praktiken des Mittelniederdeutschen. Konstruktionsgrammatik meets Kulturanalyse. In Verein für Niederdeutsche Sprachforschung, editor, *Niederdeutsches Jahrbuch*, Wachholtz Verlag, volume 138, pages 27–51.

Marie-Luis Merten. 2016. *Literater Sprachausbau kognitiv-funktional. Funktionswort-Konstruktionen in der historischen Rechtsschriftlichkeit*. Ph.D. thesis, Paderborn University. Unpublished.

Pontus Stenetorp, Sampo Pyysalo, Goran Topić, Tomoko Ohta, Sophia Ananiadou, and Jun'ichi Tsujii. 2012. BRAT: A Web-based Tool for NLP-assisted Text Annotation. In *Proceedings of the Demonstrations at the 13th Conference of the European Chapter of the Association for Computational Linguistics*. Association for Computational Linguistics, Stroudsburg, PA, USA, EACL '12, pages 102–107.

Renata Szczepaniak. 2015. Syntaktische Einheitenbildung – typologisch und diachron betrachtet. In Christa Dürscheid and Jan Georg Schneider, editors, *Handbuch Satz, Äußerung, Schema (Handbücher Sprachwissen 4)*, de Gruyter, Berlin, New York, volume 3, pages 104–124

Doris Tophinke. 2009. Vom Vorlesetext zum Lesetext: Zur Syntax mittelniederdeutscher Rechtsverordnungen im Spätmittelalter. In Angelika Linke and Helmuth Feilke, editors, *Oberfläche und Perfomanz. Untersuchungen zur Sprache als dynamischer Gestalt*, Niemeyer, Tübingen, pages 161–183.

Doris Tophinke. 2012. Syntaktischer Ausbau im Mittelniederdeutschen. Theoretisch-methodische Überlegungen und kursorische Analysen. In Angelika Linke and Helmuth Feilke, editors, *Niederdeutsches Wort*, Niemeyer, Tübingen, volume 52, pages 19–46.

Elizabeth C. Traugott and Graeme Trousdale. 2013. *Constructionalization and constructional changes*. Oxford University Press, Oxford.

Seid Muhie Yimam, Chris Biemann, Richard Eckart de Castilho, and Iryna Gurevych. 2014. Automatic Annotation Suggestions and Custom Annotation Layers in WebAnno. In *Proceedings of 52nd Annual Meeting of the Association for Computational Linguistics: System Demonstrations*. Association for Computational Linguistics, Baltimore, Maryland, pages 91–96.

Amir Zeldes, Julia Ritz, Anke Lüdeling, and Christian Chiarcos. 2009. Annis: A search tool for multi-layered annotated corpora. In *Proceedings of Corpus Linguistics*. Liverpool, UK.

Phonological Soundscapes in Medieval Poetry

Christopher Hench
University of California, Berkeley
Department of German
Berkeley, CA 94720, USA
chench@berkeley.edu

Abstract

The oral component of medieval poetry was integral to its performance and reception. Yet many believe that the medieval voice has been forever lost, and any attempts at rediscovering it are doomed to failure due to scribal practices, manuscript *mouvance*, and linguistic normalization in editing practices. This paper offers a method to abstract from this noise and better understand relative differences in phonological soundscapes by considering syllable qualities. The presented syllabification method and soundscape analysis offer themselves as cross-disciplinary tools for low-resource languages. As a case study, we examine medieval German lyric and argue that the heavily debated lyrical 'I' follows a unique trajectory through soundscapes, shedding light on the performance and practice of these poets.

1 Introduction

Research attempting to generalize medieval literary form has been severely hindered by the gap between performativity and manuscript evidence, manuscript *mouvance*, and linguistic normalization in editing practices.[1] How can formal features be identified and agreed upon if manuscripts differ significantly, and most transcriptions used by scholars today have been heavily edited? Recent scholarship has called for medievalists to move beyond such obstacles and recognize the importance of form in composition, performance, and reception (Stock, 2004; Kragl, 2011; Braun, 2013). Markus Stock focuses on sound, reasoning that if we believe these poems were primarily read

or sung aloud (with or without musical accompaniment), any insight into how they sounded to the audience would reveal a crucial aspect of the performance. Stock's reading emphasizes the sounds of words and how the repetition of words is not only a repetition of a concept, but a repetition of a sound, reinforcing an idea's connection to that sound (Stock, 2004, 195). Yet it is not necessarily about hearing and recognizing these patterns, rather that "in the sound dimension the individual rhetorical figure is blurred and a total acoustic impression emerges" (Stock, 2004, 200).

This paper proposes taking advantage of the information in syllables to gauge the aesthetic affect of a poem's soundscape by calculating the percentage of open syllables in stanzas of medieval poetry. It then attempts to correlate these "total acoustic impression[s]" with the medieval voice.

2 Soundscapes

For orientation purposes, we may first read aloud the following stanzas from the German poet Reinmar der Alte. As our focus is on the phonological sound and rhythm, we may for now set aside understanding the poem, opening up this experience to those who are not experts in medieval German.[2]

> [1] Dêst ein nôt, daz mich ein man
> vor al der werlte twinget, swes er wil.
> sol ich, des ich niht enkan,
> beginnen, daz ist mir ein swaerez spil.
> Ich hât ie vil staeten muot
> nu muoz ich leben als ein wîp,
> diu minnet und daz angestlîchen tuot.[3]

---

[1] See Paul Zumthor (1984) on the medieval voice.

[2] Each stanza is excerpted from a different poem.

[3] *Des Minnesangs Frühling* (*MF*) 192, 25-214C. "It is distressful that a man may force me before all the world to do as he wishes. Am I to begin things that I cannot, that is for me a difficult game. I've always had steadfast courage. Now I must live as a woman who loves, and does so in fear." All translations are the author's own unless otherwise noted.

Joint SIGHUM Workshop on Computational Linguistics for Cultural Heritage, Social Sciences, Humanities and Literature.
Proceedings, pages 46–56, Vancouver, BC, August 4, 2017. ©2017 Association for Computational Linguistics

[2] Swenne ich sî mit mîner valschen
    rede betrüge,
sô het ich sî unreht erkant.
Und gevâhe sî mich iemer an deheiner
    lüge,
sâ sô schupfe mich zehant
Und geloube niemer mîner klage,
dar zuo niht, des ich sage
dâ vor müeze mich got behüeten alle
    tage.[4]

It is difficult to not be immediately drawn to the unique phonological soundscapes. *Dêst ein nôt* is marked by many closed syllables, creating a short abbreviated affect, while *Swenne ich sî*, with a majority of open syllables, generates a more iambic rhythm. Although the musical settings and performance for these medieval poems and many others have not survived, we can gather from the phonology of the stanzas that they must have been very different. The great French philosopher Jean-Jacques Rousseau wrote extensively about language and music, arguing that some languages were more phonologically suitable to music than others. Rousseau believed that an unsuitable language would be "indistinct" and "piercing" when set to music (Rousseau et al., 1998, 144).[5] To avoid this, one would have to be selective with words, generating very "insipid and monotonous" music: "its progress would also be slow and tiresome for the same reason, and if one wanted to press the movement a little, its haste would resemble that of a heavy and angular body rolling along on cobblestones" (Rousseau et al., 1998, 144).[6]

Although Rousseau's description is surely exaggerated, many writers after him have shared his sentiment that vowels and open syllables are crucial to the composition of sung music and may even correlate with melismatic syllables.[7] Ger-

manic languages, including medieval Middle High German (MHG), Middle English (ME), and Old Norse (ON), would certainly be considered by Rousseau as languages phonologically less suitable when compared to medieval romance languages such as the Old Occitan of the troubadour tradition, with its many open syllables. This distinction is acknowledged in the various manifestations of the MHG word 'tandaradei', a popular interjection used to voice a bird's singing presence. Variations on 'tandaradei' all allow for significantly more sequences of open syllables than normal for MHG phonology, emphasizing the vocal quality of the singing. Heinrich von Stretelingen reimagines himself in the position of the bird, with the world needing his song, and augments the poem's soundscape by adding more open syllables to his own singing to match the bird's tune (Schweikle, 1978):

[3] Frowe, bluomen unde klê
unde heide, diu so wunneklîche grüene
    lît,
Die wen muoten unde mê,
daz diu vogellîn wol singen suozze
    widerstrît.
Des fröit sich sêre
mîn gemüete, dâz si sint fröiderîch.
al dur ir êre
singe ich mêre,
sît si ist minneklich.
Deilidurei faledirannurei
lîdundei faladaritturei![8]

Rousseau's characterization of a less-suited language can also shed light on the formal play in MHG poetry emerging in the early 13th century observed by Hugo Kuhn, Thomas Cramer, Markus Stock, and Manuel Braun (Kuhn, 1967; Cramer, 1998; Stock, 2004; Braun, 2013). Rousseau's claim that a less-suited language would be "force[d]" to exclude many words and would thus become "monotonous" is exactly what the scholarship has identified (Cramer, 1998, 45). Motifs are constantly rehashed and Kuhn claims that nothing new was contributed after the formal shift. It appears that a musical vocabulary re-

---

[4]*MF* 173, 13-96C, 53b. "If I were to ever deceive her with my false words, then I would have valued her improperly. And if she were to ever catch me in any lie, then she would immediately shake me up and never believe my lamentation, moreover anything I say. May God protect me from that every day."

[5]Rousseau understands Italian as having one of the greatest phonemic inventories due to its open syllables and bright vowels (Rousseau et al., 1998, 148).

[6]Charles Kensington argues that languages with fewer open syllables, English in particular, can remedy this if lexical breadth is sufficient to substitute words (Salaman, 1876, 123-124)

[7]See forthcoming work by Murray Schellenberg, 'Influence of Syllable Structure on Musical Text Setting.' Ross et al. (2007) suggest that preferred musical intervals are related to formants in vowel phones.

[8]MHG text from Bartsch (1964). "Lady, flowers, and clovers, and heather, which lay so wonderfully green, and who want very much that the little bird sings well and sweet in response. They are pleased by this very much, my senses, that they are joyful. All by her honor, I sing more, since she is dear. Deilidurei faledirannurei lîdundei faladaritturei!"

stricted by the phonology of a language, in addition to the natural development of the genre, led to formal play aimed at breaking these boundaries. With Konrad von Würzburg's mid-13th century infamous rhyme poem (*Schlagreimlied 26, I*), in which every word is rhymed, we understand well Rousseau's sense of "a heavy and angular body rolling along on cobblestones."[9]

3 Syllabification

To analyze phonological soundscapes on a large scale we must first be able to accurately syllabify words. The sonority sequencing principle (SSP) (Jesperson (1904)) and onset maximization and legal initials (Vennemann (1972) and Kahn (1976)) capture the fundamentals of syllabification in many languages. The SSP proposes a scale in which every phoneme in a language may be ordered. A phoneme's sonority value is based on the degree to which the lips are opened and sound is allowed to pass through the mouth (Jespersen, 1904, 186-187). Accordingly, the most sonorous phoneme is an open [ɑ]. Jesperson groups phonemes first by whether they are voiced or voiceless, then stops, fricatives, nasals, laterals, rhotic consonants, and three levels of vowels (high, medium, and low). A syllable break appears before a trough in sonority (Jespersen, 1904, 187-188). While what follows details the syllabification of MHG, this method is easily generalized to many other languages.

For the purposes of syllabifying MHG, it was determined that a three tiered sonority hierarchy was most accurate.[10] Computationally, each phoneme in a word is assigned a value from 1 to 3. Vowels, both long and short, receive a 3. Sonorants ('l', 'm', 'n', 'r', and 'w') receive a 2. All remaining consonants receive a 1. The MHG word 'werltlîchen', viz. 'worldy', is syllabified by the SSP accordingly:

werl — tlî — (ch)en[11]
2322　123　1 32

While the SSP alone can be very accurate, errors may still occur in the onset. The legality principle argues that "[m]edial syllable initial clusters should be possible word initial clusters" (Vennemann, 1972, 11). Daniel Kahn notes that this principle still leaves several possibilities if a consonant cluster could be broken up into more than one permissable word-initial grouping. To remedy this, Kahn argues that there "is a strong tendency to syllabify in such a way that initial clusters are of *maximal length*" (Kahn, 1976, 41). Because 'tlî' is not a legal onset in MHG, i.e., 'tlî' does not start any MHG word, the 't' is then drawn to the first syllable, and 'werl-tlî-chen' becomes 'werlt-lî-chen'.[12]

While some may consider this the correct syllabification, we argue that an intervocalic 'ch' should be considered ambisyllabic and thus also be split up. This and other individual fixes were informed partly by a metrical analysis.[13] MHG epic poetry generally alternates between stressed and unstressed syllables, following trochaic tetrameter (Tervooren, 1997). A typical MHG epic verse foot is two syllables in length, a stressed syllable followed by an unstressed syllable. However, feet may also consist of one or three syllables (Domanowski et al., 2009). Only phonologically heavy syllables (ending in a long vowel or a consonant) may fill an entire foot. If a foot is filled by three syllables, either the first two or the last two syllables are often phonologically light.[14] Thus the line belows necessitates the syllabification 'zec-he' so that the single syllable may be heavy and fill the entire foot:

daz |ist ein |fremdiu |zec|he[15]
× | × × | ×　×| − |× ^

The syllabification 'ze-che' would leave a light syllable to fill an entire foot, which is not permitted. Other syllabifications would break with the natural stress of the language. The final syllabification thus yields 'werlt-lîc-hen'.[16]

A similar decision had to be made for inter-

---

[9]Rousseau's thoughts on linguistic musicality has shifted focus to phonological rhythm in the field of 'rhythm metrics'. See Arvaniti (2009); Bolinger (1965); Ramus et al. (1999, 268); Grabe and Low (2002); Dasher and Bolinger (1982); Patel (2008); Palmer and Kelly (1992)

[10]When adapting to other languages, the number of tiers as well as their composition must also be adapted.

[11]For MHG, 'ch' is considered a single phoneme [x]. Other cases include 'sch' ([ʃ]) and 'ph' ([f]).

[12]For this implementation, onsets were deemed illegal if they appeared in less than .02% of all onsets in the corpus. This threshold helps reduce the acceptance of onsets in foreign words.

[13]See Estes and Hench (2016) for a computational approach to MHG phonology and meter.

[14]Excepted are several end syllables in divided falls such as '-er', '-el', and 'ez' (Domanowski et al., 2009).

[15]Wolfram von Eschenbach (1994, 17, l. 5-21) "This is a peculiar arrangement."

[16]This last change is important for our analyses in that it changes an open syllable ('lî') to a closed syllable ('lîc').

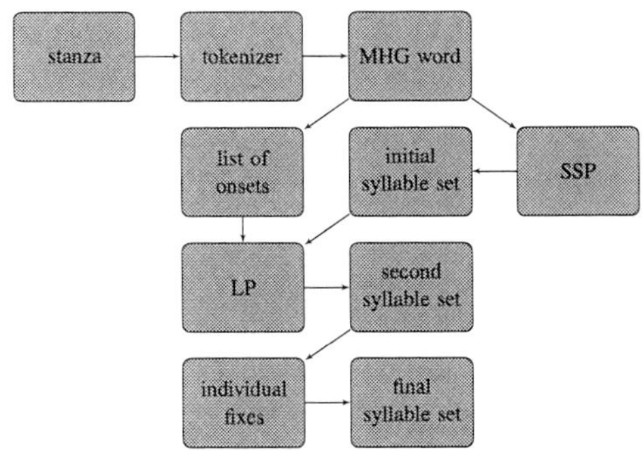

Figure 1: Flow chart for MHG syllabification.

vocalic affricates, which may be viewed as either ambisyllabic or biphonemic. For example, MHG '*sitzen*' ('sit') could be syllabified as '*si-tzen*' ([zɪ.tsən]), '*sit-zen*' ([zɪt.sən]), or '*sitz-en*' ([zɪts.ən]). The first syllabification would yield NHG [zits.ən], which is incorrect. It similarly does not correspond to manifestations in MHG meter, which deems 'sit-zen' preferable, e.g.:

sie | sêre | solde | let|zen[17]
× | × × | × × | − |×   ̂

The workflow for this process as implemented on MHG is charted in Figure 1.[18] A text is first tokenized into words, from which a list of permissable onsets is extracted. Each word is then syllabified according to the SSP and controlled for legality of onset. A final small set of language specific morphological fixes are made to yield the final syllable set.

While algorithmic computational syllabification is nothing new, previous methods have not combined syllabification principles in the manner presented here by controlling SSP syllabification with the legality principle (LP).[19] Moreover, this

method is particularly suited to languages lacking a standardized orthography. Testing the algorithm across dialects on the new *Referenzkorpus Mittelhochdeutsch* (REM) corpus (Klein et al., 2016) yielded an accuracy of 99.4% on a randomly sampled 1,000 words from the entire corpus of diplomatically transcribed texts.[20] This algorithm thus offers itself as a useful tool for the syllabification of low-resource languages, particularly those with varied orthography, a significant obstacle for computational text analysis of medieval texts.

4 Method

Returning to Reinmar's stanzas above, with such clear voice distinctions one may wonder if these soundscapes are correlated with specific content. To this end, we propose treating each stanza of poetry as a single observation. The soundscape for a stanza is quantified simply by calculating the percentage of open syllables, i.e., syllabes ending in a vowel. Reinmar's stanza [1] above has 9 open syllables and 50 closed syllables, and is thus assigned the value of 15.25%. Stanza [2] has 42 open syllables and 31 closed syllables and is assigned 57.53%. Each stanza in the corpus is then lemmatized and the lemmata are assigned to one of seven buckets at 5% intervals based solely on this percentage.[21] Finally, normalized lemmata frequencies are calculated for each bucket and are

---

[17] (Hartmann and Mertens, 2005, 250, l. 361) "[that his death] would cause them great harm."

[18] The individual fixes include: intervocalic 'ch', intervocalic 'sch', a sequence of one long vowel followed by one short vowel, and the suffixes 'lîch' and 'heit'. These morpheme boundaries interfere with the otherwise normal processes of syllabification. For example, with the fix the common MHG suffix -*lich* in *wîplich* results in the syllabification '*wîp-lich*', not '*wî-plich*', despite onset maximization preferring the latter ('*pl*' is a legal MHG onset).

[19] Early work from Bartlett et al. (2008) devised a new method for phonemic translation of English, an important step toward accurate syllabification. Bartlett et al. (2009) produced gold standard results of the SSP, LP, and OM, also creating an SVM-HMM model. Adsett and Marchand (2009) test several algorithms across multiple languages concluding that Syllabification by Analogy is most accurate. Rogova et al. (2013) develop an SCRF model for phonetic transcrip-

tions. Kondrak et al. (2016) seek to improve the gold standard syllabification by including morphological segmentation information.

[20] Syllabifying diplomatically transcribed texts introduces several orthographic obstacles for computers. Most symbols have a 1-1 signification to a standard grapheme, which for computational purposes, were resolved. The greatest obstacle was resolving 'v' and 'u' notations, as the consonant 'v' is at the other end of the sonority hierarchy than the vowel 'u'. This project assumes a conservative approach by using a corpus of standardized texts from the *Mittelhochdeutsche Begriffsdatenbank* (MHDBDB) (1992-2017) to determine permissable environments of the 'v' grapheme. If a given environment with a 'v' grapheme in the diplomatic translation does not exist in the standardized environments, the 'v' is converted to a 'u'. All other cases remain, and no other changes are made to the diplomatic transcriptions. Other spelling variations do not undermine the algorithm, as they commonly remain at the same level of the sonority hierarchy. This project therefore errs on the side of undercorrection. Note, however, that one should not compare results to Bartlett et al. (2009) as MHG is significantly easier to syllabify than English due to orthography and vocabulary. These results also include repeated words to demonstrate relevance to its application in the method.

[21] Lemmata in the MHDBDB corpus are annotated by hand for each text included in this analysis.

	stanzas
count	7856
median syllables per stanza	81
median lines per stanza	9
median syllables per line	8
median percent open syllables	32.88%

Table 1: Summary statistics for soundscape stanza analysis

percent open	stanzas
< 20%	272
< 25%	803
< 30%	1582
< 35%	2055
< 40%	1592
< 45%	974
≥ 45%	516
total	7794

Table 2: Counts of stanzas per soundscape bucket

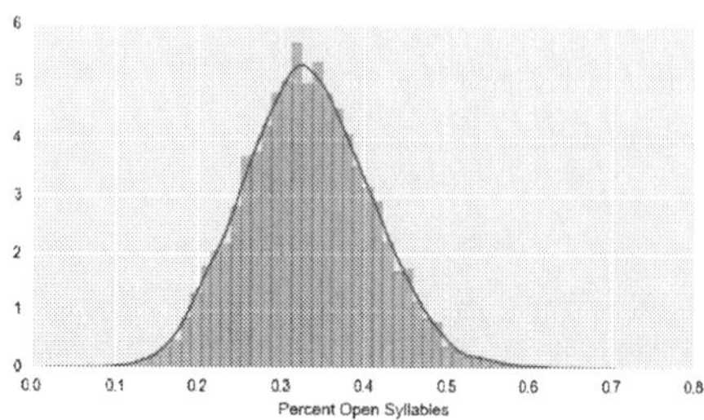

Figure 2: Distribution of soundscapes in the MHDBDB lyric corpus

examined across buckets.[22]

We take all lyric poetry from the *Mittelhochdeutsche Begriffsdatenbank* (MHDBDB) (1992-2017) corpus of medieval German texts.[23] Relevant summary statistics for this subset of the corpus are reproduced in Table 1. The distribution of soundscapes is shown in Figure 2 and the selected buckets and counts are given in Table 2.

Because the MHDBDB corpus is a collection of primarily edited texts with a range of dialects it is important to determine the degree to which editorial linguistic normalization practices might influence our measure of soundscapes. This problem is not unique to medieval German, and stands as a further significant obstacle to text analysis. A diplomatic transcription of Reinmar's stanza [1] from the Codex Manesse (Handschrift C) serves to illustrate:

D est ein not das mich ein man

vor al dˉ wˉlte twinget swes er wil.
sol ich des ich niht enkan
beginnen dc ist mir ein sweres spil.
ich hat ie vil stetē mv̊t.
nv mv̊s ich lebē als ein wib
dv̇ mīnet vñ das angestlichen tv̊t.[24]

Aside from shorthand, the primary differences are in vowel orthography and length. Unfortunately, diplomatic transcriptions of MHG lyric, as well as other traditions, are far too few to cover the breadth of the MHDBDB or to serve as the data for a large analysis of MHG lyric. Nevertheless, an impressive effort has been made by the *Lyrik des deutschen Mittelalters* (LDM) (1992-2017) project to provide a complete online edition of MHG lyric with side-by-side diplomatic transcriptions and edited editions of all extant manuscripts in which a poem survives. The LDM project has completed all of the stanzas attributed to Dietmar von Aist (42), Rubin (68), and Der wilde Alexander (35) in the largest manuscript of MHG lyric, the Codex Manesse. Across these texts we compare the soundscapes for each stanza in the diplomatic transcription and the normalized MHG. Table 3 gives the mean discrepancy in our measure (the percentage of open syllables) weighted by syllable count, demonstrating that it is unlikely that with buckets of 5% a soundscape would be placed in a bucket more than one bucket away from the correct placement. This test is an important step in building confidence to implement text analysis techniques on noisy medieval manuscripts. By abstracting from the grapheme and varied orthography, this method is still able to garner an accurate representation of a soundscape regardless of editing practices, perhaps even proxying for the other

---

[22]Lemmata frequencies are normalized by the length of the bucket. Each bucket is bootstrap resampled 1,000 times with replacement to generate 95% confidence intervals.

[23]The texts are all those designated as 'Lyrik' in the MHDBDB, with duplicate editions removed. For the purposes of this analysis, this paper considers only those stanzas > 2 lines and < 50 lines. While some poems have extended stanzas, especially in the longer political or social commentary poems, considering a stanza > 50 lines distracts from the focus of studying a smaller unified group generating a clear soundscape.

[24]Transcription from Pfaff (1898, 197).

	stanzas	sound diff.
Dietmar von Aist	42	.79% ± 1.00 %
Rubin	68	.82% ± .89%
Der wilde Alexander	35	1.09% ± .99%
lyric total	145	.86% ± .95%

Table 3: Comparison of soundscape measure in diplomatic transcriptions and normalized editions in manuscript C, weighted by syllable count in stanza.

layers of mediation inherent in medieval literature.

5 Soundscapes and Voice

Returning to Reinmar's stanzas, it is noteworthy that *Dêst ein nôt* is a male voice and *Swenne ich sî* is a female voice. Reinmar was not the only one to distinguish speaker roles through soundscapes:[25]

[4] Owê,
si kuste âne zal
in dem slâfe mich.
dô vielen hin zetal
ir trehene nider sich.
iedoch getrôste ich sie,
daz si ir weinen lie
und mich alumbe vie.
dô tagte ez.[26]

[5] Owê,
daz er sô dicke sich
bî mir ersehen hât!
als er endahte mich,
sô wolt er sunder wât
mîn arme schouwen blôz.
ez was ein wunder grôz,
daz in des nie verdrôz.
dô tagte ez.[27]

It is no coincidence that Heinrich von Morungen uses this soundscape difference to highlight

the 'Wechsellied', viz. 'alternating song', quality of his dawn song. This change in soundscape is a feature that largely goes unnoticed by modern readers, as these songs are no longer performed or read aloud. Manuel Braun, describing Ulrich von Liechtenstein's *Wizzet frouwe wol getan*, similarly shows a clear formal distinction between male and female voices: "The man speaking in the first stanza demonstrates his abilities by using only a single rhyme. The woman in the second stanza does the opposite, not rhyming at all. Thus her speech appears artless and inferior [...]" (Braun, 2013, 223). Thomas Cramer illuminates the same poem, emphasizing that such formal mastery would not have been understood by the average audience member, especially not in a purely oral tradition (Cramer, 1998, 16). Yet this paper argues that these formal distinctions would have been experienced as such by an audience accustomed to such performances, and that these soundscapes have thematic and voice associations.

Among the many possibilities of correlating thematics and voice with soundscapes, we choose here to investigate voice through one of the most common groups of words in the entire corpus: pronouns. Figure 3 shows the relative frequency of the lemmatized pronouns for 'I' ('ich'), 'he' ('er'), and 'she' ('sie') for each soundscape grouping. Shaded regions depict 95% confidence intervals determined by bootstrap resampling 1,000 stanzas from each bucket. Among the pronouns there is a clear trend in 'ich' and 'er'. To reiterate, 'ich' in this analysis includes all inflected forms—'ich', 'mich' (me, acc.), 'mir' (me, dat.), etc. Figure 3 implies that with a greater share of open syllables in any given stanza, the share of all words referring to a first person subject 'I' increases. The opposite holds true for 'he', while 'she' remains relatively constant across buckets.[28]

For further confirmation of this method, we also chart the trends of each grammatical gender's definite article with the hypothesis that due to the definite article inflections and nominal adjective endings attributed to each gender, the feminine article lemma would increase as the mascu-

---

[25]Heinrich von Morungen, *MF* 143,22-93C ff.

[26]59.18% open syllables. "Woe, she kissed me innumerable times in my sleep. Then her tears fell downward. Yet I comforted her, that she let her crying be, and embraced me. Then the day dawned."

[27]27.08% open syllables. "Woe, that he falls for me over and over! As he discovered me, he wanted to see my arms uncovered and bare. It was a great wonder that he never stopped. Then the day dawned."

[28]Several tests were conducted to further ensure and explore the accuracy of these results. The most obvious potential complication from the above analysis is that the size, content, and style of these texts vary significantly, and larger texts will inevitably have a larger influence on the analysis. The analysis was rerun holding out a different text each iteration, producing similar results. The five largest texts were also removed, yielding similar results.

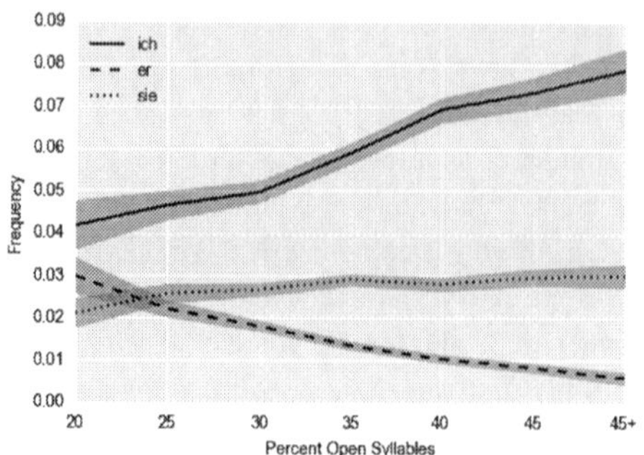

Figure 3: Lemmatized pronouns by soundscape bucket

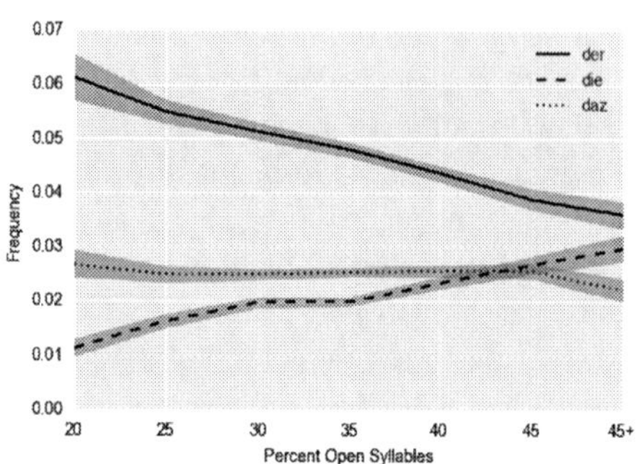

Figure 4: Lemmatized definite articles by soundscape bucket

line article lemma decreases, and the neuter article lemma would remain relatively stable across soundscape buckets.[29] Figure 4 confirms this hypothesis and demonstrates the inevitability that underlying grammatical genders have a significant impact on the soundscape of a MHG stanza.

The duration of this study will focus on the soundscapes of the first person pronoun and the lyrical 'I'.[30] 'ich' and all of its inflected forms are unambiguous in MHG in their reference to a first person speaker. Moreover, save the feminine accusative possessive pronouns, each form of 'ich' is a closed syllable. To be growing in presence inside of a soundscape with a greater share of open syllables implies that it must be counteracting itself with more open syllables to offset its own closed quality.

6 The Medieval German Lyrical 'I'

In MHG lyric there are two opposing interpretations of the lyrical 'I', with a wide spectrum in between.[31] One interpretation claims that the lyrical 'I' and all other roles are entirely fictional, created for entertainment or pedagogical purposes. It follows that we know nearly nothing about the real authors and performers. Günther Schweikle, while not assuming this extreme stance, argues that *Minnesang* (medieval German love lyric) is a constructed realm of stage play (Schweikle, 1995, 92).[32]

Schweikle's position has been softened significantly by Jan-Dirk Müller, who, while acknowledging and emphasizing the fictional aspect of *Minnesang*, seeks to reconcile this aspect with the many attempts by the *Minnesänger* (the poets of *Minnesang*) to integrate a very real aspect of their life, society, and work into their poems. Elements of reality, Müller argues, are necessary to convince and captivate the audience. One great difference in *Minnesang* from other forms of poetry is that the poets commonly represent not a single fictional or non-fictional person, but an entire community (ladies, knights, singers, etc.), as these roles often collapse into one through an abundance of references, not hinting at reality, but at what reality could or should be (Müller, 2001, 110, 113, 127). Müller argues for an inclusive interpretation of this

---

[29]Following *Mittelhochdeutsche Grammatik* (Paul et al., 1982), all masculine definite article inflections are closed syllables, only a nominative nominal adjective ending is open. Feminine neuter and accusative article inflections are open syllables, as is the pronominal nominative adjective ending. All neuter definite article inflections are closed syllables, both the nominative and dative nominal adjective endings are open syllables.

[30]Admittedly, 'er' and 'sie' are complicated cases, as MHG can refer to non-human objects using the masculine and feminine pronouns for the gender, though in this genre of lyric that is rather uncommon. While stanzas with a female voice have not been separately annotated, Katharina Boll's thorough study *Also redete ein vrowe schoene* identifies two characteristics marking a stanza in a female voice: "For one, the extreme distinction through a male first-person singer with the 'Inquit' formula. The gender specific status of the speaker can also be shown internally, for example through

the apostrophization of the male partner" (Boll, 2007, 117). This 'Inquit' formula, "sprach diu vrouwe" ("the lady said"), is not measured in the preceding analysis. However, the common internal pronoun reference ('er' and its inflections) is captured clearly and is consistent in soundscapes with a lower share of open syllables, exemplified by Reinmar and Heinrich above. While we hesitate to make any stronger claims due to referential ambiguity, this line should be further investigated and the groundwork for constructing a supervised classifier has been laid.

[31]This debate began with Warning (1979). See also Strohschneider (1996) and Müller (2001), (2004).

[32]Horst Brunner adopts a similar stance for MHG lyric outside the *Minnesang* genre (Brunner and Tervooren, 2000, 7). Sabine Obermaier argues that even when speaking self-reflexively, these poets recreate themselves many times over in different professions (Obermaier, 2000).

'I' as an individual, an author, a singer, and community, also emphasizing the *agenda* behind the 'ich'.

Intensifying some of Müller's claims, Harald Haferland maintains that the fiction of *Minnesang* is actually much closer to reality and that the *Minnesänger*, through situational references, often speak directly to the audience as themselves (Haferland, 2004, 77). Haferland argues that *Minnesang*'s success was contingent upon believability. The effect of the poems would be much stronger if the poet could relate situations directly to the audience without a fictive role.

What consequences do these soundscapes have for the configuration of the first person in MHG poetry? Considering Stock's recent research on sound, we recognize that repeating the first person pronoun is not only repeating a semantic concept, but the actual sounds of 'ich', 'mich', 'mir', etc. Stock's example is Gottfried von Neifen, one of the lead poets in shifting the genre toward more formalist ambitions. He is interested in Gottfried's use of sound through word repetition, specifically through the repetition of 'fröide' ('joy') and 'liebe' ('love'), in the sense of Vickie Ziegler's 'Leitwort', viz. 'leading-' or 'guiding word' (Ziegler, 1975). While the 'Leitwort' is generally understood to have semantic importance due to its high frequency relative to the rest of the corpus or song, what if the ubiquitous lyrical 'I', this heavily controversial figure, is elevated to 'Leitwort', or perhaps 'Leitklang' ('leading sound'), via its unique soundscape presence?

[6] **Ich** solt aber dur die süezen
grüezen meien walt heid ouwe
und der kleinen vogel süezez singen,
lieze eht **mir** an ir gelingen
trût **mîn** trôst, **mîs** herzen frouwe,
daz si **mînen** kumber wolde büezen:
seht, sô wurde **ich** noch an fröiden rîche.
truter lip, nu tuot genæedecliche:
rôter munt, du maht **mîn** leit verdrin-
gen.[33]

[7] Süeziu minne, sît dîn minne

sinne krenket zallen stunden,
wie sold **ich** dan iemer frô belîben?
lieber lîp vor allen lîben,
heilet **mir mîns** herzen wunden,
daz **mîn** fröide lige an dem gewinne.
tuot ir daz, sô wirde **ich** froidebære.
sælic wîp, nu scheidet **mich** von swære.
Minne, dû maht **mir mîn** leit
vertrîben.[34]

[8] **Ich** hân fröide von ir eine:
seine troestet **mich** ir güete.
dâ von muoz **mir** spilndiu fröide
swinden.
lieze sie **mich** gnâde vinden,
seht, so fröite **mîn** gemüete,
daz **mir** wurde ir rôter kus, ein kleine;
so wær **ich** vil manger sorgen âne.
triutelehter lîp, **ich** lebe in wâne
daz **ich** fröide von iu müge enpfinden.[35]

Formal play is clearly on display in Gottfried's song through rhyme, alliteration, and soundscape. The percentage of open syllables gradually increases in each stanza, taking on an entirely new soundscape in the last stanza, while retaining nearly the same number of syllables per line and presumably the same metrical scansion. While we clearly see the increased presence of the 'Leitwort' 'fröide', it is easy to overlook the simultaneous increased presence of the first person (following the trend in Figure 3). Not only does this subject increase in count, but also in space and time intervals, both crucial aspects of the performance. In the first two stanzas the subject appears in more concentrated sections, while Gottfried leaves himself (or his fictive role) out of consecutive verses to describe nature, a bird, and love. Not so in the final stanza, in which Gottfried's subject asserts himself in every verse, refocusing the audience's attention on the subject before them, not only through these self-references, but also by intensifying the sound-

---

[33]Text from Kraus (1951-1958). 35.71% open syllabes. "I should but sing sweetly through the sweet, welcoming May forest, heather, water, and to the small birds. May it only reach her as comfort, my dear, lady of my heart, that she would wish to relieve my suffering: see, so will I be rich in joy. My dear, now do so graciously: red mouth, you drive away my suffering."

[34]39.29% open syllables. "Sweet love, since your love weakens the senses at all hours, how should I then ever be left happy? My dear above all others, heal me of my heart's wounds, that my happiness is won. If this is done, so will I be joyful. Fortunate lady, part me now from grief. Love, you drive away my suffering."

[35]49.41% open syllables. "I had joy from her alone: her goodness comforted me, from which the playful joy must vanish. If she allowed me to find grace, you see, so would my disposition be joyed, that I would receive her red kiss, a small one; so would I be without many worries. My dear, I live in hope that I may feel joy from you."

scape. Each self-reference throughout the entire poem is itself a closed syllable for which Gottfried must compensate further as the song progresses. The clear increased presence of 'fröide' is certainly one solution. Stock hesitantly borrows from Kuhn's terminology, that the 'fröide' 'Leitwort' in Gottfried's complementary KLD song 3 through its repeated employment in formal moves becomes "objective".[36] The objective 'fröide' becomes the central theme of the poem, superseding the singer himself. Yet in his poem above, Gottfried appears to struggle with the objectivisation of 'fröide' in order to maintain the singer as the central reference, in fact it is the subject, to which this increased presence of the sound (and 'reality') of 'fröide' is constantly subjected. Although as we have now come to learn, it is not only the sound of 'fröide', rather the sonorous sound of open syllables, with which the subject is temporally and sequentially surrounded, and which may simply serve as a counter-weight to the increased presence of the ego-centric subject.

7 Conclusion

This paper has demonstrated that abstracting from orthographic variation and individual graphemes to the building blocks of language can help unite a diverse corpus for analysis. Testing this method on various levels of mediation demonstrates its potential for text analysis on the heavily mediated medieval corpus. Implementing this method reveals unique soundscape experiences of a medieval audience. This paper thus answers calls for new formal approaches to sound across disciplines, and provides a generalizable workflow for the syllabification of low-resource languages. The results from a case study of medieval German lyric support a counter-intuitive trend in the positioning of the lyrical 'I', and paves the way for feature extraction and classification of gendered voice.[37]

Acknowledgments

We would like to thank the *Mittelhochdeutsche Begriffsdatenbank* and Klaus Schmidt, Digital Humanities at Berkeley, and David Bamman for their continued support of this project.

---

[36]See Stock (2004, 188) and Kuhn (1967).

[37]The source code for this project is available at `https://github.com/henchc/ACL-LaTeCH-CLfL-2017`.

References

Connie R Adsett and Yannick Marchand. 2009. A comparison of data-driven automatic syllabification methods. In *International Symposium on String Processing and Information Retrieval*. Springer, pages 174–181.

Amalia Arvaniti. 2009. Rhythm, Timing and the Timing of Rhythm 66(1):46–63. https://doi.org/10.1159/000208930.

Susan Bartlett, Grzegorz Kondrak, and Colin Cherry. 2008. Automatic syllabification with structured svms for letter-to-phoneme conversion. In *ACL 2008*. pages 568–576.

Susan Bartlett, Grzegorz Kondrak, and Colin Cherry. 2009. On the syllabification of phonemes. In *Proceedings of Human Language Technologies: The 2009 Annual Conference of the North American Chapter of the Association for Computational Linguistics*. Association for Computational Linguistics, pages 308–316. http://dl.acm.org/citation.cfm?id=1620799.

Karl Bartsch. 1964. *Die Schweizer Minnesänger*. Huber.

D. L. Bolinger. 1965. Pitch accent and sentence rhythm. In *Abe, Kanekiyo, Forms of English: accent, morpheme, order*, Harvard University Press, pages 139–180.

Katharina Boll. 2007. *Also redete ein vrowe schoene: Untersuchungen zu Konstitution und Funktion der Frauenrede im Minnesang des 12. Jahrhunderts*. Number 31 in Würzburger Beiträge zur deutschen Philologie. Königshausen & Neumann.

Manuel Braun. 2013. Aufmerksamkeitsverschiebung. Zum Minnesang des 13. Jahrhunderts als Form- und Klangkunst 21:203–230.

Horst Brunner and Helmut Tervooren. 2000. Einleitung: Zur situation der sangspruch- und meistergesangsforschung 119(2000):1–9.

Thomas Cramer. 1998. *Waz hilfet âne sinne kunst?: Lyrik im 13. Jahrhundert Studien zu ihrer Ästhetik*. Number Heft 148 in Philologische Studien und Quellen. E. Schmidt.

Richard Dasher and Dwight Bolinger. 1982. On pre-accentual lengthening 12(2):58–71. https://doi.org/10.1017/S0025100300002462.

Anna Domanowski, Yochanan Rauert, Hanno Rüther, and Tomas Tomasek. 2009. Mittelhochdeutsche Metrik Online. https://www.uni-muenster.de/MhdMetrikOnline/.

Alex Estes and Christopher Hench. 2016. Supervised machine learning for hybrid meter http://www.aclweb.org/anthology/W/W16/W16-0201.pdf.

E. Grabe and E. Low. 2002. Durational variability in speech and the rhythm class hypothesis Vol. 7:515–546.

Harald Haferland. 2004. Minnesang als posenrhetorik. In Albrecht Hausmann, Cornelia Logemann, and Christian Rode, editors, *Text und Handeln: zum kommunikativen Ort von Minnesang und antiker Lyrik*, Winter, number Heft 46 in Beihefte zum Euphorion, pages 65–105.

Hartmann and Volker Mertens. 2005. *Der arme Heinrich*. Bibliothek des Mittelalters. Chadwyck-Healey, Cambridge, England.

Otto Jespersen. 1904. *Lehrbuch der Phonetik;*. Leipzig, Teubner. http://archive.org/details/lehrbuchderphone00jespuoft.

Daniel Kahn. 1976. Syllable-based generalizations in english phonology.

Thomas Klein, Klaus-Peter Wegera, Stefanie Dipper, and Claudia Wich-Reif. 2016. Referenzkorpus mittelhochdeutsch (1050-1350). https://www.linguistics.ruhr-uni-bochum.de/rem/.

Garrett Nicolai Lei Yao Grzegorz Kondrak. 2016. Morphological segmentation can improve syllabification. *ACL 2016* page 99.

Florian Kragl. 2011. wort unde wîse. Formen des sangbaren Verses in der deutschen Literatur des Mittelalters 52:31–80.

Carl von Kraus. 1951-1958. *Gottfried von Neifen*, volume Deutsche Liederdichter. M. Niemeyer.

Hugo Kuhn. 1967. *Minnesangs Wende*. Hermaea n.F., Bd. 1. Niemeyer.

Hugo Moser, Helmut Tervooren, and Carl von Kraus, editors. 1977. *Des Minnesangs Frühling*. Hirzel, 36., neugestaltete u. erw. aufl edition.

Jan-Dirk Müller. 2001 "ir sult sprechen willekomen": Sänger, sprecherrolle und die anfänge volkssprachlicher lyrik. In Ute von Bloh and Armin Schulz, editors, *Minnesang und Literaturtheorie*, Niemeyer, pages 107–128.

Jan-Dirk Müller. 2004. Die fiktion höfischer liebe und die fiktionalität des minnesangs. In *Text und Handeln. Zum kommunikativen Ort von Minnesang und antiker Lyrik*, pages 47–64.

Sabine Obermaier. 2000. Der dichter als handwerker - der handwerker als dichter. autorkonzepte zwischen sangspruchdichtung und meistersang. 119(2000):59–72.

Carloline Palmer and Michael Kelly. 1992. Linguistic prosody and musical meter in song 31(4):525–542. https://doi.org/10.1016/0749-596X(92)90027-U.

Aniruddh D. Patel. 2008. *Music, language, and the brain*. Oxford University Press.

Hermann Paul, Hugo Moser, Ingeborg Schröbler, and Siegfried Grosse. 1982. *Mittelhochdeutsche Grammatik*. Max Niemeyer, Tübingen.

Fridrich Pfaff. 1898. *Die grosse Heidelberger Liederhandschrift, in getreuem textabdruck*. C. Winter. https://catalog.hathitrust.org/Record/100607933.

F. Ramus, M. Nespor, and J. Mehler. 1999. Correlates of linguistic rhythm in the speech signal 73(3):265–292.

Kseniya Rogova, Kris Demuynck, and Dirk Van Compernolle. 2013. Automatic syllabification using segmental conditional random fields. *Comput. Linguist. Neth. J* 3:34–48.

Deborah Ross, Jonathan Choi, and Dale Purves. 2007. Musical intervals in speech 104(23):9852–9857. http://www.pnas.org/content/104/23/9852.short.

Jean-Jacques Rousseau, John T. Scott, and Jean-Jacques Rousseau. 1998. *Essay on the origin of languages and writings related to music*. Number vol. 7 in The collected writings of Rousseau. University Press of New England.

Charles Kensington Salaman. 1876. On the English Language as a Language for Music 3(1):120–139. https://doi.org/10.1093/jrma/3.1.120.

Günther Schweikle. 1978. Heinrich von stretelingen. In *Die deutsche Literatur des Mittelalters, Verfasserlexikon*, W. de Gruyter, volume 3. Zweite, völlig neu bearbeitete auflage edition.

Günther Schweikle. 1995. *Minnesang*, volume 244. Metzler.

Margerete Springeth, Nikolaus Morocutti, and Daniel Schlager. 1992-2017. Mittelhochdeutsche begriffsdatenbank (mhdbdb). universität salzburg. http://www.mhdbdb.sbg.ac.at/. Accessed: 2016-10-01.

Markus Stock. 2004. Das volle wort - sprachklang im späteren minnesang. In Albrecht Hausmann, Cornelia Logemann, and Christian Rode, editors, *Text und Handeln: zum kommunikativen Ort von Minnesang und antiker Lyrik*, Winter, number Heft 46 in Beihefte zum Euphorion, pages 65–105.

Peter Strohschneider. 1996. "nu sehent, wie der singet!": vom hervortreten des sängers im minnesang. In *"Aufführung" und "Schrift" in Mittelalter und früher Neuzeit*, pages 7–30.

Helmut Tervooren. 1997. *Minimalmetrik zur Arbeit mit mittelhochdeutschen Texten*. Kümmerle Verlag, Göppingen.

Theo Vennemann. 1972. On the Theory of Syllabic Phonology. *Linguistische Berichte* 18:1–18

Rainer Warning. 1979. Lyrisches ich und öffentlichkeit bei den trobadors. In *FS Hugo Kuhn (1979)*, pages 120–159.

Wolfram, Karl Lachmann, Eberhard Nellmann, and Dieter Kuhn. 1994. *Parzival*. Bibliothek deutscher Klassiker. Deutscher Klassiker Verlag, Frankfurt am Main, 1 edition.

Vickie L. Ziegler. 1975. *The leitword in Minnesang: stylistic analysis and textual criticism*. The Penn State series in German literature. Pennsylvania State University Press.

Paul Zumthor. 1984. *La poésie et la voix dans la civilisation médiévale*, volume 9. Julliard.

An End-to-end Environment for Research Question-Driven Entity Extraction and Network Analysis

Andre Blessing[♡] and **Nora Echelmeyer**[♣] and **Markus John**[◇] and **Nils Reiter**[♡]

[♡] Institute for Natural Language Processing
[♣] Institute for Literary Studies
[◇] Institute for Visualization and Interactive Systems
Stuttgart University

`{andre.blessing@ims, nora.echelmeyer@ilw}.uni-stuttgart.de`
`{markus.john@vis, nils.reiter@ims}.uni-stuttgart.de`

Abstract

This paper presents an approach to extract co-occurrence networks from literary texts. It is a deliberate decision not to aim for a fully automatic pipeline, as the literary research questions need to guide both the definition of the nature of the things that co-occur as well as how to decide co-occurrence. We showcase the approach on a Middle High German romance, *Parzival*. Manual inspection and discussion shows the huge impact various choices have.

1 Introduction

The main contribution of this paper is the presentation of a conceptualized and implemented workflow for the study of relations between entities mentioned in text. The workflow has been realized for multiple, diverse but structurally similar research questions from Humanities and Social Sciences, although this paper focuses on one from literary studies in particular. We see this workflow as exemplary for research involving Natural Language Processing (NLP) and Digital Humanities (DH), in which operationalization and modularization of complex research questions often has to be a first step. It is important to realize that this modularization can not be guided by NLP standards alone – the interests of the respective humanities discipline need to be considered, and practical considerations regarding timely availability of analyses as well: If a large portion of the funding period is spent with developing, adapting and fine-tuning NLP tools, the analysis of the results (with often leads to new adaptation requests) risks being missed out.

Our workflow combines clearly defined tasks for which we follow the relatively strict NLP paradigm (annotation guidelines, gold standard, evaluation) with elements that are more directly related to specific Humanities research questions (that often are not defined as strictly). The final module of this workflow consists in the manual exploration and assessment of the resulting social networks by literary scholars with respect to their research questions and areas. In order to enable scholars to explore the resulting relations, we make use of interactive visualization, which can also show developments and changes over time.

More generally, this workflow is the result of ongoing work on the modularization and standardization of Humanities research questions. The need for modularization is obvious for computer scientists (and computational linguists), as they are often consciously restricting their tasks to clearly defined problems (e.g., dependency parsing). However, this opposes typical Humanities research style, which involves the consideration of different perspectives, contexts and information sources – ignoring the big picture would be a no-go in literary studies. This makes research questions seemingly unique and incomparable to others, which in turn leaves little room for standards applied across research questions.

Our ultimate goal is to develop methodology that supports the work of humanities scholars on their research questions. This in turn makes interpretability of the results of NLP-tools an important constraint, which sometimes goes against the tendency of NLP research to produce methods that are solely judged on their prediction performance. However, we intentionally do not focus on tool development: The appropriate use of tools and adequate interpretation of their results is of utmost importance if these form the basis of hermeneutical interpretations. To that end, scholars need to understand fundamental concepts of quantitative analysis and/or machine learning.

The trade-off between interpretability and pre-

Joint SIGHUM Workshop on Computational Linguistics for Cultural Heritage, Social Sciences, Humanities and Literature.
Proceedings, pages 57–67, Vancouver, BC, August 4, 2017. ©2017 Association for Computational Linguistics

diction performance has also been discussed in other projects, e.g. in Bögel et al. (2015). In our project we follow two strategies: (i) Offering visualization and inspection tools as well as a close feedback loop and (ii) integrating humanities scholars early into the development cycle, such that they are involved in the relevant decisions.

Parzival We will use *Parzival* as an example in this paper, because it involves a number of DH-related challenges. The text is an Arthurian grail novel and has been written between 1200 and 1210 CE by Wolfram von Eschenbach in Middle High German. The text comprises of 25k lines and is divided into 16 books. The story of the books mainly follows the two knights Parzivâl and Gâwân and their interaction with other characters. One of the key characteristics of *Parzival* is a large inventory of characters that have complex genealogical patterns and familial relations. This led to an ongoing discussion about the social relations in *Parzival* (Bertau, 1983; Delabar, 1990; Schmidt, 1986; Sutter, 2003), which are much more complex than in other Arthurian romances (*Erec*, *Iwein*). The systematic comparison of the social/spatial relations in different narrations of a similar story is one of our goals. With that in mind, we investigate various operationalization options for these networks.

2 Workflow

Given the above discussion about *Parzival*, we are aiming to establish a workflow to extract social networks from text, such that scholarly/domain experts are enabled to compare the resulting networks from different narrations. Therefore, the steps in this workflow need to be reasonably transparent, errors traceable and the overall results interpretable for scholars without deep technical background.

Next to our example case *Parzival*, we believe that many research questions in Humanities and Social Sciences can be cast as such a network/relation extraction task, at least on a structural level: Studying the relation of characters in narrative texts is structurally similar to the relation of concepts in philosophical texts, for instance. The workflow we employ consists of the following steps:

1. Identification of textual references to entities of various types (Sect. 3),

2. Grounding of detected entity references (e.g.,

identifying "the knight" as a reference to the main character Parzivâl; Sect. 4),

3. Segmentation of the texts in appropriate parts (e.g., story taking place at a specific location; Sect. 5),

4. Manual, interactive exploration of proto-networks for validation (Sect. 6), and

5. Creation and analysis of networks of entities that co-occur within a segment (e.g., the characters that take part in a great feast; Sect. 7).

It is important to note that this workflow is impacted by the Humanities research question at multiple stages. The notion of **entity** is relatively generic and we have applied it to a number of different genres. However, in order to group entity references into entity types, one has to determine what entity types are actually relevant in the text at hand and for the specific research question. While we assume intersubjective agreement on entity annotations, we make no such assumption for **segment** annotations. Different segmentation criteria can be tested and the resulting networks compared.

In general, we make no assumptions on every step being automatic. Semi-automatic, manual, interpretative or other kinds of work packages can be integrated in such workflows (and, given the nature of (Digital) Humanities, often need to be).

The *Parzival* corpus is preprocessed by several webservices from the CLARIN infrastructure[1] (Mahlow et al., 2014) to obtain a sentence splitted, tokenized and part-of-speech tagged corpus for the previously described workflow steps.

3 Detecting Entity References

3.1 Conceptualisation and Annotation

We define entities as individually distinguishable objects in the real or a fictional world. Words in texts may refer to entities and are thus called entity references (ERs). Linguistically, entity references can be expressed as proper names, pronouns and appellative noun phrases (which together are typically called *mentions* within coreference resolution). Our annotations include only proper names and appellative noun phrases, pronouns have been excluded by definition. Therefore, the task described here is situated in between

---

[1] European Research Infrastructure for Language Resources and Technology: https://www.clarin.eu/

the well-known NLP tasks of named entity recognition (NER) and coreference resolution. This was a pragmatic decision, in order to avoid the most difficult coreference resolution challenges (as pronouns are the most ambiguous mentions) and still include more occurrences than just names. In addition, the referents for appellative noun phrases can be resolved with only a limited amount of context, which makes their grounding (cf. Sec 4) faster for Humans and more promising to automatically support. Our annotation scheme distinguishes between different types of entities. Entity references are marked with the type of the entity they refer to.

We annotate manually five books of *Parzival*, following the annotation guidelines developed in parallel with the annotation process[2]. The manual annotation is done in parallel by two different annotators. Annotation differences have been adjudicated by a third person, after discussion with the annotators. Difficult cases have been discussed with annotation groups for different texts.

In *Parzival*, two different types are actually appearing: Persons and locations. Table 1 shows the distributions of the entity types across the five books that constitute our gold standard. As can be seen, the variance across the books is quite low.

Book	Lines	Tokens	PER	LOC
III	1,898	12,015	610	120
IV	1,338	8,035	464	122
V	1,682	10,441	472	140
VI	1,740	10,918	594	144
VII	1,800	11,358	687	134
Mean	1,691.6	10,553.4	565.4	132
SD	213.2	1,522.5	95.7	10.7

Table 1: Corpus Statistics. PER/LOC: References to persons or locations, SD: Standard deviation.

3.2 Automatic Entity Reference Detection

Our entity reference tagger is built using ClearTK (Bethard et al., 2014), which in turn employs mallet CRF (McCallum, 2002) and the BIO scheme.

Feature set The features presented in Table 2 are extracted for the current, two preceding and one succeeding tokens. Since we are applying this

tagger to different corpora in different languages, we use language-, genre- or text-specific resources only in two, clearly defined cases: part of speech and names gazetteers. Part of speech taggers are available even for many low resource languages (or are among the first being created), gazetteers can often be created by domain experts.

Id	Feature	Description
F_1	Surface	The surface form of the token
F_2	PoS	The part of speech tag of the token. For *Parzival*, we are using a fairly new, publicly available model (Echelmeyer et al., 2017) for tree-tagger (Schmid, 1994).
F_3	Case lookup	Do tokens written in upper case also exist in lower case?
F_4	Unicode character pattern	A canonicalized list of Unicode character properties that appear in the token. "Obilôte", for instance, is represented as LuLl, signaling upper case letters followed by lower case letters.
F_3	Gazetteer	A list of names. The gazetteer in our experiment has been collected from various MHG texts by extracting tokens with upper case letters and manually removing the non-names. Generally, this feature allows the inclusion of domain knowledge in a simple and broadly applicable manner.

Table 2: Feature set

3.3 Evaluation

The entity reference tagger is evaluated using book-wise cross-validation (i.e., 5-fold CV). In the **strict** setting, we only count exactly matching boundaries as correct, while in the **loose** setting, we count a true positive as long as there is a one-token overlap between system and reference.

Baselines We compare the entity reference tagger against two baselines: The Stanford named entity recognizer for Modern German (BL_{NER}) and marking every upper case word as a majority class reference (i.e., Person; BL_{Case}).

---

[2]The (German) guidelines are available on the project web site http://www.creta.uni-stuttgart.de.

		Person		Location	
		Prec	Rec	Prec	Rec
strict	BL$_{NER}$	27.3	1.2	27.6	2.4
strict	BL$_{Case}$	36.2	19	0	0
strict	ERT	71.2	56.8	71.8	48
loose	BL$_{NER}$	72.9	3.6	41.9	3.9
loose	BL$_{Case}$	74.8	38.5	0	0
loose	ERT	91.6	76.1	85.3	57.9

Table 3: Evaluation results for the entity reference tagger (ERT), compared with two baselines (NER and case-based).

Discussion The results achieved purely automatically can be seen in Table 3. As expected, evaluation scores for the loose setting are higher than for the strict setting. The loose setting in fact is more representative for the actual performance of the tagger in our workflow. As the domain experts perform semi-manual grounding anyway, the exact boundaries of the found entity reference are not that important. In addition, manual inspection revealed that in many cases the entity tagger in fact marked the head of the noun phrase.

Performance scores are higher for Person references, which can be attributed to their frequency. Both baselines are clearly outperformed, although both have their presumed strengths for the proper noun references. Manual inspection also revealed that most of the remaining recall errors are appellative noun phrases (e.g., "des burcgrâven tohterlîn"/"the burgrave's daughter").

3.4 Semi-Automatic Labeling

Although automatic labeling of entity references is an important part of our workflow, a recall error of about 25% of the persons severely limits its usefulness for applications in digital literary studies. We therefore implemented a user interface (not shown) in which scholars can inspect the found entity references on unseen texts and mark them as either *correct*, *incorrect*, or *boundary-incorrect*, for span errors as well as subsequently annotate missing entity references (recall errors). For once, these annotations are then stored as manual annotations that can be used in subsequent workflow steps and secondly, they can be employed as additional training material.

This procedure also gives clear guidance on where to focus the improvements of the tagger:

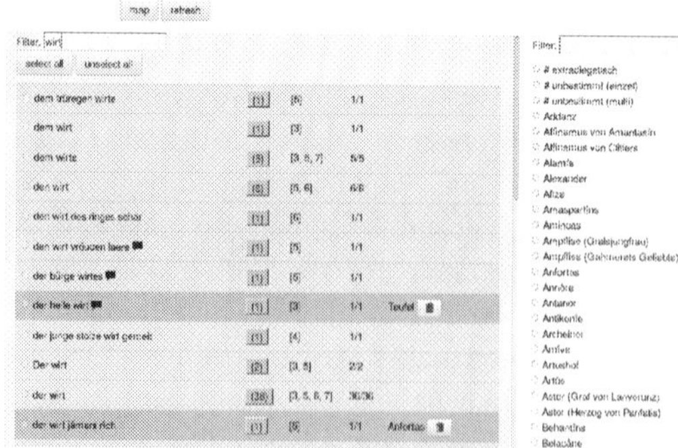

Figure 1: Grounding view: Annotated entity reference types (left) mapped to characters (right)

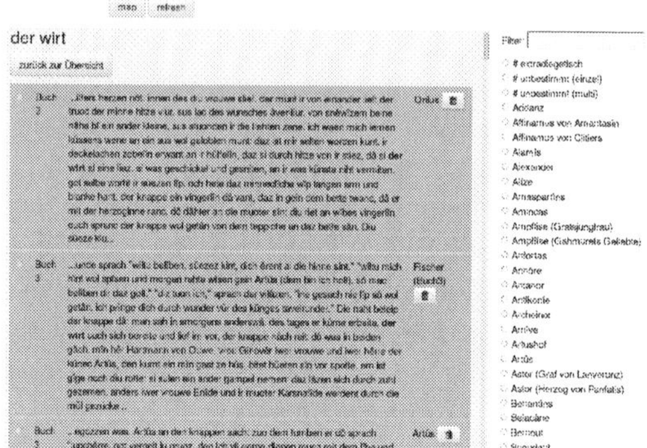

Figure 2: For each mention type all occurrences including textual context can be shown

Precision errors are much easier to spot and correct in this fashion, making improvements in terms of recall our priority.

4 Entity Grounding

Each annotated entity reference is mapped to a pre-defined list of characters[3]. This task can be seen as entity linkage or entity grounding (Ji and Grishman, 2011). In this paper we restricted the mapping to persons but it can easily be applied to other entity classes. While the entity reference detection task was supported automatically, grounding is done manually. Fig. 1 displays the user interface of the mapping tool. The detected entity references are listed on the left, and the characters on the right. Each surface form can appear more than once in the text (e.g., 36 times "der wirt"). The user has two options for the grounding: a) map all occurrences to one character; b) consider

---

[3]The character list was created in several iterations by merging already existing lists and automatically extracted candidates from the corups.

Character	#ER	#Proper nouns	Ratio
Parzivâl	427	111	25.8
Gâwân	185	118	63.8
Artûs	128	88	68.8
Jeschûte	103	30	29.1
Clâmidê	74	47	63.5
Herzeloyde	69	9	13

Table 4: Ratio of proper nouns among references

each textual context and map each occurrence differently (Fig. 2).

Table 4 shows the grounding result for some main characters. These characters can be divided into two classes: i) characters which are often refered by their name (Gâwân, Artûs, Clâmidê); ii) characters (Parzivâl, Jeschûte, Herzeloyde) which are mainly referred to by appellative noun phrases.

5   Text Segmentation

For the later network analysis a segmentation is needed to define windows in which relations between characters are extracted. In contrast to the task of entity reference detection, we do not cast text segmentation as a 'real' NLP task, for which we create annotation guidelines, train annotators etc. The reason for this is that this task is directly related to the research question a scholar wants to investigate. It is difficult to imagine context- and text-independent criteria for the segmentation. Annotation guidelines created for *Parzival* might not generalise to other texts.

We therefore explore segmentation approaches based on linguistic and structural criteria and with regards to the content. For all segmentation settings, we (manually) removed non-narrative sections (in which the heterodiegetic narrator gives comments; cf. Coste and Pier (2014)).

Linguistics   Straightforwardly, one can segment according to sentences. Sentence boundaries have been detected automatically using rules based on punctuation. The lack of abbreviations in *Parzival* also removes the most frequent error source for punctuation-based sentence splitting. Each sentence is considered an individual segment.

Structure   *Parzival* is structured into strophes of 30 lines each. There is no apparent meaning to these strophes, and sometimes sentences are split over multiple strophes. In this segmentation setting, each strophe is used as a segment.

Content   Content-based segments are designated as episodes. An episode is a self-contained and homogenous segment of the story. Typical indicators of an episode break are changes in character constellations, time and/or space. Episodes have been annotated manually by one of the authors.

6   Interactive Visual Exploration

To inspect and verify automatic results we use a web-based tool that supports close and distant reading. It provides different views including word clouds, plot views, and graph visualizations that allow analyzing entities and exploring their relationships. Each view allows to directly access the corresponding text passage(s).

In this context particularly relevant is the interactive graph visualization, through which processing errors become apparent quickly. The graph visualization uses a force-directed graph layout and represents the relations between entities, as depicted in Fig. 3 (on the left side). The nodes represent characters/persons and the edges the relations between them. The view is complemented by a fingerprint visualization (A) that indicate where the characters are mentioned in the text. A range slider (B) enables users to select a certain range of the text, for example a single chapter. This way, users can analyze not only the overall text but also the development of the relationships between characters. In a list view (C) users can dynamically adapt the network by selecting or deselecting the entities in the list. Furthermore, they can select an edge in the network view to highlight the co-occurrences of two related entities in the fingerprint visualization. By selecting an occurrence, users can jump to the corresponding text passage as depicted in Fig. 3 (right side).

In the text view the selected entities are highlighted in their assigned color. The background color (orange) represent the respective text segmentation. Next to the scrollbar, a vertical fingerprint displays the further co-occurrences. By hovering over an occurrence the corresponding text passage is displayed in a tooltip, as depicted in (D). After clicking on one, the text view jumps to the corresponding position. This way, users can easily analyze and compare the relevant text passages of the selected entities. With the aid of both views, users can determine incorrect relationships

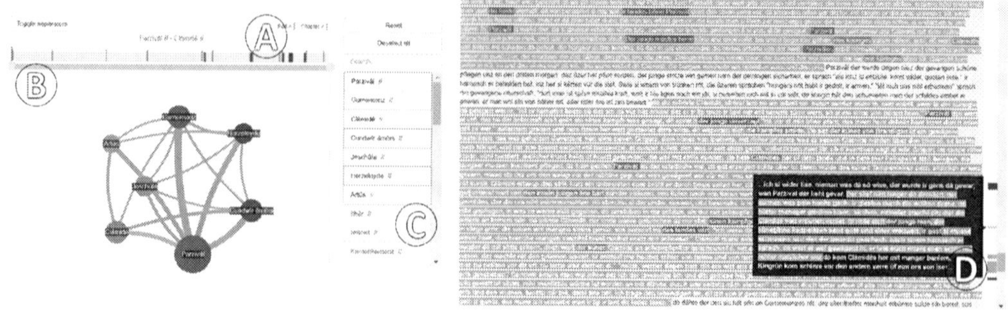

Figure 3: Graph visualization and the text view with selected entities Parzivâl and Clâmidê.

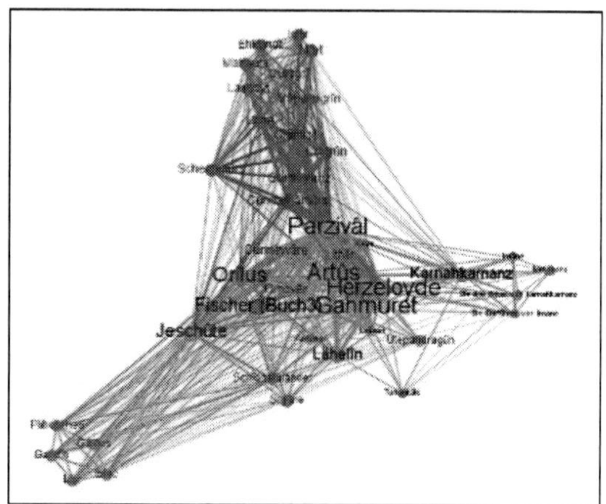

(a) including embedded entity references and direct speech

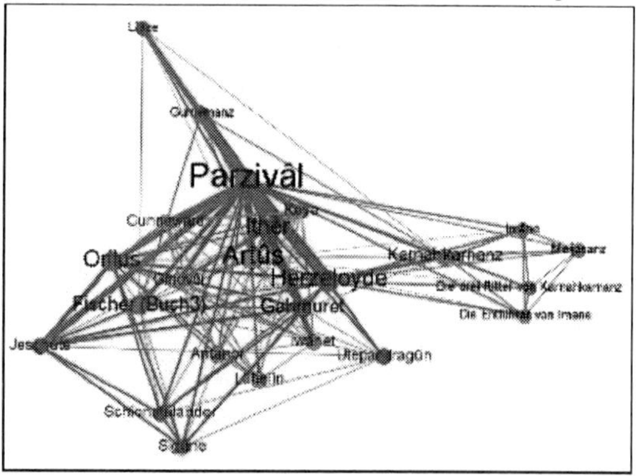

(b) without embedded entity references and direct speech. Several nodes and sub-networks (around Gurzgrî or Gâlôes) disappear; some characters (Gahmuret) become less important because they are often embedded in other entities' expressions.

Figure 4: Entity network of Book III, using content-based segmentation

(graph visualization) and inspect or verify them in detail (text view).

| | Direct speech | + | − | − |
	Embedded ERs	+	+	−
Nodes		41	24	24
Edges		431	144	130
Density		0.526	0.522	0.47
Avgerage degree		21	12	10.8

Table 5: Influence of removing direct speech and embedded entity references on network parameters. Density: Edges / Possible edges; degree: Number of edges in a node.

7 Network Analysis

In this section we compare different parameters of network visualization and analyze their interdependencies and influences on the network results. In the moment, we focus on person-based networks and leave aside the spatial information, which can be used in further analysis, e.g., to distinguish between static and dynamic characters or to detect events (cf. Lotman, 1977).

All network graphs are created with Gephi (Bastian et al., 2009), which provides various layout algorithms, offers statistics and network metrics, and supports dynamic graph visualization. Plots and tables in this section are based on Book III of *Parzival*.

7.1 Embedded entities and direct speech

As a first step, we explore the influence of ERs within a) other ERs (embedded) and b) direct speech. This is due to the fact that neither embedded entities (as Gahmuret in "vil li roy Gahmuret"/"son of the king Gahmuret") nor entities mentioned in (direct) speech are neccesarily taking part in the narrated story or event.

Fig. 4 demonstrates the influence of embedded

Segmentation	by sentence		by strophe		by content	
Entity grounding	+	−	+	−	+	−
Edges	24	18	24	19	130	74
Nodes	65	25	79	26	24	20
Density	0.18	0.15	0.27	0.16	0.47	0.39
Avgerage degree	5.4	2.74	6.48	2.84	10.83	7.4
Connected components	1	3	1	3	1	1
Network diameter	4	4	3	6	2	3

Table 6: Influence of the different segmentation types on the network parameters. Comparison of the network parameters with and without entity grounding. Connected components: Isolated groups of nodes (lower number: stronger connectivity); diameter: Largest distance between two nodes.

entites and direct speech visually, Table 5 provides a numerical view. The network without embedded ERs or direct speech is less dense (0.47 vs. 0.526), the average degree is much lower (10.8 vs. 21), and the number of nodes and edges decreases from 41 nodes and 431 edges to 24 nodes and 130 edges.

7.2 Segmentation

Figures 5a-c show the effects of the different segmentation criteria (cf. Sect. 5) on the networks, quantitative network properties are displayed in Table 6. First we observe a decrease in density from the largest content-based segmentation (0.47) to the medium-sized segmentation in strophes (0.27) to the smallest segmentation in sentences (0.177), which comes along with a reduction of the number of edges (from 130 to 79 to 65). The highest average degree can be found in the content-based network (10.8), in the strophe-based network it is reduced to 6.5 and in the sentence-based network it decreases further to 5.5. As the nodes are less and less connected, the network diameter becomes bigger the smaller the segmentation gets. Since the chosen segmentation serves as basis for the extraction of co-occurrences of characters, it has a huge impact on the network properties which is important to reflect for later interpretations of the network.

7.3 Entity grounding

To estimate the influence of entity grounding on the networks we compare networks based on entity grounding (Sect. 4) to those only based on proper names. We identify an interdependency between entity grounding and segmentation. The sentence-based and strophe-based segmentation are relatively small and therefore more dependent on entity grounding. The co-occurrence of two proper names in a sentence is rare (in Book III of *Parzival*: 25 co-occurrences in over 750 sentences), even in a strophe it rarely appears (26 co-occurrences in 63 strophes). As we see in Fig. 5, the sentence- and strophe-based networks without entity grounding disintegrate into three components, they become less dense and most of the relations get lost.

The last example (Fig. 6) shows the high influence of entity grounding and its importance for an appropriate representation of the character configurations of a narrative text. The unequal ratio of proper names and nouns (cf. Table 4) underlines the importance: By only taking into account the proper names, we found that Parzivâl is mentioned 111 times (in Books III-VII) and that Gâwân is mentioned 118 times. Whereas the consideration of other references to both characters leads to the fact that Parzivâl amounts to 427 mentions and Gâwân to 185 mentions. This means that the primacy of Parzivâl only becomes apparent by including entity grounding.

Thus, being aware of the chosen parameters is a precondition for an adequate analysis and interpretation of the networks. To represent the plot and narrative structure of *Parzival* by analyzing the development of character configurations over time, for instance, it is necessary to exclude embedded entities and direct speech as well as to include entity grounding. The appropriate way of segmentation still needs to be reconsidered.

8 Related Work

Several researchers have extracted co-occurrence networks from dramatic texts or screen plays (Moretti, 2011; Trilcke et al., 2016; Wilhelm et al.,

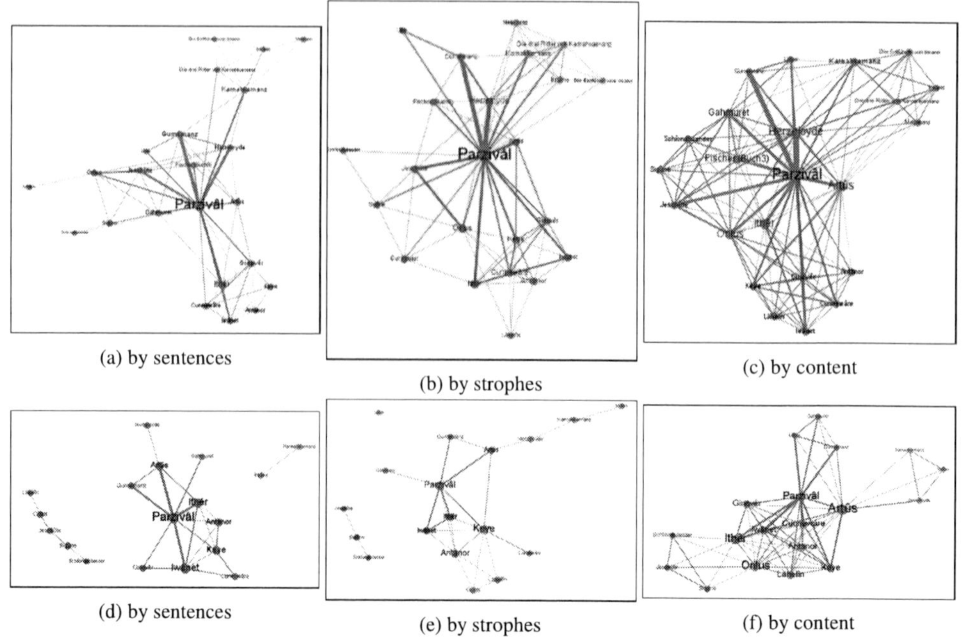

(a) by sentences   (b) by strophes   (c) by content

(d) by sentences   (e) by strophes   (f) by content

Figure 5: Different segmentation options. (a)-(c): With entity grounding; (d)-(f): Without grounding.

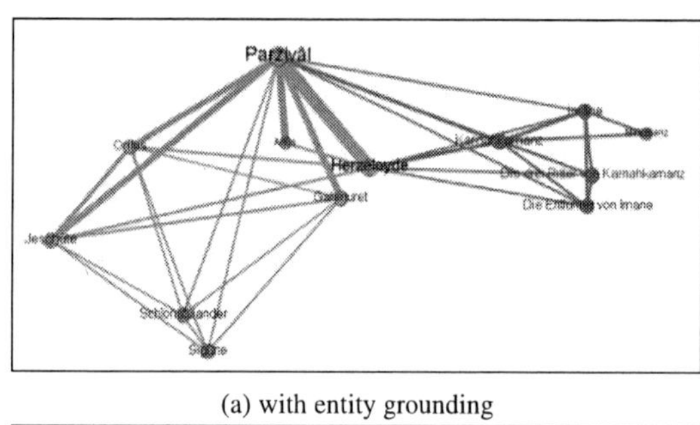

(a) with entity grounding

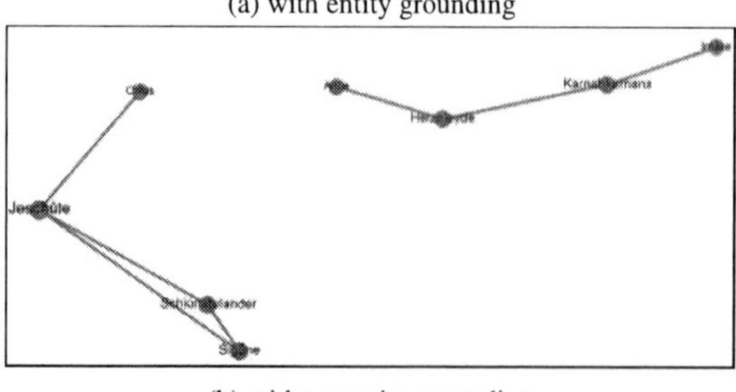

(b) without entity grounding

Figure 6: Parzivâls childhood, content-based segmentation with and without entity grounding. Without entity grounding (b) he is not present despite being a central character (a).

2013; Agarwal et al., 2014b). The strong structuring of such texts (scenes, acts) and clearly defined speakers make identifying co-occurring characters simple. The networks extracted from narrative texts by Elson et al. (2010) only include conversational relations: If two characters appear together in a dialogue, they are connected in a network. The work has been conducted on 19th century British novels and is based on named entities only, with a rule-based co-reference resolution. Agarwal et al. (2012) identify 'social events' in *Alice in Wonderland* and extract different types of networks (interaction- and observation-network) to investigate the roles/profiles of the characters. Using Mouse and Alice as an example they demonstrate the limitations of static networks and the need for dynamic networks that can display change over time. In later publications, they employ automatically created FrameNet frames as a basis to detect social events between named entities (Agarwal et al., 2014a).

Recently, several approaches for visualizing social networks have been introduced. For example, Oelke et al. (2013) analyze prose literature by using the pixel-based literature fingerprinting technique (Keim and Oelke, 2007). The approach visualizes relationships between characters and their evolution during the plot. A related technique is used in FeatureLens (Don et al., 2007), which has been designed to support analysts in finding interesting text patterns and co-occurrences in texts.

There are quite a number of approaches (Vuillemot et al., 2009; Stasko et al., 2008) that provide node-link diagrams to represent social networks. In general, nodes represent entities and edges relations between them. An alternative method is a matrix-based representation which shows relationships among a large number of items where rows and columns represent the nodes of the network (Henry and Fekete, 2007). Both approaches have their drawbacks respective the readability of the structure of the overall network and also for detailed analysis (Ghoniem et al., 2005). Therefore, Henry et al. (2007) introduced a hybrid representation for social networks which combines the benefits of both approaches. It supports a set of interactions which allow users to flexibly change the representation to and from node-link and matrix forms of certain areas in the network.

9   Conclusions

We have presented an end-to-end environment for the extraction of co-occurrence networks based on criteria guided by literary research questions. This guidance not only informs the kinds of entities we are taking into account, but also the different ways of segmenting the text and even the fact that we are including non-named entities in the networks. The given examples in Section 7 demonstrate the influence of these choices on the networks of one and the same narrative text, thus it is important to make these decisions in close collaboration with the domain experts who will use the results. Ultimately, relying solely on named entities can lead to highly skewed impressions of the relative importance of characters in a text, to misleading interpretations of networks and thus, of literary texts. This becomes even more dangerous when large text collections are analyzed, for which a manual inspection is simply not possible. Allowing interactive exploration of aggregated data (networks) mitigates this issue: Domain experts interactively working with a network of a text become aware of such issues quickly. The early integration of scholarly experts even into primarily technical modules is therefore of utmost importance.

The collaboration with experts from different disciplines from Humanities and Social Sciences not only greatly benefits the conceptual development of, e.g., entity reference annotation guidelines: Difficult cases that appear frequently in one text type might appear rarely in another – Researchers working on the latter benefit from the collaboration because it would have taken much longer to come across rare cases. But in addition, this collaboration helps to ensure that technical and methodological developments are not too specialized for one particular text or text type. Too specialized software is relatively expensive to develop and will be outdated quickly. It also runs counter to the often purely methodological computer science goals of 'generic problem solving'. We therefore also concentrate on the fundamental methodological questions rather than on tool development.

We have focused here on one particular research question and corpus, but the above described workflow has been applied to narrative (modern and medieval) texts, theoretical philosophical texts (with the goal of establishing relations between philosophical networks) and parliamentary debates (with the goal of connecting political parties to political issues). We believe that it is worthwhile and feasible to search for common interests across multiple Humanities and Social Sciences disciplines and research questions. The identification of – at least structurally – common research questions allows to develop workflows that are supported by NLP and visualization methods that otherwise would just not pay off due to the development efforts.

Acknowledgments

This research has been conducted within the CRETA project[4] which is funded by the German Ministry for Education and Research (BMBF).

---

[4]http://www.creta.uni-stuttgart.de

References

Apoorv Agarwal, Sriramkumar Balasubramanian, Anup Kotalwar, Jiehan Zheng, and Owen Rambow. 2014a. Frame semantic tree kernels for social network extraction from text. In *Proceedings of the 14th Conference of the European Chapter of the Association for Computational Linguistics*. Association for Computational Linguistics, Gothenburg, Sweden, pages 211–219. http://www.aclweb.org/anthology/E14-1023.

Apoorv Agarwal, Sriramkumar Balasubramanian, Jiehan Zheng, and Sarthak Dash. 2014b. Parsing screenplays for extracting social networks from movies. In *Proceedings of the 3rd Workshop on Computational Linguistics for Literature (CLFL)*. Association for Computational Linguistics, Gothenburg, Sweden, pages 50–58. http://www.aclweb.org/anthology/W14-0907.

Apoorv Agarwal, Augusto Corvalan, Jacob Jensen, and Owen Rambow. 2012. Social network analysis of alice in wonderland. In David K. Elson, Anna Kazantseva, Rada Mihalcea, and Stan Szpakowicz, editors, *Proceedings of the NAACL-HLT 2012 Workshop on Computational Linguistics for Literature*. Association for Computational Linguistics, Montréal, Canada, pages 88–96. http://www.aclweb.org/anthology/W12-2513.

Mathieu Bastian, Sebastien Heymann, and Mathieu Jacomy. 2009. Gephi: An open source software for exploring and manipulating networks. In *Proceeding of International AAAI Conference on Weblogs and Social Media*.

Karl Bertau. 1983. Wolfram von Eschenbach. Versuch über die Verhaltenssemantik von Verwandten im "Parzival". In Karl Bertau, editor, *Neun Versuche über Subjektivität und Ursprünglichkeit in der Geschichte*, München, Germany, pages 190–240.

Steven Bethard, Philip Ogren, and Lee Becker. 2014. Cleartk 2.0: Design patterns for machine learning in uima. In Nicoletta Calzolari (Conference Chair), Khalid Choukri, Thierry Declerck, Hrafn Loftsson, Bente Maegaard, Joseph Mariani, Asuncion Moreno, Jan Odijk, and Stelios Piperidis, editors, *Proceedings of the Ninth International Conference on Language Resources and Evaluation (LREC'14)*. European Language Resources Association (ELRA), Reykjavik, Iceland.

Thomas Bögel, Michael Gertz, Evelyn Gius, Janina Jacke, Jan Christoph Meister, Marco Petris, and Jannik Strötgen. 2015. Gleiche Textdaten, unterschiedliche Erkenntnisziele? Zum Potential vermeintlich widersprüchlicher Zugänge zu Textanalyse. In *Proceedings of DHd*. Digital Humanities im deutschsprachigen Raum, Graz, Austria.

Didier Coste and John Pier. 2014. Narrative levels (revised version; uploaded 23 april 2014). In Peter Hühn, editor, *the living handbook of narratology*, Hamburg University Press. http://www.lhn.uni-hamburg.de/article/narrative-levels-revised-version-uploaded-23-april-2014.

Walter Delabar. 1990. *Erkantiu sippe unt hoch geselleschaft: Studien zur Funktion des Verwandtschaftsverbandes in Wolframs von Eschenbach "Parzival"*. Kümmerle, Göppingen, Germany.

Anthony Don, Elena Zheleva, Machon Gregory, Sureyya Tarkan, Loretta Auvil, Tanya Clement, Ben Shneiderman, and Catherine Plaisant. 2007. Discovering interesting usage patterns in text collections: Integrating text mining with visualization. In *Proceedings of the 16th ACM Conference on Conference on Information and Knowledge Management*. ACM, CIKM '07, pages 213–222. https://doi.org/10.1145/1321440.1321473.

Nora Echelmeyer, Nils Reiter, and Sarah Schulz. 2017. Ein PoS–Tagger für "das" Mittelhochdeutsche. In *Book of Abstracts of DHd 2017*. Bern, Switzerland, pages 141–147. https://doi.org/10.18419/opus-9023.

David K. Elson, Nicholas Dames, and Kathleen McKeown. 2010. Extracting social networks from literary fiction. In Jan Hajič, Sandra Carberry, Stephen Clark, and Joakim Nivre, editors, *Proceedings of the 48th Annual Meeting of the Association for Computational Linguistics*. Association for Computational Linguistics, Uppsala, Sweden, pages 138–147. http://www.aclweb.org/anthology/P10-1015.

Mohammad Ghoniem, Jean-Daniel Fekete, and Philippe Castagliola. 2005. On the readability of graphs using node-link and matrix-based representations: a controlled experiment and statistical analysis. *Information Visualization* 4(2):114–135.

Nathalie Henry and Jean-Daniel Fekete. 2007. Matlink: Enhanced matrix visualization for analyzing social networks. *Human-Computer Interaction–INTERACT 2007* pages 288–302.

Nathalie Henry, Jean-Daniel Fekete, and Michael J McGuffin. 2007. Nodetrix: a hybrid visualization of social networks. *IEEE transactions on visualization and computer graphics* 13(6):1302–1309.

Heng Ji and Ralph Grishman. 2011. Knowledge base population: Successful approaches and challenges. In *Proceedings of the 49th Annual Meeting of the Association for Computational Linguistics: Human Language Technologies-Volume 1*. Association for Computational Linguistics, pages 1148–1158.

D. Keim and D. Oelke. 2007. Literature fingerprinting: A new method for visual literary analysis. In *Proceedings of the IEEE Symposium on Visual Analytics Science and Technology*. VAST '07, pages 115–122. https://doi.org/10.1109/VAST.2007.4389004.

Juri Lotman. 1977. *The Structure of the Artistic Text*. Oxon Publishing Ltd. Translated by Ronald Vroom.

Cerstin Mahlow, Kerstin Eckart, Jens Stegmann, Andre Blessing, Gregor Thiele, Markus Grtner, and Jonas Kuhn. 2014. Resources, Tools, and Applications at the CLARIN Center Stuttgart. In *Proceedings of the 12th Konferenz zur Verarbeitung natrlicher Sprache (KONVENS 2014)*. pages 11–21.

Andrew Kachites McCallum. 2002. Mallet: A machine learning for language toolkit. Http://mallet.cs.umass.edu.

Franco Moretti. 2011. Network theory, plot analysis. Pamphlets of the Stanford Literary Lab 2, Stanford Literary Lab.

D. Oelke, D. Kokkinakis, and D. A. Keim. 2013. Fingerprint matrices: Uncovering the dynamics of social networks in prose literature. *Computer Graphics Forum* 32(3pt4):371–380. https://doi.org/10.1111/cgf.12124.

Helmut Schmid. 1994. Probabilistic part-of-speech tagging using decision trees. *Proceedings of the conference on New Methods in Language Processing* 12.

Elisabeth Schmidt. 1986. *Familiengeschichten und Heilsmythologie. Die Verwandtschaftsstrukturen in den französischen und deutschen Gralromanen des 12. und 13. Jahrhunderts*. Tübingen, Germany.

John Stasko, Carsten Görg, and Zhicheng Liu. 2008. Jigsaw: Supporting investigative analysis through interactive visualization. *Information Visualization* 7(2):118–132. https://doi.org/10.1057/palgrave.ivs.9500180.

Rolf Sutter. 2003. *mit saelde ich gerbet han den gral: Genealogische Strukturanalyse zu Wolframs von Eschenbach "Parzival"*. Ph.D. thesis, Eberhard-Karls-Universität, Tübingen, Germany.

Peer Trilcke, Frank Fischer, Mathias Göbel, and Dario Kampkaspar. 2016. Theatre plays as 'small worlds'? network data on the history and typology of german drama. In *Digital Humanities 2016: Conference Abstracts*. Jagiellonian University & Pedagogical University, Kraków, pages 385–387. http://dh2016.adho.org/abstracts/360.

R. Vuillemot, T. Clement, C. Plaisant, and A. Kumar. 2009. What's being said near "martha"? exploring name entities in literary text collections. In *Proceedings of the IEEE Symposium on Visual Analytics Science and Technology, 2009*. VAST '09, pages 107–114. https://doi.org/10.1109/VAST.2009.5333248.

Thomas Wilhelm, Manuel Burghardt, and Christian Wolff. 2013. "To See or Not to See" - An Interactive Tool for the Visualization and Analysis of Shakespeare Plays. In *Kultur und Informatik: Visual Worlds & Interactive Spaces*. Verlag Werner Hülsbusch, Glückstadt, Germany, pages 175–185.

Modeling intra-textual variation with entropy and surprisal: topical vs. stylistic patterns

Stefania Degaetano-Ortlieb
Saarland University
Campus A2.2
66123 Saarbrücken
s.degaetano@mx.uni-saarland.de

Elke Teich
Saarland University
Campus A2.2
66123 Saarbrücken
e.teich@mx.uni-saarland.de

Abstract

We present a data-driven approach to investigate intra-textual variation by combining entropy and surprisal. With this approach we detect linguistic variation based on phrasal lexico-grammatical patterns across sections of research articles. Entropy is used to detect patterns typical of specific sections. Surprisal is used to differentiate between more and less informationally-loaded patterns as well as types of information (topical vs. stylistic). While we here focus on research articles in biology/genetics, the methodology is especially interesting for digital humanities scholars, as it can be applied to any text type or domain and combined with additional variables (e.g. time, author or social group) to obtain insights on intra-textual variation.

1 Introduction

While there is an abundance of studies on linguistic variation according to domain, register and genre, text-internal variation, i.e. variation based on changing micro-purposes within a text (Biber and Finegan, 1994), has received much less attention. As such internal shifts occur in all kinds of discourse — be it in spoken (such as spontaneous conversation or speeches) or written mode (such as literary texts, written editorials, research articles) — there has been recently a growing interest in this type of variation. In general, knowledge on intra-textual variation leads to a more comprehensive understanding of the data underlying computational modeling, analysis, interpretation, etc.

In the field of NLP, there is a growing need in the development of applications that consider variation also at the textual level to improve perfor-

mance. Considering research articles, approaches within BioNLP, for instance, have moved from focusing on abstracts as sources of text mining to using also full-text articles (Cohen et al., 2010), not least because this data is made available through repositories such as PubMedCentral (PMC). To obtain good performance, corpora created from such resources are highly annotated with linguistic as well as semantic categories characterizing e.g. gene names. From these, specific features are selected with a trade-off between ease of extraction and desired type of information. In the field of DH, intra-textual variation is considered especially in literary studies, computational stylistics, and authorship attribution. Hoover (2016) shows, for example, how knowledge about differences between text parts helps to improve computational stylistic approaches. In corpus linguistics, the common approach to intra-textual variation is to start with a set of pre-defined linguistic features (Biber and Finegan, 1994). While the choice of features is clearly linguistically informed, this initial step in analysis is manual and needs to be carried out anew for every new text type or register considered. Also, analysis is restricted to frequency (i.e. unconditioned probabilities).

We present a methodology for investigating intra-textual variation that is data-driven and based on conditional probabilities which are calculated using two information-theoretic measures, entropy and surprisal. Being data-driven, our approach can be applied to any text type or domain, avoiding extensive annotations and manual selection of features possibly involved in variation. Based on probabilities conditioned on ambient and extra-linguistic context, it allows to capture variation in a more fine-grained manner than by considering mere frequencies.

As a testbed for our approach, we use scientific research articles in genetics, as they clearly

Joint SIGHUM Workshop on Computational Linguistics for Cultural Heritage, Social Sciences, Humanities and Literature.
Proceedings, pages 68–77, Vancouver, BC, August 4, 2017. ©2017 Association for Computational Linguistics

exhibit the typical IMRaD (Introduction, Methods, Results and Discussion) structure of scientific articles, with internal shifts in purpose (see e.g. Swales (1990)).

We use *relative entropy* (Kullback-Leibler Divergence) to detect features typical of specific sections. By considering *surprisal* (i.e. probabilities of features in their ambient context), we are able to detect the amount and type of information these typical features convey, e.g. more informationally-loaded expressions (e.g. terminology) vs. less informationally-loaded expressions (e.g. linguistic formula, such as *These results show that*). Thus, besides possible topical variation within articles across sections, we are able to detect also variation of stylistic lexico-grammatical patterns. While our focus is on research articles, the methodology can be applied to any text type or domain to detect (intra-textual) variation in a data-driven way.

2   Related work

Related work in (corpus) linguistics has mainly focused on variation across domains, registers or genres (represented by corpora) and less on variation within text. Among the few approaches to intra-textual variation is Swales' work on moves, discourse-structuring units with specific communicative purposes (Swales, 1990), which he applies to the analysis of research articles. A different approach is taken by Biber and colleagues (e.g. Biber et al. (2007)), who use multi-dimensional analysis considering detailed, pre-defined linguistic features to observe intra-textual variation across research article sections. Gray (2015) applies the same approach to observe features of 'elaborated' vs. 'compressed' grammatical structures (e.g. finite complement clauses such as *that*-clauses vs. adjectives as nominal pre-modifiers) across disciplines and research article sections. While quite detailed and linguistically informed, these approaches are clearly biased towards the pre-selection of features to be investigated.

In computational stylistics, there is related work on style variation of literary works, where it has been recently shown that knowledge on intra-textual variation among literary texts possibly improves computational stylistic tasks (Hoover, 2016). In terms of methods, similar work is done especially in the field of authorship attribu-

tion. These approaches aim to determine probable authors of disputed texts, ranging from considering frequencies of words, keywords and keyness to measures such as Burrow's Delta and Kullback-Leibler Divergence (see e.g. Burrows (2002); Hoover (2004); Jannidis et al. (2015); Pearl et al. (2016); Savoy (2016)). While we also use Kullback-Leibler Divergence to obtain typical features (here: of specific sections of research articles), in our approach we also account for the amount and type of information typical features provide, allowing a more fine-grained differentiation between topical vs. stylistic features.

In computational linguistics, a related problem is discourse segmentation. For an early approach see e.g. TEXTTILING (Hearst, 1997), a cohesion-driven approach for segmentation of multi-paragraph subtopic structure. More recently, topic modeling (notably LDA) has been applied to discourse segmentation as well (e.g. Misra et al. (2011); see also Riedl and Biemann (2012) for an overview). The dominant interest is on topical shifts in text as indicator of discourse structure, however topic modeling estimation is computationally expensive and needs domain-adaptation.

Recently, there is also an increasing interest in argumentative and rhetorical structure (e.g. Gou et al. (2011); Séaghdha and Teufel (2014)). While recent approaches in this field achieved promising results, they rely on highly annotated data and have to be adapted for different domains.

Further, there is work on intra-textual variation within the BioNLP community, motivated by the need to extract biomedical knowledge not only from abstracts, but also from full-text articles (Cohen et al., 2010). Besides the use of a pre-defined linguistic feature set, in BioNLP also ontologies are widely employed. This again involves a bias towards feature selection, use of highly annotated data combined with a restricted use to specific domains.

More recently, information-theoretic notions have been employed to analyze intra-textual variation. For example, Verspoor and colleagues employ Information Gain to measure the difference between conditional probabilities of tokens being part of a term within an ontology (Groza and Verspoor, 2015). The intuition behind this is to model the amount of information a token such as *activity* provides when being part of a term such as *alpha-1, 6-mannosyltransferase activity*. In this example, *activity* provides a low amount of information, as it is also widely used within other entries (over 25,000) in the Gene Ontology. Others combine entropy with a Bayesian approach to unsupervised topic segmentation (Eisenstein and Barzilay, 2008).

We propose here to employ entropy and surprisal to model intra-textual variation. First, this allows us to detect linguistic features typical of specific sections (rather than using pre-defined ones), modeling intra-textual variation in a data-driven way. Second, by considering the amount of information (i.e. more or less informationally-loaded) and the type of information these typical features provide (i.e. topical vs. stylistic), we obtain a more comprehensive picture of the type of variation. Moreover, while the majority of approaches relies on lexical features, we take a step of abstraction, focusing also on grammatical patterns, which adds to the genericity of our approach.

3 Methodology

3.1 Data

As a dataset, we use a subsection of the SCITEX corpus (Degaetano-Ortlieb et al., 2013) with research articles from genetics, amounting to approx. 2.5 million tokens (see Table 1), and covering the years 2004 to 2006. For tokenization, lemmatization and part-of-speech (POS) tagging, we use TreeTagger (Schmid, 1994) with an updated list of abbreviations specific to academic writing. Sentence splitting is based on labels of punctuations from POS information.

journal	tokens	texts
Gene	1,972,206	280
Nucleid Acids Research	612,988	71

Table 1: Journals with corpus size and number of texts

The two selected journals have the advantage of having a relatively systematic section labeling, which allows us to automatically detect sections by trigger words (e.g. Abstract, Introduction). The automatic annotation is revised manually to ensure a high quality section labeling. Table 2 shows the amount of tokens across sections[1].

---

[1] As the body of an article can be split into a variety of sections, rather than trying to match these into methods and result sections, we opted for putting this material into one MAIN part.

section	tokens
Abstract	33,577
Introduction	143,863
Main (Methods/Results)	2,136,679
Conclusion	271,075

Table 2: Section size

3.2 Methods

To observe differences in phrasal lexico-grammatical patterns across sections of research articles, we consider part-of-speech (POS) trigrams as features[2], as they have shown to perform best in inspecting lexico-grammatical patterns[3]. To consider whether a phrasal pattern transports more or less information, we also consider the amount of information in bits being transmitted by the lexical fillers of POS trigrams in a running text. For this, we use a model of *average surprisal* (AvS), i.e. the (negative log) probability of a given unit (e.g. a word) in context (e.g. its preceding words) for all its occurrences, measured in bits:[4]

$$AvS(w) = \frac{1}{|w|} \sum_i -\log_2 p(w_i|w_{i-1}w_{i-2}w_{i-3}) \quad (1)$$

where w_i is a word, w_{i-1} to w_{i-3} its three preceding words with $p(w_i|w_{i-1}w_{i-2}w_{i-3})$ being the probability of a word given its preceding three words. To obtain AvS values for POS trigrams, we take the mean of the AvS of the three lexical fillers:

$$AvS(trigram_i) = \frac{AvS(w_1) + AvS(w_2) + AvS(w_3)}{3} \quad (2)$$

This allows us to measure the amount of information in bits each instance i, i.e. each lexical realization of a POS trigram, conveys. The distribution of $AvS(trigram_i)$ is divided up into three quantiles, categorizing the data into low, middle and high AvS ranges, a methodology that already

---

[2] We exclude POS trigrams consisting of characters constituting sentence markers (e.g. fullstops, colons), brackets, and symbols (e.g. equal sign).

[3] Note that bi-grams proved to be too short to capture grammatical information (e.g. passives), four- and five-grams lead to sparse data.

[4] For a similar approach see Genzel and Charniak (2002).

phrase type	example trigram (POS.AvS)	example
AdjP mod	JJ.NN.NN.high	**paa2 gene cluster**
Citation	NP.CC.NP.high	*Indeed,* **Wolner and Gralla** *(12) showed that*
Compound	NP.NN.NP.high	**TbR-I inhibitor SB-431542**
Gerund	VVG.MD.VV.high	**silencing should prove**
NP demonstrative	DT.NNS.VHP.low	**these studies have**
Passive	NNS.VHP.VBN.high	*In plants,* **polyamines have been** *reported to play a crucial role in morphogenesis*
Past participle	VVN.IN.DT.low	**Based on the** *data presented in Figure 5*
PP mod	NN.IN.JJ.middle	**use of alternative**
Semi-modal	VVP.TO.VB.low	*more detailed studies* **need to be** *done*
that-clause	IN.PP.MD.low	*but it was possible* **that they could** *be transcribed*
to-inf evaluative	JJ.TO.RB.middle	**useful to finally**
V coordination	NNS.CC.VV.high	*to functionally characterize the identified* **mutations and distinguish** *between polymorphisms*
Evaluative *it*-pattern	PP.VBZ.JJ.low	**it is remarkable** *that*
VP existential	EX.VBP.JJ.low	**There are several** *hypotheses about*
VP interactant	PP.VVP.IN.low	**we show that**
VP modal	MD.VV.DT.middle	**could explain the**
VP reporting	NNS.VVP.IN.low	**data suggest that**

Table 3: Typical phrase types with examples of POS trigrams with AvS range and examples

proved to be useful in capturing diachronic variationDegaetano-Ortlieb and Teich (2016)[5]. We then combine for each instance i information about the POS trigram and the AvS range it belongs to. At the same time, this also provides for each POS trigram the number of i with low, middle and high AvS, i.e. how many times a POS trigram occurs with low, middle or high AvS. These POS trigrams with AvS ranges serve then as features, providing a set of 19,776 features.

Detection of typical features from this feature set is based on Kullback-Leibler Divergence (KLD; or *relative entropy*), a well-known measure of (dis)similarity between probability distributions (Kullback and Leibler, 1951) used in NLP, speech processing, and information retrieval. Based on work by Fankhauser et al. (2014a,b), we create KLD models for each section (ABSTRACT, INTRODUCTION, MAIN, CONCLUSION), calculating the average amount of additional bits per feature (here: POS trigrams with AvS ranges) needed to encode features of a distribution A (e.g. ABSTRACT) by using an encoding optimized for a distribution I (e.g. INTRODUCTION). The more additional bits are needed, the more distinct or distant A and I are. This is formalized as:

$$D(A||I) = \sum_i p(feature_i|A) log_2 \frac{p(feature_i|A)}{p(feature_i|I)} \quad (3)$$

where $p(feature_i|A)$ is the probability of a feature in a section A (e.g. ABSTRACT) and $p(feature_i|I)$ is the probability of that feature in a section I (e.g. INTRODUCTION). The $log_2 \frac{p(feature_i|A)}{p(feature_i|I)}$ relates to the difference between the probability distributions $(log_2 p(feature_i|A) - log_2 p(feature_i|I))$, giving the number of additional bits. These are then weighted with the probability of $p(feature_i|A)$ so that the sum over all $feature_i$ gives the average number of additional bits per feature, i.e. the relative entropy. This allows us to determine whether any two sections are distinct or not and if they are, to what degree and by which features. For this, we inspect the ranking (based on KLD values) of features for one section vs. the other sections. In terms of typicality, the more additional bits are used to encode a feature, the more typical that feature is for a given section vs. another section. For instance, in a comparison between two sections (e.g. ABSTRACT vs. INTRODUCTION), the higher the KLD value of a features for a section (e.g. ABSTRACT), the more typical that feature is for that given section. In addition, we test for significance of a feature by an unpaired Welch's t-test. Thus, features considered typical are distinctive according to KLD and show a p-value below a given threshold (e.g. 0.05).

We thus obtain typical features for each section, i.e. typical POS trigrams combined with AvS ranges, allowing us to see whether a typical POS trigram carries more or less information (i.e. the amount of information) as defined by AvS.

For analysis, we then categorize typical POS trigrams into phrase types. Table 3 shows examples

---

[5]We also considered a division into quartiles, but it proved to be too narrow.

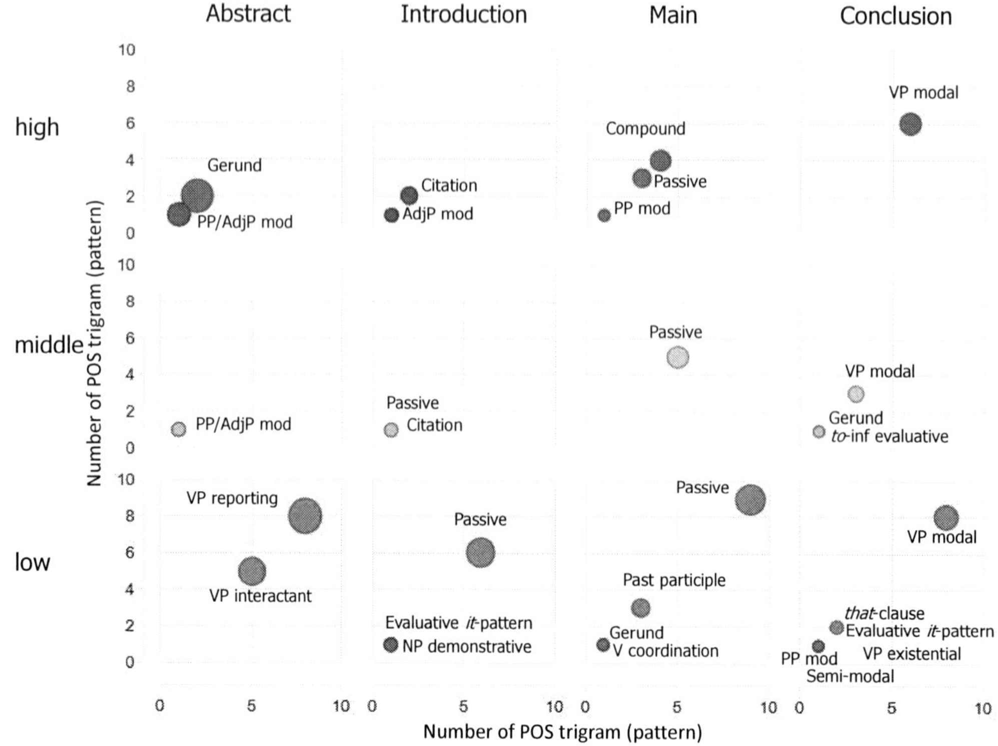

Figure 1: Typical phrase types across sections and AvS range

of POS trigrams with AvS range by their phrase type with examples of lexical realizations.

4 Analysis

In the analysis, we aim to explore intra-textual variation taking a variationist approach (rather than a text segmentation approach) and pursue the following questions:

(a) *Typical features*: Which phrasal lexico-grammatical patterns are typical of specific sections?

(b) *Amount of information*: How much information (by means of AvS) do phrasal lexico-grammatical patterns convey?

(c) *Type of information*: What type of information do phrasal lexico-grammatical patterns convey?

4.1 Typical phrase types across sections

For better comparison across sections, Figure 1 shows the number of POS trigrams (patterns) for a specific phrase type (on the x and y-axis) and

the frequency per million (fpM) of the phrase type by circle size across sections with respect to high (red), middle (yellow) and low (blue) AvS values. For examples of each phrase type consider Table 3.

Considering ABSTRACT and low AvS (lower left part of Figure 1), it is strongly characterized by reporting patterns, mainly used with *that*-clauses and relatively general nouns (e.g. *data suggest that*, *analysis showed that*), and by interactant patterns (such as *we show that* and *we report here*). Considering the high AvS range (red), gerunds (see Example 4) as well as adjectival and prepositional modification are typical (see Examples 5 and 6, respectively).

(4) **Considering** *some severe limitations of viral systems [...] synthetic nonviral systems are highly desirable in the above applications.* (ABSTRACT; VVG.DT.JJ)

(5) *The T. maritima rpoA gene coding the subunit does not complement the* **thermosensitive rpoA112 mutation** *of E. coli.* (ABSTRACT; JJ.NN.NN)

(6) *The minichromosome maintenance (MCM) proteins are thought to function as the replicative helicases **in eukarya and archaea**.* (ABSTRACT; IN.NN.CC)

INTRODUCTION is characterized by passives (e.g. *been used with*), especially with low AvS, followed by citation with middle and high AvS (e.g. *Wolner and Gralla*). Also typical is the evaluative *it*-pattern (see Example 7) and a demonstrative pattern (e.g. *these studies/proteins have*) both in the context of presenting previous work/knowledge.

(7) ***It has become evident*** *in the last decade that many, if not the majority, of genes are regulated post-transcriptionally* [...]. (INTRODUCTION, low AvS; PP.VHZ.VVN)

MAIN is strongly characterized by passives (e.g. *analysis was performed*), especially with low AvS, but also with middle and high AvS. Also typical in the low AvS range are past participle patterns (e.g. *performed as described, based on the*), gerund (e.g. *purified by using*), and coordination (e.g. *and visualized with*). In addition, compound patterns are typical in the high AvS range, being clearly terminological (such as *TbR-I inhibitor SB-431542, SG parallel G-quadruplex, GC12/ GC3 correlation*).

In CONCLUSION modal verb patterns are most typical across all three AvS ranges (e.g. *units might result, could explain the*). In addition, with low AvS *that*-clauses are typical (e.g. *suggests that it may require*), evaluative *it*-patterns (e.g. *it is important to note, it is possible that*) as well as semi-modals (e.g. *seem/appear to be*), existentials (e.g. *there are several/other*) and prepositional post-modification (e.g. *present/useful in the*). Thus, modality and evaluation are quite typical for CONCLUSION sections in genetics.

Comparing typical phrase types across sections, we see that while for INTRODUCTION and MAIN passives are quite typical (especially with low AvS for both), ABSTRACT and CONCLUSION are marked by relatively unique typical phrase types (e.g. reporting verb phrases for ABSTRACT vs. modal verb phrases for CONCLUSION).

While this is in line with observations made by Biber and Finegan (1994), who have shown e.g. a preference of passives in the main part of articles as well as a common use of modal verbs in conclusions, besides other features (such as evaluative patterns) we also show the amount of information these features transmit (by AvS). Typical phrase types with high AvS values belong mostly to nominal groups (compounds and nouns modified by adjectives (AdjP mod) and prepositional phrases (PP mod)) conveying topical information, while those with low AvS values mostly to verb groups (passives and verb phrases with different functions such as reporting, evaluative, etc.) conveying a more stylistic type of information.

4.2 Amount of information and type of information of typical phrase types

Zooming into the most frequent lexical realizations of specific patterns, gives a clearer picture of the type of information conveyed by different ranges of AvS.

Here, we present two examples: First, we zoom into typical patterns of ABSTRACT, showing how the type of information differs from topical to stylistic based on the AvS range. Second, we look at CONCLUSION considering its typical modal verb phrase across AvS ranges.

Figure 2 shows lexical realizations of typical phrase types within ABSTRACT across AvS ranges (high: reddish, middle: yellowish, low: blueish) with the size relating to frequency for each range.

Typical reporting verb patterns (VP reporting) with low AvS values (blueish) make use of relatively general nouns (*data, analysis, results*) with verbs such as *suggest, show* and *indicate*. For VP interactional, the phrase *we show that* is the dominant lexical realization, followed, for example, by phrases such as *we characterized the/demonstrate that/report here*. The amount of information transmitted by these phrases is relatively low. The purpose of use of these phrases is more style-oriented rather than topic-oriented.

Comparing this to lexical realizations of high AvS values (reddish) for ABSTRACT (see again Figure 2), we see that these are clearly related to quite compact linguistic forms expressing either processes with the gerund form (*lining the gastrovacular*) or scientific terms with adjectival (e.g. *multiple gene cassette*) and prepositional modification (e.g. *helicases in eukarya and archaea*[6]). Clearly, the amount of information these phrases

---

[6]Note that for this pattern we have shown more context for better understanding, as the pattern would only show Preposition-Noun-Conjunction, which in the example is realized as *in eukarya and*.

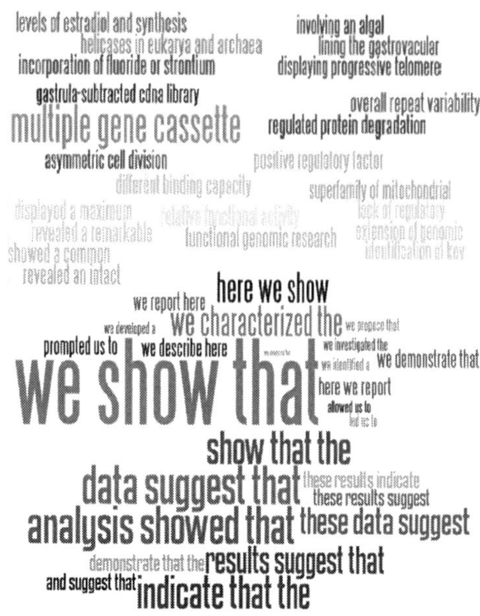

Figure 2: Lexical realizations of typical patterns with high, middle and low AvS in ABSTRACT

transmit is relatively high and the type of information is topic-oriented.

Lexical realizations of middle AvS lie in between, i.e. terms seem to be more generic (e.g. by adjectival modification such as *positive regulatory factor* or prepositional modification such as *lack of regulatory*) and reporting verb phrases are used in a less confined ambient context (e.g. *showed a common* instead of *showed that*). Thus, these phrases transmit a relatively moderate amount of information and can be style- or topic-oriented.

In Figure 3 we zoom into CONCLUSION, showing how the same typical phrase type (here: VP modal; compare also with Figure 1) can differ in the information type it conveys depending on its AvS range. Here, lexical realizations of verb patterns with modal verbs are shown for high (reddish), middle (yellowish), and low (blueish) AvS values. With high AvS, the modal verb is used in combination with specific terms (e.g. *tlh genes*, *tRNA isodecoders*). From Examples 8 and 9, we can see how within the whole sentences assumptions are put forward about the two terms *tlh genes* and *tRNA isodecoders*. In the middle range, the modal verb patterns are used with a variety of verbs. Examples 10 and 11 show relatively

generic preceding contexts (*the structure of the substrate* in 10 and *subtle changes* in 11), which are used with modal expressions of middle AvS. In the lower range, the modal verbs are used with a confined set of verbs (*suggest, result*), in relatively formalized lexical phrases (*may/might be due*), and in relational phrases (*may be an, might be the*). Example 12 to 14 show a quite vague preceding context realized by the use of referring expressions such as *this* and *there* for modal verbs used with low AvS.

Figure 3: Lexical realizations of modal verb patterns (VP modal) with high, middle and low AvS in CONCLUSION

(8) *A possibility suggested by the presence of transposable elements in the pericentromeric heterochromatin of higher eukaryotes is that the **tlh genes might** be parts of transposons that preferentially transpose to heterochromatic regions.* (CONCLUSION)

(9) *One can envision that **tRNA isodecoders may** be more harmful than useful in translation.* (CONCLUSION)

(10) *This assay is performed in the absence of dNTP, so that the structure of the substrate*

cannot be affected by polymerization .
(CONCLUSION)

(11) *PAX 7 gene expression levels are highly
controlled during tissue development and
subtle **changes could lead** to important
effects.* (CONCLUSION)

(12) *Our work does not suggest that gene
expression contributes to the asymmetric
evolution of paralogs that we observed but
again **this may be due** to small sample size.*
(CONCLUSION)

(13) ***This may be due** to the short length (11 bp)
of the primer [...].* (CONCLUSION)

(14) ***There may be a** few possible reasons for
why hix-AG is not bound by Hin [...].*
(CONCLUSION)

Given that this is just one type of phrase, i.e.
modal verb phrase being typical for CONCLUSION
in genetics, by considering AvS we clearly see
how it still differs in the type of information it
transmits, depending on the ambient context it occurs with, being either topical or stylistic.

5 Section classification

While in the analysis we have taken a variationist approach, we also test how well sections can
be distinguished by typical features obtained by
our approach. Our baseline is a classifier using
all POS trigrams without AvS ranges. In Table 5
we report the F-Measure of three classifiers (Naive
Bayes, Support Vector Machine (SVM) and RandomForest (RF)). Adding AvS ranges improves
classification for all classifiers. Using only typical
POS trigrams obtained by our approach improves
the model considerably. A further improvement is
achieved by considering typical POS trigrams with
AvS ranges. The random forest classifier achieving the best result with 86.0 of F-Measure.

set	BL (NaiveBayes)	SVM	RF
POS 3grams	76.6	78.2	72.9
POS 3grams+AvS	77.0	80.3	74.2
typPOS	80.3	82.5	85.6
typPOS+AvS	81.1	81.0	**86.0**

Table 4: Classification results with typical POS trigrams and AvS ranges.

Considering classification performance of sections with Random Forest, ABSTRACT and MAIN

can be best predicted with 94.5 and 92.5 of F-
Measure, followed by INTRODUCTION with 82.8.
CONCLUSION is less well distinguishable, but still
achieves a considerable improvement when considering typical POS trigrams (from 17.4 to 61.2
of F-Measure).

set	ABS	INTRO	MAIN	CONC
POS 3grams	84.1	71.2	88.2	17.4
POS 3grams+AvS	84.8	75.5	87.9	20.1
typPOS	93.3	81.0	92.7	61.2
typPOS+AvS	**94.5**	82.8	92.5	60.5

Table 5: Classification results by F-Measure for
each section (RandomForest)

6 Conclusion

This paper has presented a novel data-driven approach to intra-textual variation. We have shown
how sections of research articles from genetics differ with respect to the phrasal lexico-grammatical
patterns used across sections (see Section 4.1).
We used *relative entropy* to obtain typical lexico-
grammatical patterns for each section. Moreover,
we have modeled the amount and type of information these lexico-grammatical patterns convey (see
Section 4.2) by using *average surprisal* (AvS),
showing that sections vary in topical as well as
stylistic type of information. In future work, we
plan to model different scientific domains to investigate which of these lexico-grammatical patterns would generalize across domains and which
are domain-specific.

Being data-driven and using part-of-speech information to generate features (see Section 3.2),
our approach can be applied to any other domain,
text type and even other languages (given a good
quality POS annotation), since it is not biased by
topical variation. While here we have modeled
intra-textual variation, additional variables such as
time, author, social group, production type, language etc. can be integrated into the model. For
an application on diachronic data see Degaetano-
Ortlieb et al. (2016) and Degaetano-Ortlieb and
Teich (2016). As long as the variables are known
(e.g. publication dates for time, author names for
author, etc.), our approach allows to investigate
variation at a more abstract linguistic level than
topical variation. Thus, our approach is directly
relevant to studies in sociolinguistics, historical
linguistics and digital humanities in general.

Assessing the amount and type of information

of typical lexico-grammatical patterns is relevant for more sophisticated text analysis. For example, historical linguists might be interested in the whole AvS range, as specific linguistic features might move across time between high, middle and low AvS. A linguistic feature might have high AvS in one time period (e.g. when it enters language use its ambient context may be expected to vary a lot), and low AvS in a later time period (where the feature is well-established in language use and might be more confined to a specific ambient context). The transition period would be seen in the use of the feature in the middle AvS range. In information retrieval, instead, features with high AvS are more relevant as they convey more information and are topic/content-related. AvS ranges could also be more fine-grained in this scenario to distinguish relatively established from new terms. Considering more fine-grained ranges of high AvS combined with time as a variable might be a possible way to explore knowledge change.

7 Acknowledgments

This work is funded by *Deutsche Forschungsgemeinschaft* (DFG) under grants SFB 1102: Information Density and Linguistic Encoding (www.sfb1102.uni-saarland.de) and EXC 284: Multimodal Computing and Interaction (www.mmci.uni-saarland.de). We are also indebted to Stefan Fischer for his contributions to corpus processing and Peter Fankhauser (IdS Mannheim) for his support in statistical analysis. Also, we thank the anonymous reviewers for their valuable comments.

References

Douglas Biber, Ulla Connor, and Thomas A. Upton. 2007. *Discourse on the Move: Using Corpus Analysis to Describe Discourse Structure*. Benjamins, Amsterdam.

Douglas Biber and Edward Finegan. 1994. Intratextual Variation within Medical Research Articles. In Susan Conrad and Douglas Biber, editors, *Variation in English: Multi-dimensional Studies*, Routledge Taylor & Francis Group, pages 108–123.

John Burrows. 2002. Delta: a Measure of Stylistic Difference and a Guide to Likely Authorship. *Literary and Linguistic Computing* 17(3):267–287. https://doi.org/10.1093/llc/17.3.267.

K. Bretonnel Cohen, Helen L. Johnson, Karin Verspoor, Christophe Roeder, and Lawrence E. Hunter. 2010. The Structural and Content Aspects of Abstracts versus Bodies of Full Text Journal Articles are Different. *BMC Bioinformatics* 11(492):1–10.

Stefania Degaetano-Ortlieb, Hannah Kermes, Ashraf Khamis, and Elke Teich. 2016. An Information-Theoretic Approach to Modeling Diachronic Change in Scientific English. In Carla Suhr, Terttu Nevalainen, and Irma Taavitsainen, editors, *Selected Papers from Varieng - From Data to Evidence (d2e)*, Brill, Language and Computers.

Stefania Degaetano-Ortlieb, Hannah Kermes, Ekaterina Lapshinova-Koltunski, and Elke Teich. 2013. SciTex - A Diachronic Corpus for Analyzing the Development of Scientific Registers. In Paul Bennett, Martin Durrell, Silke Scheible, and Richard J. Whitt, editors, *New Methods in Historical Corpus Linguistics*, Narr, volume 3 of *Corpus Linguistics and Interdisciplinary Perspectives on Language - CLIP*, pages 93–104.

Stefania Degaetano-Ortlieb and Elke Teich. 2016. Information-based Modeling of Diachronic Linguistic Change: From Typicality to Productivity. In Nils Reiter, Beatrice Alex, and Kalliopi A. Zervanou, editors, *Proceedings of the 10th SIGHUM Workshop on Language Technology for Cultural Heritage, Social Sciences, and Humanities*. Association for Computational Linguistics (ACL).

Jacob Eisenstein and Regina Barzilay. 2008. Bayesian Unsupervised Topic Segmentation. In *Proceedings of the Conference on Empirical Methods in Natural Language Processing (EMNLP)*. Association for Computational Linguistics, Stroudsburg, PA, USA, EMNLP '08, pages 334–343. http://dl.acm.org/citation.cfm?id=1613715.1613760.

Peter Fankhauser, Hannah Kermes, and Elke Teich. 2014a. Combining Macro- and Microanalysis for Exploring the Construal of Scientific Disciplinarity. In *Digital Humanities*. Lausanne, Switzerland. URL: http://dharchive.org/paper/DH2014/Poster-126.xml.

Peter Fankhauser, Jörg Knappen, and Elke Teich. 2014b. Exploring and Visualizing Variation in Language Resources. In *Proceedings of the Ninth International Conference on Language Resources and Evaluation (LREC '14)*. European Language Resources Association (ELRA), Reykjavik, pages 4125–4128. http://nbn-resolving.de/urn:nbn:de:bsz:mh39-26224.

Dmitriy Genzel and Eugene Charniak. 2002. Entropy Rate Constancy in Text. In *Proceedings of the 40th Annual Meeting on Association for Computational Linguistics (ACL)*. Association for Computational Linguistics, Philadephia, Pennsylvania, USA, pages 199–206. http://dl.acm.org/citation.cfm?id=1073117.

Yufan Gou, Anna Korhonen, and Thierry Poibeau. 2011. A Weakly-supervised Approach to Argumentative Zoning of Scientific Documents. In *Proceedings of the Conference on Empirical Methods in Natural Language Processing (EMNLP)*. Edinburgh, UK, pages 273–283.

Bethany Gray. 2015. On the Complexity of Academic Writing. Disciplinary Variation and Structural Complexity. In Viviana Cortes and Eniko Csomay, editors, *Corpus-based Research in Applied Linguistics. Studies in Honor of Doug Biber*, John Benjamins Publishing Company, Amsterdam / Philadelphia, volume 66 of *Studies in Corpus Linguistics (SCL)*, pages 49–77.

Tudor Groza and Karin Verspoor. 2015. Assessing the Impact of Case Sensitivity and Term Information Gain on Biomedical Concept Recognition. *PLoS One* 10(3):1–22.

Marti A. Hearst. 1997. TextTiling: Segmenting Text into Multi-paragraph Subtopic Passages. *Computational Linguistics* 23(1):33–64.

David L. Hoover. 2004. Testing Burrows's Delta. *Literary and Linguistic Computing* 19(4):453–475. https://doi.org/10.1093/llc/19.4.453.

David L. Hoover. 2016. Textual Variation, Text-Randomization, and Microanalysis. In *Proceedings of Digital Humanities Conference (DH)*. Kraków, Poland, pages 223–225.

Fotis Jannidis, Steffen Pielström, Christof Schöch, and Thorsten Vitt. 2015. Improving Burrows' Delta - An Empirical Evaluation of Text Distance Measures. In *Digital Humanities Conference (DH)*. Sydney, Australia.

Solomon Kullback and Richard A. Leibler. 1951. On Information and Sufficiency. *The Annals of Mathematical Statistics* 22(1):79–86.

Hemant Misra, François Yvon, Olivier Cappé, and Joemon Jose. 2011. Text Segmentation: A Topic Modeling Perspective. *Information Processing & Management* 47(4):528 – 544. https://doi.org/http://dx.doi.org/10.1016/j.ipm.2010.11.008.

Lisa Pearl, Kristine Lu, and Anousheh Haghighi. 2016. The Character in the Letter: Epistolary Attribution in Samuel Richardsons Clarissa. *Digital Scholarship in the Humanities* https://doi.org/https://doi.org/10.1093/llc/fqw007.

Martin Riedl and Chris Biemann. 2012. Text Segmentation with Topic Models. *Journal for Language Technology and Computational Linguistics (JLCL)* 27(1):47–70.

Jacques Savoy. 2016. Estimating the Probability of an Authorship Attribution. *Journal of the Association for Information Science and Technology* 67(6):1462–1472. https://doi.org/10.1002/asi.23455.

Helmut Schmid. 1994. Probabilistic Part-of-Speech Tagging Using Decision Trees. In *International Conference on New Methods in Language Processing*. Manchester, UK, pages 44–49.

Diarmuid Ó Séaghdha and Simone Teufel. 2014. Unsupervised Learning of Rhetorical Structure with Un-topic Models. In *Proceedings of the 25th International Conference on Computational Linguistics (COLING)*. Dublin, Ireland, pages 2–13.

John M. Swales. 1990. *Genre Analysis: English in Academic and Research Settings*. Cambridge Applied Linguistics. Cambridge University Press, Cambridge.

Finding a Character's Voice: Stylome Classification on Literary Characters

Liviu P. Dinu, Ana Sabina Uban
Faculty of Mathematics and Computer Science,
Human Language Technologies Research Center,
University of Bucharest
liviu.p.dinu@gmail.com, ana.uban@gmail.com

Abstract

We investigate in this paper the problem of classifying the stylome of characters in a literary work. Previous research in the field of authorship attribution has shown that the writing style of an author can be characterized and distinguished from that of other authors automatically. In this paper we take a look at the less approached problem of how the styles of different characters can be distinguished, trying to verify if an author managed to create believable characters with individual styles. We present the results of some initial experiments developed on the novel "Liaisons Dangereuses", showing that a simple bag of words model can be used to classify the characters.

Keywords: authorship attribution, stylome classification, literary characters, bag of words

1   Previous Work and Motivation

Automated authorship attribution has a long history (starting from the early 20th century (Mendenhall, 1901)) and has since then been extensively studied and elaborated upon. The problem of authorship identification is based on the assumption that there are stylistic features that can help distinguish the real author of a text from any other theoretical author. One of the oldest studies to propose an approach to this problem is on the issue of the *Federalist Papers*, in which Mosteller and Wallace (Mosteller and Wallace, 1963) try to determine the real author of a few of these papers which have disputed paternity. This work remains iconic in the field, both for introducing a standard dataset and for proposing an effective method for distinguishing between the author's

styles, that is still relevant to this day, based on function words frequencies. Many other types of features have been proposed and successfully used in subsequent studies to determine the author of a text. These types of features generally contrast with the content words commonly used in text categorization by topic, and are said to be used unconsciously and harder to control by the author. Such features are, for example, grammatical structures (Baayen et al., 1996), part-of-speech n-grams (Koppel and Schler, 2003), lexical richness (Tweedie and Baayen, 1998), or even the more general feature of character n-grams (Kešelj et al., 2003; Dinu et al., 2008). Having applications that go beyond finding the real authors of controversial texts, ranging from plagiarism detection to forensics to security, stylometry has widened its scope into other related subtopics such as author verification (verifying whether a text was written by a certain author) (Koppel and Schler, 2004) or author profiling (extracting information about an author's age, gender, etc).

A related problem that has barely been approached in the scientific literature is that of distinguishing between the writing styles of *fictional* people, namely literary characters. This problem may be interesting to study from the point of view of analyzing whether an author managed to create characters that are believable as separate people with individual styles, especially since style is a feature of speech that is said to be hard to consciously control.

One of the first studies that analyzes literary characters stylistically appeared in John Burrow's "Computation into Criticism" (Burrows, 1987), where he shows that Jane Austen's characters in particular show strong individual styles, which the author distinguishes by comparing lists of the most frequent 30 function words. One more recent study by the same author (Burrows and Craig,

Joint SIGHUM Workshop on Computational Linguistics for Cultural Heritage, Social Sciences, Humanities and Literature.
Proceedings, pages 78–82, Vancouver, BC, August 4, 2017. ©2017 Association for Computational Linguistics

2012) looks at a corpus of seventeenth-century plays and tries to cluster them by character and by playwright, finding in the end that the author signal is stronger than the character one. Another recent study (van Dalen-Oskam, 2014) analyzes the works of two epistolary novels authors, who are known to have written their books together, and tries to solve at the same time the problem of distinguishing between passages written by each author, and between styles of each character in the novel. Using a simple word frequency method to distinguish between the characters, the author finds some of the characters were easier to distinguish than others and concludes that further research is needed.

In this paper we attempt to further the answer to the questions of the best way to solve this problem, and propose some new questions to be approached by future research.

2 Data and Methodology

2.1 Liaisons Dangereuses

The corpus used for this experiment was the 18th century epistolary novel "Liaisons Dangereuses" by Pierre Choderlos de Laclos. The plot of the book is built around two main characters, the Vicomte de Valmont, and the Marquise de Merteuil, who engage with various other characters especially as part of games of seduction, deceit or revenge. The other characters act as their victims, in various roles: Cécile, the innocent young girl who Merteuil plans to corrupt, Danceny, her young passionate admirer, Madame de Tourvel, a faithfull wife who Valmont intends to seduce.

The choice of this text was mainly motivated by the structure of the novel, which is fitting to our problem - as an epistolary novel, it is organized into letters, each written by a different character, which is ideal for easily labelling our text samples with the characters that the text is attributed to. We used the original French version of the text so that we can work on its purest form, unaltered by any noise introduced by translation.

The book consists of 175 letters, sent between the characters; the lengths of the letters vary from 100 to 3600 words, with an average of ~800 words. The routes of the letters sent by and to the main characters can be seen in Table 1 below: the rows correspond to letter senders and the columns to recipients. Table 2 lists the legend for the abbreviations used for the characters' names.

	CV	MM	VV	MV	CD	PT	MR	O
CV		3	2		8			11
MM	1		21	2	2			
VV	2	34			2	12		2
MV		1			1	2	8	
CD	9	3	4	1			2	
PT			9	5			9	
MR				1	1	6		1

Table 1: Letter authors and recipients

Abv.	Character full name
CV	Cécile Volanges
MM	Marquise de Merteuil
VV	Vicomte de Valmont
MV	Madame de Volanges
CD	Chevalier Danceny
PT	Présidente Tourvel
MR	Madame de Rosemonde
O	other

Table 2: Character name legend

2.2 Methodology

We constructed our set of labelled text samples by first splitting the novel into individual letters labelled with their respective "authors". We then only selected the characters who were authors of at least two letters and excluded the rest. We were left with seven main characters: the Marquise de Merteuil, the Vicomte de Valmont, the Présidente de Tourvel, Cécile Volanges, Madame Volanges, the Chevalier Danceny and Madame de Rosemonde. Preprocessing the text involved also removing the first row of each letter, which often contained explicitly the writer and recipient of the letter, so as not to bias the classifier.

3 Text Classification

In order to classify the letters and distinguish between the characters, we used a simple linear support vector machine classifier. We represented the text of the letters starting from a basic bag-of-words model, at first using all words as features in our classifier, then experimenting with additional feature selection, focusing on features that proved to be successful for authorship attribution. In one experiment, we used only content words, using their tf-idf scores as features, after which we tried limiting the features to the k-best features, by using chi^2 feature selection. In another experiment we tried including only stopwords in the feature set - which are widely used in authorship attribution. Verifying whether these features are still relevant for classifying characters is interesting especially considering they should be harder to consciously manipulate by the author. In a separate experiment, we also tried a feature set of character n-grams, which were previously shown to work for authorship attribution (Dinu et al., 2008), and that are also a very general (and language independent) and versatile type of features that are successfully used in various other natural language processing tasks.

Classification accuracy was measured for each character separately, in a series of leave-one-out experiments. For each character, we built a dataset contaning all letters, from which we excluded at a time one letter written by the target character, to be labelled by our classifier. The dataset was then artificially balanced to contain an equal number of letters pertaining to each character, by only keeping for each character a number of letters equal to the smallest total number of letters written by any character (among the ones we considered). The classification accuracy per character was calculated in the end as the percent of letters written by the character that were correctly classified; the overall accuracy was obtained by averaging the per character accuracy scores (since for character we considered the same number of letters, a simple average results in the overall accuracy).

4   Results and Analysis

Table 3 below illustrates the results (average overall accuracy) for each of the feature sets used, showing that the simple bag-of-words model, including all content words in the text as features, works well for this problem, and additional feature selection do not improve upon these results. The accuracy per character (using the most successful of the models) is shown in Table 4.

This result may look encouraging, as such a simple model is able to obtain a reasonable classification accuracy. On the other hand, it is interesting and worth further investigating that the features demonstrated to work best for authorship attribution do not perform as well on character classification.

We take a closer look at how the characters were classified by showing the confusion matrix containing the misclassified characters, as seen in Ta-

Features	Overall accuracy
content words	72.1%
k-best (1000)	69.9%
stopwords	46.6%
char 3-grams	48.5%
char 5-grams	53.3%

Table 4: Overall accuracy for each featureset

Character	Accuracy
CV	95.8%
MM	84.6%
VV	50.0%
MV	75.0%
CD	68.4%
PT	91.3%
MR	55%

Table 5: Classification accuracy per character

ble 6. For the same purpose we show an illustration of how the letters, color-coded by author, are grouped together in 2D space, by drawing a scatterplot of the representation of each letter (with content words' tf-idfs as features) after applying 2-dimensional PCA on the feature vectors, shown in Figure 1 below.

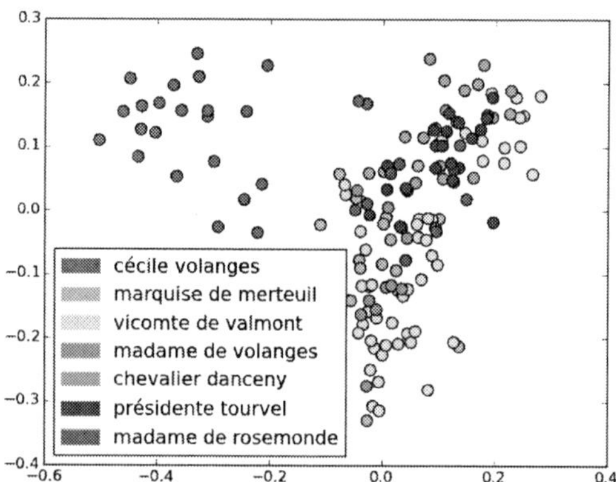

Figure 1: The letters in 2D space of word vector space

Finally, in order to make sense of the importance of each feature for the problem of character classification on our test case, we look at the discriminant features, by taking the list of the highest weighted features from the trained classifier (SVM), shown in table 5 below.

The scatterplot, as well as the confusion matrix, show some interesting insights into how the

Character	Features
CV	aime clef voudrais triste harpe merteuil monsieur petite vicomte maman
MM	sais voudrais merteuil valmont belle harpe aime monsieur danceny maman
VV	présent voudrais aime sais harpe ami amie danceny fille maman
MV	chagrin chose triste clef voudrais harpe amour danceny cécile maman
CD	mal voudrais triste chagrin ami harpe clef aime danceny maman
PT	triste mal aime voudrais harpe ami danceny belle maman neveu
MR	vis faute présidente gercourt danceny madame petite bonne belle vicomte

Table 3: Most discriminating features (bag-of-words)

classifier distinguishes between the letters and the mistakes it makes. In the plot, as well as in the confusion matrix, we can see that the Vicomte de Valmont, the central character of the book, as well as the one involved with most of the other characters, is the character that is hardest to classify. Additionally, he most often gets confused with the Marquise de Merteuil, who is his main interlocutor and "partner in crime". This may point to a common style, but possibly also to common topics of conversation. This hypothesis is enforced by the poor classification results obtained using stopwords as features, as compared to using content words.

	CV	MM	VV	MV	CD	PT	MR
CV	23					1	
MM		22	1			2	1
VV	1	10	26		7	8	
MV				9		1	2
CD	1		1		13	4	
PT			2			21	
MR			1			3	5

Table 6: Confusion matrix for character classification

5 Conclusions and Future Directions

We have shown that a simple bag of words model using a linear support vector machine as a classifier can be used to distinguish between characters of a literary work. It is unclear though whether the classifier captures style in the same sense as in authorship attribution, or rather characters' preferred ideas or topics of conversation for example. From this point of view it may be interesting to compare these results to a topic modelling approach on the same dataset, as well as further explore the attributes of the most useful features.

In the future it may also be interesting to look at how various authors pertaining to different periods and literary currents compare in terms of their ability (and desire) to create individual, stylistically independent characters. Literary theory (Wellek and Warren, 1956) tells us that the practice of giving characters strongly individual voices is a rather modern idea, which may be interesting to confirm experimentally. In theory, literary characters evolved with time and literary current from the classical figures, who represented a typology, to the realist characters, who are pictured with strong individualities.

Further, the analogous problem to author profiling could be tackled with regard to literary characters. Separately of whether characters are easy to distinguish stylistically from one another, it may be interesting to see if an author managed to belivably build a character's style that is consistent with features of the character's personality: such as age or gender. Can older authors write from the point of view of teenagers (a notable example of this is Salinger's *Catcher in the Rye*), can males create consistent female characters? These are questions that we intend to approach in further experiments on this topic.

References

Harald Baayen, Hans Van Halteren, and Fiona Tweedie. 1996. Outside the cave of shadows: Using syntactic annotation to enhance authorship attribution. *Literary and Linguistic Computing* 11(3):121–132.

John Burrows and Hugh Craig. 2012. Authors and characters. *English studies* 93(3):292–309.

John Frederick Burrows. 1987. *Computation into criticism: A study of Jane Austen's novels and an experiment in method.* Clarendon Pr.

Liviu Petrisor Dinu, Marius Popescu, and Anca Dinu. 2008. Authorship identification of romanian texts with controversial paternity. In *LREC*.

Vlado Kešelj, Fuchun Peng, Nick Cercone, and Calvin Thomas. 2003. N-gram-based author profiles for authorship attribution. In *Proceedings of the conference pacific association for computational linguistics, PACLING*. volume 3, pages 255–264.

Moshe Koppel and Jonathan Schler. 2003. Exploiting stylistic idiosyncrasies for authorship attribution. In *Proceedings of IJCAI'03 Workshop on Computational Approaches to Style Analysis and Synthesis*. volume 69, page 72.

Moshe Koppel and Jonathan Schler. 2004. Authorship verification as a one-class classification problem. In *Proceedings of the twenty-first international conference on Machine learning*. ACM, page 62.

Thomas Corwin Mendenhall. 1901. A mechanical solution of a literary problem. *Popular Science Monthly* .

Frederick Mosteller and David L Wallace. 1963. Inference in an authorship problem: A comparative study of discrimination methods applied to the authorship of the disputed federalist papers. *Journal of the American Statistical Association* 58(302):275–309.

Fiona J Tweedie and R Harald Baayen. 1998. How variable may a constant be? measures of lexical richness in perspective. *Computers and the Humanities* 32(5):323–352.

Karina van Dalen-Oskam. 2014. Epistolary voices. the case of elisabeth wolff and agatha deken. *Literary and Linguistic Computing* page fqu023.

Rene Wellek and Austin Warren. 1956. *Theory of literatures*. Harcourt, Brace & World New York.

An Ontology-Based Method for Extracting and Classifying Domain-Specific Compositional Nominal Compounds

Maria Pia di Buono
TakeLab
Faculty of Electrical Engineering and Computing
University of Zagreb, Croatia
mariapia.dibuono@fer.hr

Abstract

In this paper, we present our preliminary study on an ontology-based method to extract and classify compositional nominal compounds in specific domains of knowledge. This method is based on the assumption that, applying a conceptual model to represent knowledge domain, it is possible to improve the extraction and classification of lexicon occurrences for that domain in a semi-automatic way. We explore the possibility of extracting and classifying a specific construction type (nominal compounds) spanning a specific domain (Cultural Heritage) and a specific language (Italian).

1 Introduction

In the Cultural Heritage domain, as in many other specific domains of knowledge, phrases and word sequences present recursive formal structures. Some of these structures may form lists of compounds that have specific meanings only when used with reference to that domain and, for this reason, constitute the terminology of that domain. This means that if such compounds present a certain degree of polysemy, it will be possible to disambiguate usages according to the different specific domains they belong to. Thus, taking into account a specific domain of knowledge, compounds become unambiguous and clear terms, useful for conceptualizations, which contribute to outline formalizations. In this sense, we can assert that domain-specific compounds present two levels of representation, which are separated but interlinked: a conceptual-semantic level, pertaining to the knowledge domain and its ontology, and a syntactic-semantic level, pertaining to sentence and word production. We adopt the expression atomic linguistic units (ALUs) to indicate any kind of lemmatizable terminological compound words which, even being very often semantically compositional, can be lemmatized due to their particular non-ambiguous informational content (Vietri and Monteleone, 2013). In this paper, we explore the possibility of extracting and classifying a compositional ALU type (nominal compounds) spanning a specific domain (Cultural Heritage) and a specific language (Italian).

This paper is organized as follows, section 2 describes the background and related work. Our approach is detailed in section 3. The description of testing and results is given in section 4. Section 5 concludes the paper and points to future work.

2 Related Work

The task of dealing with ALUs attracts the interest of several researches, due to the issue of consistently recognizing those groups of words, able to carry a different semantic expressiveness and charge than single words. Thus, the prediction of these linguistic phenomena in natural language processing (NLP) applications has been investigated by several scholars from different point of views. Due to the success for simple words, a growing attention concerns the application of distributional approaches for coping with compositional compounds (McCarthy et al., 2003; Reddy et al., 2011; Salehi et al., 2014). Likewise, different scholars aim at achieving distributed representations of word meanings using word embeddings for various purposes (Mikolov et al., 2013; Patel and Bhattacharyya, 2015).

We will see that, being both ontology and dictionary based, our identification and classification of ALUs is founded on a systematic and exhaustive formalization of natural language.

Joint SIGHUM Workshop on Computational Linguistics for Cultural Heritage, Social Sciences, Humanities and Literature.
Proceedings, pages 83–88, Vancouver, BC, August 4, 2017. ©2017 Association for Computational Linguistics

3 Methodology

Our method lays its foundations in the Lexicon-Grammar (LG) framework (Gross, 1984, 1986). LG considers lexicon as a group of terminal values, in a formal grammar of natural languages, which have to be associated to ordered sequences on the basis of independent combinatory behaviours and rules. Thus, lexicon is not separable from syntax, namely every lexical element, occurring in a sentence context, holds a grammatical function which combines with grammatical functions of other constituents. Combinatory behaviours are driven by co-occurrency and restriction-selection rules. Furthermore, we deal with compositional ALUs also according to semantic expansion mechanisms, firstly attested by Harris (1946). These mechanisms are useful to fully account for compositional ALUs, or better for free word groups. Due to the fact that this kind of phenomena may have some possibility to be automatically and successfully parsed by means of regular expressions[1].

In our research, we focus on a specific construction type, which may be described and retrieved as ALUs: nominal compounds which present a restricted semantic expansion. It means that such ALUs are formed by a head phrase, generally fixed or semi-fixed, followed by variable elements which belong to specific grammatical categories. These variable elements are characterized by a selection restriction, which is determined by the head phrase, which functions as a predicate, and by the semantic provisions which they represent. We define such ALUs as semi-open nominal compounds, namely word sequences formed by one or more (semi)fixed elements and a restricted selection of co-occurring elements. As in the example it follows:

(palmetta+semipalmetta+rosetta) + Adjective + Preposition + DNUM *(petali + lobi + foglie)*.

In the previous ALU, we can recognize a restricted head *palmetta+semipalmetta+rosetta* followed by an adjective and a preposition, and

a numeral, characterized by a high variability, and a restricted selection of nouns, i.e., *petali+lobi+foglie*.

In other words, in such lexical phenomena the fixed or semi-fixed head defines grammatical and semantic types of all variable elements. This phenomenon is mainly observable inside the lexicons of specific knowledge domains, even if it presents features belonging to both common-usage lexicon and terminology. Indeed, such semi-open ALUs are characterized by a variability of non-fixed elements but, at the same time, they are also characterized by a non-ambiguous meaning as a result of the compositional process.

In the following sections, we will show how we can recognize and, subsequently, classify by means of a domain ontology, such linguistic phenomena through a set of finite state automata (FSA), basing our method on co-occurrence likelihood of elements in semi-open ALUs.

3.1 Linguistic and Semantic Features

The high variability of non-fixed elements is related to the possibility of selecting elements from non-restraint sets of lexical items, the grammatical categories of which are predictable thanks to components constituting the head. On a lexical level, such a feature is correlated to the paradigmatic relationship which indicates words belonging to the same part of speech (POS) class. On the other hand, constraints deriving from heads components are associated to the syntagmatic relationship among words, that means to semantic aspects of ALUs. Thus, for example, in the Cultural Heritage domain, we may observe this phenomenon of semi-open ALUs in Coroplastic descriptions, as the following example shows:

- (1) *statua di* (statue of) [NPREP]+N

- (2) **statua di* (statue of) [NPREP]+A

'Statue of' represents the head, which determines the type of the element which comes afterwards, that must be a noun (1), and not an adjective (2). Indeed, if the head is composed by a noun, belonging to a specific semantic category, as *statua* (statue), followed by a preposition, like *di* (of), the element which comes afterwards must belong to noun POS. Similarly, the head works as a constraint for the type of noun selected, which means that we have a restricted semantic expansion concerning the semantic type of noun. Thus, the semi-

---

[1]On the contrary, non-compositional ALUs, as the result of a continuous interaction between *langue* and *parole* (De Saussure, 1989), are formed according also to linguistically motivated, manifold, deep-logic contiguous juxtapositions, and they present unpredictable formation routines. For this reason, they cannot be stochastically coped with, and must be necessary lexicalized if they present the even slightest non-compositional link among their components.

open NP 'statue of' may select a proper noun as 'Silenus', or a noun as 'woman', but not a noun as 'table'.

As far as syntactic aspects are concerned, some semi-open ALUs, especially referred to Coroplastic description, are sentence reductions in which a present participle construction is used. For instance,

- (3) *statua raffigurante Sileno* (statue representing Silenus) is a reduction (Gross, 1975; Harris and Gross, 1976) of the sentence:

    (3a) *Questa statua raffigura Sileno* (This statue represents Silenus)

    (3b) [relative] *Questa è una statua che raffigura Sileno* (This is a statue which represents Silenus)

    (3c) [pr. part.] *Questa è una statua raffigurante Sileno* (This is a statue representing Silenus)

These semi-open ALUs, which present sentence reductions, may be retrieved using FSA which recognize specific verb role-sets. Therefore, such an FSA recognizes sentence structures as they follow:

- NP(Head)+VP+NP

- NP(Head)+VP+NP+AP

- NP(Head)+VP+AP+NP

- NP(Head)+PREP+NP

- NP(Head)+PREP+NP+AP

- NP(Head)+PREP+AP+NP.

In the previous sample, the noun phrase (NP) which stands for the head of semi-open ALUs is composed by a group of non-restricted nouns related to Coroplastics. It means that in such a group we insert nouns as statue, bust, figure and so on.

As for semantics, we also observe the presence of semi-open ALUs in which the head does not occur in the first position. For example, the open series *frammenti di* (*terracotta*+*anfora*+*laterizi*+N) (fragments of (clay+amphora+bricks+N)), places the heads at the end of the compounds, being *frammenti* used to explicit the notion 'N0 is a part of N1'.

On the basis of our theoretical premises, and applying these selection restriction rules, we may

identify syntactic and semantic sets of lexical elements which may co-occur in specific semi-open ALUs. Such recursive formal structures allow the development of non-deterministic FSA, suitable to recognize all the elements of a specific open list (di Buono et al., 2013).

3.2 Ontology-based Extraction and Classification

In order to recognize and extract this kind of semi-open ALUs, we develop a set of FSA, which takes advantage from the semantic information stored in electronic dictionaries developed by means of NooJ (Silberztein, 2008). NooJ allows to formalize natural language descriptions and to apply them to corpora. NooJ is used by a large community, which developed linguistic modules, including Finite State Automata/Transducers and Electronic Dictionaries, for more than twenty languages. The Italian linguistic resources (LRs) have been built by the Computational Linguistic group of University of Salerno, which started its study of language formalization from 1981 (Elia et al., 1981). Our analysis is based on the Italian module for NooJ (Vietri, 2014), enriched with the LRs for the Archaeological domain (di Buono et al., 2014). The Italian LRs are composed of simple and compound word electronic dictionaries, inflectional, syntactic and morphological grammars, annotated with cross-domain semantic tags (e.g., 'Human' and 'Animal' label). The LRs for the Archaeological domain present a taxonomic tagging, derived from the the Italian Central Institute for the Catalogue and Documentation (ICCD) guidelines, which indicate how to classify an object, and a reference to the CIDOC Conceptual Reference Model (CRM), defined by the Conseil International des Musees (Doerr, 2003) . The CIDOC CRM is an object-oriented semantic model, compatible with RDF, which stands for a domain ontology which may be applied to describe Cultural Heritage items and the relations among them. In this conceptual model, entity classes are described by means of pertaining information about the taxonomic relation among entity classes (i.e., Subclass of), a description of class essential properties (i.e., Scope note), sentences which exemplify natural language representations used to denote an element belonging to the class, and the properties which may co-occur with the given entity class.

Entry	Kylix a labbro risparmiato
POS	N
Int. Str.	NPREPNA
FLX	C610
SYN	lip cup
DOM	RA1SUOCR
CCL	E22

Table 1: Sample of a semantic and taxonomic annotated entry from the Archaeological Italian Electronic Dictionary.

Each entry in the LRs presents taxonomic and ontological information, as it follows (Table 1):

- Its POS, internal structure and inflectional code (+FLX), which recall a local grammar suitable for generating and recognizing inflected forms.

- Its variants (VAR) or synonyms (SYN), if any;

- With reference to the taxonomy, the pertaining knowledge domain (DOM), e.g., RA1SUOCR stands for Archaeological Remains/Tools/Kitchen Utensil;

- Finally, we insert a tag referring to the ontological entities derived from the CIDOC CRM, e.g., E22 refers to Man-Made Object class, that is a subclass of E19 Physical Object.

In order to create the role sets suitable to extract and classify the ALUs, we use these semantic information to apply a series of domain constraints. Thus, we firstly employ information which refer to the domain taxonomic hierarchy. For instance, in the sample (1), our first selection restriction is constrained by the tag value which indicates Sculpture class in the taxonomy. Therefore, we extract all ALUs, labeled with this tag, through a semi-automatic method. Consequently, a manual procedure is employed to identify nouns which fit to the meaningful sentence context.

In compounds containing present participle forms, i.e., sample (3), semantic features can be identified using local grammars built on specific verb classes (semantic predicate sets); in such cases, co-occurrence restrictions can be described in terms of lexical forms and syntactic structures. For these occurrences, we apply the specific semantic set, descriptive predicates, in order to put into evidence elements extracted from specific verbal classes (i.e., 20A and 47B[2]). We also employ grammatical and syntactic constraints referred to tense and number of verb phrase; thus, we select just present 3rd persons singular and plural (sample 3a and 3b) and present participle (sample 3c). Due to the complexity of Coroplastic descriptions, sub-graphs presents many recursive nodes, mainly in noun phrases.

4 Testing and Results

Our methodology has been tested on Italian Cultural Heritage texts. The corpus has been built merging different datasets of catalographic data provided by ICCD[3]. We refer to Archaeological Remains datasets, classified according to the guidelines of ICCD and released as open data[4]. The total amount of the dataset is about 123K records. Each record contains different information, structured according to the Functional Requirements for Authority Data (Patton, 2009). An evaluation of the results produced by our approach is given in Table 2. Our method is evaluated by means of Precision, Recall and F-score results in the extraction of the main entity classes, i.e. Building, Clothing, Furniture, Sculpture, and Tools. For this evaluation we consider some of the higher classes in the taxonomic classification of ICCD. This choice is justified by the compositional structures of ALUs, which are comparable for the subclasses related to the same main class. Anyway, the ontological tags used to classify them are fine-grained, so a distinction between these categories is performed any time. As we can notice, the values present a variability with reference to the different categories. Generally speaking, the cause of mismatching results can be retrieved in the use of too broad terms, which determines ambiguity hard to solve, i.e., *bitronconico*, that can be referred to an *askos*, belonging to the class of Tools, or to a kind of necklace, an element in the class of Clothing. Furthermore, another source of mismatching is related to the presence of references to the inventory number, or other information related to the ICCD classification, merged in the definition field, e.g., description of materials used.

---

[2]Classes refer to Italian Lexicon-Grammar Tables, available at http://dsc.unisa.it/composti/tavole/combo/tavole.asp.

[3]http://www.catalogo.beniculturali.it/opendata/?q=dataset.

[4]http://www.catalogo.beniculturali.it/opendata/?q=dataset.

Class	Precision	Recall	F-score
Building	0.87	0.77	0.81
Clothing	0.88	0.72	0.79
Furniture	0.79	0.66	0.72
Sculpture	0.89	0.68	0.77
Tools	0.85	0.75	0.80

Table 2: Evaluation for the main classes.

5 Conclusion and Future Work

In this paper, we have presented our preliminary study on an ontology-based strategy to extract and classify compositional nominal compounds in the Cultural Heritage domain for Italian. This FSA-based system allows to retrieve a very large amount of expressions and ALUs among those present in the analysed corpus. The highly productive formal structures are the following ones:

- Noun(Head) + Preposition + Noun + Preposition +Noun, i.e., *fibula ad arco a coste* (ribbed-arch fibula), in which the fixed component is represented by *fibula* (fibula);

- Noun(Head) + Preposition + Noun + Adjective, i.e., *anello a capi ritorti* (twisted-heads ring), the head is represented by *anello* (ring);

- Noun(Head)+ Preposition + Noun + Adjective + Adjective, i.e., *punta a foglia larga ovale* (oval broadleaf point).

The main hypothesis, leading the development of our system, is that the precision and the recall of extraction and classification systems for compositional compounds can be improved by representing linguistic and semantic features in a more consistent way. We consider the average results quite satisfying, nevertheless we are already planning to enrich our research outcomes with many other improvements in order to solve ambiguity and classification issues.

Acknowledgments

This work has been funded by the Unity Through Knowledge Fund of the Croatian Science Foundation, under the grant 19/15: EVEnt Retrieval Based on semantically Enriched Structures for Interactive user Tasks (EVERBEST).

References

Ferdinand De Saussure. 1989. *Cours de linguistique générale: Édition critique*, volume 1. Otto Harrassowitz Verlag.

Maria Pia di Buono, Mario Monteleone, and Annibale Elia. 2014. Terminology and knowledge representation. italian linguistic resources for the archaeological domain. In *Workshop on Lexical and Grammatical Resources for Language Processing*. page 24.

Maria Pia di Buono, Mario Monteleone, Federica Marano, and Johanna Monti. 2013. Knowledge management and cultural heritage repositories: Cross-lingual information retrieval strategies. In *Digital Heritage International Congress (DigitalHeritage), 2013*. IEEE, volume 2, pages 295–302.

Martin Doerr. 2003. The cidoc conceptual reference module: an ontological approach to semantic interoperability of metadata. *AI magazine* 24(3):75.

Annibale Elia, Maurizio Martinelli, and Emilio D'Agostino. 1981. *Lessico e strutture sintattiche: introduzione alla sintassi del verbo italiano*. Liguori.

Maurice Gross. 1975. *Méthodes en syntaxe*. Hermann.

Maurice Gross. 1984. Lexicon-grammar and the syntactic analysis of french. In *Proceedings of the 10th International Conference on Computational Linguistics and 22nd annual meeting on Association for Computational Linguistics*. Association for Computational Linguistics, pages 275–282.

Maurice Gross. 1986. Lexicon-grammar: the representation of compound words. In *Proceedings of the 11th coference on Computational linguistics*. Association for Computational Linguistics, pages 1–6.

Zellig S. Harris. 1946. From morpheme to utterance. *Language* 22(3):161–183.

Zellig S. Harris and Maurice Gross. 1976. *Notes de Cours de Syntaxe: Traduit de l'anglais par Maurice Gross*. Seuil.

Diana McCarthy, Bill Keller, and John Carroll. 2003. Detecting a continuum of compositionality in phrasal verbs. In *Proceedings of the ACL 2003 workshop on Multiword expressions: analysis, acquisition and treatment-Volume 18*. Association for Computational Linguistics, pages 73–80.

Tomas Mikolov, Ilya Sutskever, Kai Chen, Greg S Corrado, and Jeff Dean. 2013. Distributed representations of words and phrases and their compositionality. In *Advances in neural information processing systems*. pages 3111–3119.

Dhirendra Singh Sudha Bhingardive Kevin Patel and Pushpak Bhattacharyya. 2015. Detection of multiword expressions for hindi language using word embeddings and wordnet-based features .

Glenn E. Patton. 2009. *Functional requirements for authority data: A conceptual model*, volume 34. Walter de Gruyter.

Siva Reddy, Diana McCarthy, and Suresh Manandhar. 2011. An empirical study on compositionality in compound nouns. In *IJCNLP*. pages 210–218.

Bahar Salehi, Paul Cook, and Timothy Baldwin. 2014. Using distributional similarity of multi-way translations to predict multiword expression compositionality. In *EACL*. pages 472–481.

Max Silberztein. 2008. Nooj v2 manual.

Simona Vietri. 2014. The italian module for nooj. In *Proceedings of the First Italian Conference on Computational Linguistics, CLiC-it*.

Simona Vietri and Mario Monteleone. 2013. The english nooj dictionary. In *Proceedings of NooJ 2013 International Conference, June*. pages 3–5.

Speeding up corpus development for linguistic research: language documentation and acquisition in Romansh Tuatschin

Géraldine Walther
University of Zürich
Plattenstrasse 54
8032 Zürich, Switzerland
geraldine.walther@uzh.ch

Benoît Sagot
Inria
2 rue Simone Iff
75 012 Paris, France
benoit.sagot@inria.fr

Abstract

In this paper, we present ongoing work for developing language resources and basic NLP tools for an undocumented variety of Romansh, in the context of a language documentation and language acquisition project. Our tools are designed to improve the speed and reliability of corpus annotations for noisy data involving large amounts of code-switching, occurrences of child speech and orthographic noise. Being able to increase the efficiency of language resource development for language documentation and acquisition research also constitutes a step towards solving the data sparsity issues with which researchers have been struggling.

1 Introduction

Contemporary linguistic research relies more and more heavily on the exploration of statistical patterns in language. The non-categorical distribution and variety of linguistic units has become a focus for understanding complex variations across patterns, such as dative alternations (Bresnan et al., 2007) or cases of optionality (Wasow et al., 2011). Studies like these require the availability of large consistently annotated corpora.

For lesser or undescribed languages however, such resources are not readily available. What is worse, the current rate of language extinction could lead to the disappearance of 20-90% of today's spoken languages by the end of the 21st century (Krauss, 1992). Documenting endangered languages will allow us to preserve traces of the current language diversity, a part of the world's cultural heritage. Building reliable linguistic resources will allow us to study them according to fast evolving research standards.

Similarly, studies on language acquisition are based on recorded, transcribed, and annotated data of parent-child interactions. Language acquisition research has produced significant databases, such as the CHILDES project (McWhinney, 2000), yet mainly manually and at enormous costs.

Relying solely on manual annotators is too costly an option. Minimising resource development costs is crucial. Manual language resource development for language documentation and language acquisition projects should be sped up, as soon as technically possible, by employing NLP tools such as spelling correction/normalisation tools and part-of-speech (POS) taggers. For instance, POS taggers used as pre-annotators have been shown to increase both annotation speed and annotation quality, even when trained on limited amounts of data (Marcus et al., 1993; Fort and Sagot, 2010).

Yet language acquisition and language documentation data presents specific challenges for automatic linguistic annotation. Firstly, such data usually consists of transcriptions of spontaneous speech. Secondly, previously undescribed languages are often not written and lack established orthographies, resulting in noisy transcriptions. Thirdly, acquisition data consists of recordings of child-parent interactions. The recorded target children's language production can differ dramatically from adult language, adding another layer of linguistic variation. Finally, as new data is usually still being collected, available raw and even more so annotated data is rare, which significantly limits the available training data for annotation tools.

In this paper, we show the interaction between manual resource development (morphological lexicon, spelling and POS-annotated corpus) and automatic tools on current annotation experiments for a language documentation and acquisition project on the undocumented and previously

Joint SIGHUM Workshop on Computational Linguistics for Cultural Heritage, Social Sciences, Humanities and Literature.
Proceedings, pages 89–94, Vancouver, BC, August 4, 2017. ©2017 Association for Computational Linguistics

non-written Romansh dialect of Tuatschin.

2 Romansh Tuatschin

The term Romansh denotes a set of Romance languages with important Germanic lexical and grammatical influence, mostly spoken in the canton of the Grisons in South-Eastern Switzerland. Although Romansh is considered one of the four official national languages of Switzerland, the term Romansh covers in fact a variety of languages and dialects with significantly differing features. The dialect we focus on in present paper corresponds to a previously undocumented dialect of the Romansh Sursilvan variety called Tuatschin. It is spoken by approximately 1,500 speakers in the Val Tujetsch area. Contrary to the neighbouring main Sursilvan dialect, which is also the main language in local schools, Tuatschin is at this point an unwritten language. It is however still natively spoken and transmitted both in the local area and within families who have left and settled in larger cities within the country. Speakers are proud of their language and culture and promote it through a local cultural association and occasional, non-normalised, publications in the local newspaper.

The development of the resources described here is part of a project which combines language documentation and acquisition research. One aim of this project is to gain better understanding of intergenerational language transmission in endangered language contexts, which might contribute to eventually slowing down, if not reversing, linguistic and cultural erosion of minority languages. The data used in this project is mostly original data from fieldwork in the Val Tujetsch, original recordings within five Tuatschin speaking families with at least one child aged between 2 and 3 years, and updated and normalised lexical data from the Tuatschin word-list by Caduff (1952).

Adult speakers of Tuatschin are usually multilingual, natively speaking at least two, if not more, Romansh dialects (Tuatschin and Sursilvan), as well as German (both High German and the local variety of Swiss German), and often a fair amount of Italian and French. Everyday conversations in the Tuatschin speaking area comprise a high amount of code-switching. Conversations between speakers of neighbouring dialects more often than not result in each speaker speaking their own variety, accommodating the other person's dialect to varying degrees. Insertion of German lexical items or full utterances is ubiquitous.

As a result, our recorded Tuatschin data comprises a high amount of German and standard Sursilvan. This is even more acute in the acquisition corpus data used within present experiments, as the children's families tend to be natively bilingual. While the children's mothers are all native Tuatschin speakers, the fathers are Sursilvan, Swiss German or Italian speakers. The children therefore produce a significant amount of mixed utterances. In addition to the high amount of code-switching due to this particular language setting, language acquisition data also comprises intrinsic noise due to the differences between child and adult language, including nonce-words or specific child-speech. The variation observed in our corpus data ranges from language and dialectal variation to adult/child register differences. Developing automated tools for such a corpus requires coping with noisy, heterogeneous corpus data.[1]

3 Developing guidelines

3.1 Orthography

The first challenge in developing linguistic resources and automated tools for a previously unwritten language like Tuatschin consists in developing an orthography that can be used for transcribing recorded data, and training future transcribers (native speakers) in using this new orthography. We wanted this orthography to also be usable by native speakers outside the project. In collaboration with two native speakers within the Val Tujetsch, we developed a new orthography for Tuatschin, which is mainly based on the orthography for the neighbouring written dialect Sursilvan, but accommodates the phonetic and morphological differences of Tuatschin, from the pronunciation of specific vowels and diphthongs to diacritic marking of infinitive forms. Once the main principles of the orthography had been established, we started training our native corpus transcribers. However, without complete resources (such as a full lexicon or grammar) at their disposal, each one of them still had their own interpretation of the overall principles for the tran-

---

¹Note that while Sursilvan does have an established orthography and is used a a language of instruction in schools, there are no automatic tools available for the language. The existing online lexicon can only be queried online but is not freely available. Despite the languages' similarity there are no existing resources that could be leveraged to facilitate automatic work on Tuatschin at this point.

scription of individual words, adding an additional transcriber-related layer to the variation within the data. Developing the new orthography also required several passes, based on feedback from our transcribers and progress in our own understanding of the language data through our ongoing field work. Subsequent changes contributed to variation even within an individual transcriber's orthography, however reducing the differences between different transcribers' orthographic strategies.

3.2 Annotation tagset inventories

For our corpus annotation, we developed two separate tagsets, one for part-of-speech (POS) annotation and one for morphosyntactic features. Just as for our orthographic conventions, our tagset evolved alongside field work progress while annotation was already ongoing, adding further noise to our corpus data. This kind of noise is a common problem in language documentation projects where data collection, annotation, and analysis are conducted in parallel. Without the availability of automatic tools, it normally requires several passes of manual post-cleaning and adds to the overall cost of language resource development.

Our POS tagset comprises a fine-grained and a coarse POS inventory. The full coarse-grained inventory, used for our POS tagging experiments (see Section 5.2) is the following: ADJ, ADV(erb), COMPL(ementiser), CONJ(unction), DET(erminer), INTER(jection), N(oun), PN (proper noun), PREP(osition), PRN (pronoun), PUNCT(uation), QW (question word), SOUND, V(erb). Fine-grained tags add information such as DET_def for definite articles or PREP_loc for locative prepositions. It also comprises a specific _childspeech refinement of all POS for words that are specific to child-speech. The morphosyntactic features follow the Leipzig Glossing Rule conventions commonly used in language documentation projects and comprise distinctions for number and gender, as well as tense, mood and person.

Although we have designed this language-specific inventory as a means to better model the morphological and morphosyntactic properties of Tuatschin, we recognise the relevance and importance of the Universal Dependency (UD) initiative,[2] whose aim is to "develo[p] cross-linguistically consistent treebank annotation for many languages, with the goal of facilitating mul-

tilingual parser development, cross-lingual learning, and parsing research from a language typology perspective." In the current version (2.0), several dozen languages are already covered, sometimes with more than one treebank. What is more, the UD website announces a Romansch and a (distinct) Sursilvan Romansch treebank. Our initiative is not related to these treebank development efforts—we had independently decided to develop a deterministic mapping between our language-specific label inventory and a UD-compatible annotation scheme, in order to pave the way for a future Romansch-Tuaschin UD corpus. Together with the dependency annotation of our data, this will be the focus of future work.

4 Manual ressource development

4.1 TuatLex

We manually developed a morphological lexicon for Tuatschin. For that, we devised an explicit grammatical description of Tuatschin nominal and verbal morphology based on our own field work data. We implemented this description within the Alexina$_{PARSLI}$ lexical framework (Sagot and Walther, 2013). In addition to the implemented morphological description, our Tuatschin lexicon, TuatLex, comprises a list of 2,176 lemmas, based on an updated version of the Tuatschin word-list by Caduff (1952) complemented with our newly collected data, among which 780 verbs, 949 nouns, and 146 adjectives. The Alexina inflection tool uses the grammar to produce 46,089 inflected entries, among which 29,361 verbal, 15,137 nominal, and 762 adjectival forms.

4.2 Manual corpus annotation

After devising the tagset, we trained advanced linguistic undergraduate students to manually annotate our corpus data. The students were no native speakers of Romansh. They were asked to annotate each token for (fine-grained) POS and morphosyntactic information and to indicate an English translation for each token's base form.[3] Using the WebAnno annotation tool (Eckart de Castilho et al., 2014), annotators took approximately 15 to 25 hours for annotating files containing typically 1,000 to 2,000 words. Difficulties for annotators mainly came from orthographic vari-

---

[2]http://universaldependencies.org

[3]For example, for the Tuatschin token *nûrsas*, they would have provided the following annotations: POS = N, Morphosyn = pl, and the English translation 'EWE'.

ation, variation in the representation of word to-kens,[4] and dialectal variation.[5] Weekly meetings between two trained linguists, among whom one Sursilvan native speaker, and all annotators were organised to compare notes, discuss recurrent difficulties, and adapt the tagsets whenever necessary.[6]

4.3 Manual corpus normalisation

In order to simplify the annotation task, we set up a procedure for systematic orthographic correction. We first asked one of the native speakers, who had been involved in the development of the orthographic conventions, to manually correct already transcribed corpus data for orthographic errors and individual-word-based code-switching in a separate *normalised* tier within the corpus.[7] We then manually introduced an additional tier indicating for each 'normalised' token whether it had been corrected for orthography, code-switching, child-speech, or actual pronunciation errors. This intermediate layer, in addition to being useful for subsequent acquisition or code-switching studies, is meant to help the development of an automatic spell-checker. Aside from variation in the usage of diacritics, some of the most frequent errors in the transcribed data involved the amalgamation of words meant to be written as separate tokens.[8]

5 Automation and tools

5.1 Tokenisation and orthographic correction

In order to speed up the manual development of orthographically normalised corpora based on new transcriptions, but also to prepare the fully automatic processing of non-annotated text, we first developed an automatic tokenisation and spelling standardisation/correction tool. It is implemented

---

in the form of a Tuatschin-specific parametrisation of the SxPipe shallow processing architecture (Sagot and Boullier, 2008).

Note that the spelling standardisation/correction tool is not meant to be used as a standalone tool. It has been designed and developed only for speeding up future corpus development and for serving as a cleaning step before applying the POS tagger, whose results are obviously better on (even only partially) normalised data.

Our spelling standardisation/correction tool relies on a list of deterministic rewriting patterns that we automatically extracted and manually selected based on the data described in Section 4.3. More precisely, we applied standard alignment techniques for extracting n-to-m correspondences between raw and normalised text. Among the extracted rules, 695 were deterministic, which means that there was a unique output in the corpus for a given input. Out of these 695 candidate rules, we manually selected 603, whose systematic application could not result in any over-correction.[9] Several others are non-deterministic. However, a careful manual examination of these candidate ambiguous rules showed that most of the ambiguity is an artifact of the rule extraction process, and that true ambiguities can be resolved in context.[10] As a result, contextual information was included in our standardisation/correction patterns, thus resulting in a fully deterministic standardisation/correction module.

5.2 POS tagger

In order to assess and improve the quality of the POS annotation, but also to have a POS pre-annotation tool for speeding up future manual annotation, we trained the MElt POS tagger (Denis and Sagot, 2012) on the manually POS-annotated data available so far, using coarse POS to reduce sparsity (see Section 3.2). The 2,571 already annotated sentences, containing 9,927 tokens, were divided in training, development and test sets by randomly selecting sentences with re-

---

[4]E.g. *vegni* instead of *vegn i* 'it comes' (lit. 'comes it').

[5]For example, unexpected morphological forms that prevented the recognition of inflected forms such as verbs ending in Sursilvan *-el* instead of Tuatschin *-a* in the first person singular.

[6]The project being mainly a documentation project on a previously undescribed language, data collection, annotation, and data analysis are currently being carried out in parallel. Data annotation in particular has been performed as a collaborative task rather than as a task conducted by individual annotators, that would have to be evaluated for inter-annotator agreement.

[7]The purpose of this normalised layer is solely to help automatic (and, to a lesser extent, manual) annotation of the data. It is not meant to replace the original transcription layer, which remains the relevant layer for subsequent linguistic analysis.

[8]Cf. the *vegni/vegn i* example from previous footnote.

[9]A few examples: *stù→stu, sèl→sè'l, schia→schéia*.

[10]For instance, *vegnì* and all other verbs from TuatLex's inflection class Vi can produce ambiguous tokens such as *vegni*, which must be changed into *vegnì* (infinitive) before pronouns such as *ju, té, el, ella, el, i, nus, vus, els, ellas, ins*, but, in most other contexts, must be rewritten as *vegn i* (V+PRN) with an expletive pronoun *i*. We applied the latter to those verb tokens likely to appear with expletive subjects like *vegnì* 'to come' while inserting the infinitive diacritic on all other verb instances (such as *capì* 'understand').

spective probabilities 0.8, 0.1 and 0.1. We also extracted from the TuatLex lexicon described above a set of 19,771 unique (form, POS) pairs, to be used by MElt as a complementary source of information, in addition to the training corpus.

We trained a first version of MElt, and applied the resulting POS tagger on the training data themselves. Annotation mismatches allowed us to identify several systematic errors in the training data. Some of them came from individual errors or annotator disagreement. But most were due to changes made in the annotation guidelines while manual annotation was already ongoing, and of which some had not yet been correctly retroactively applied to already annotated data.[11] We applied a series of POS correction rules to the whole corpus (train+dev+test) as a result of this training-corpus-based study, and re-trained MElt on the corrected data. The result is a POS tagger trained on 2,062 sentences (7,901 words) with a 91.7% accuracy overall and a 65.3% accuracy on words unknown to the training corpus. Interestingly, if trained without TuatLex lexical information, accuracy figures do not drop as much as usually observed (Denis and Sagot, 2012): respectively 91.6% and 62.5%. This suggests that lexical information might not be as important for improving POS taggers for child-related speech as it is for tagging standard text, a fact likely related to the more limited vocabulary size in such corpora.

6 Conclusion

We have described ongoing efforts for developing language resources (lexicon, annotated corpus)[12] and basic NLP tools for the Romansh variety of Tuatschin, in the context of a project on language description and language acquisition dedicated to a previously non-written language. Our next step will consist in using our tools for pre-annotating new raw data, in order to speed up annotation while increasing its quality and consistency. They will also be used for creating automatically annotated data, which will complement the manually annotated corpus.

On a longer term, our tools are also meant to be used for automatically categorising tokens and sequences of tokens into occurrences of child-speech or various types of code-switching, relying on the information comprised within the intermediate tier introduced during the normalisation procedure (see Section 4.3). This intermediate layer is meant to be ultimately automatically generated by SxPipe. The richer and more accurate information that our tools will be able to provide will also facilitate subsequent quantitative linguistic studies on Romansh Tuatschin, its acquisition by children and its influences by surrounding languages, especially Sursilvan and (Swiss) German.

7 Acknowledgements

The authors gratefully acknowledge the SNF project number 159544 "The morphosyntax of agreement in Tuatschin: acquisition and contact" whose funding has been instrumental to the work presented here. We also thank our project collaborators and especially our annotators Nathalie Schweizer, Michael Redmond, and Rolf Hotz for their help in annotating the data, and Claudia Cathomas for her extremely valuable help and native expertise on Romansh data. For their help in developing a new Tuatschin orthography we would like to express our warmest thanks to Ciril Monn and Norbert Berther.

References

Joan Bresnan, Anna Cueni, Tatiana Nikitina, and Harald Baayen. 2007. Predicting the dative alternation. In G. Boume, I. Kraemer, and J. Zwarts, editors, *Cognitive Foundations of Interpretation*, Royal Netherlands Academy of Science, Amsterdam, pages 69–94.

Léonard Caduff. 1952. *Essai sur la phonétique du parier rhétoroman de la Vallée de Tavetsch (canton des Grisons - Suisse)*. Francke, Bern.

Pascal Denis and Benoît Sagot. 2012. Coupling an annotated corpus and a lexicon for state-of-the-art POS tagging. *Language Resources and Evaluation* 46(4):721–736.

Richard Eckart de Castilho, Chris Biemann, Iryna Gurevych, and Seid Muhie Yimam. 2014. Webanno: a flexible, web-based annotation tool for clarin. In *Proceedings of the CLARIN Annual Conference (CAC) 2014*. CLARIN ERIC, Utrecht, Netherlands, page online. Extended abstract.

Karën Fort and Benoît Sagot. 2010. Influence of pre-annotation on POS-tagged corpus development. In *Proceedings of the Fourth ACL Linguistic Annotation Workshop (LAW IV)*. Uppsala, Sweden, pages 56–63.

---

[11]For instance, the previously defined POS "V_particle" had been discarded at some point during corpus development, yet it still had a number of occurrences in the training data.

[12]The lexicon and tools will all be made freely available.

Michael Krauss. 1992. The worlds language in crisis. *Language* (68).

Mitchell Marcus, Béatrice Santorini, and Mary Ann Marcinkiewicz. 1993. Building a large annotated corpus of English: The Penn Treebank. *Computational Linguistics* 19(2):313–330.

Bryan McWhinney. 2000. *The CHILDES Project: Tools for analyzing talk.*. Lawrence Erlbaum Associates, Mahwah, NJ, 3 edition.

Benoît Sagot and Pierre Boullier. 2008. SxPipe 2: architecture pour le traitement pré-syntaxique de corpus bruts. *Traitement Automatique des Langues* 49(2):155–188.

Benoît Sagot and Géraldine Walther. 2013. Implementing a formal model of inflectional morphology. In Cerstin Mahlow and Michael Piotrowski, editors, *Proceedings of the Third International Workshop on Systems and Frameworks for Computational Morphology (SFCM 2013)*. Humboldt-Universität, Springer-Verlag, Berlin, Germany, volume 380 of *Communications in Computer and Information Science (CCIS)*, pages 115–134.

Thomas Wasow, T. Florian Jaeger, and David Orr. 2011. Lexical variation in relativizer frequency. In H. Simon and H. Wiese, editors, *Expecting the Unexpected: Exceptions in Grammar*, de Gruyter, Berlin, pages 175–195.

Distantly Supervised POS Tagging of Low-Resource Languages under Extreme Data Sparsity: The Case of Hittite

Maria Sukhareva[†], Francesco Fuscagni[‡], Johannes Daxenberger[†],
Susanne Görke[¶], Doris Prechel[‡] and Iryna Gurevych[†]

[†] Ubiquitous Knowledge Processing Lab (UKP)
Department of Computer Science, Technische Universität Darmstadt
www.ukp.tu-darmstadt.de
sukhareva@ukp.informatik.tu-darmstadt.de

[‡] Altorientalische Philologie, Institut fr Altertumswissenschaften
Johannes Gutenberg-Universität Mainz

[¶] Akademie der Wissenschaften und der Literatur Mainz
Philipps-Universität Marburg

Abstract

This paper presents a statistical approach to automatic morphosyntactic annotation of Hittite transcripts. Hittite is an extinct Indo-European language using the cuneiform script. There are currently no morphosyntactic annotations available for Hittite, so we explored methods of distant supervision. The annotations were projected from parallel German translations of the Hittite texts. In order to reduce data sparsity, we applied stemming of German and Hittite texts. As there is no off-the-shelf Hittite stemmer, a stemmer for Hittite was developed for this purpose. The resulting annotation projections were used to train a POS tagger, achieving an accuracy of 69% on a test sample. To our knowledge, this is the first attempt of statistical POS tagging of a cuneiform language.

1 Introduction

Natural Language Processing (NLP) for historical languages is a challenging task. The mere digitization of historical texts can take several years as the original data vary from ancient manuscripts to clay tablets which only a trained historical linguist can read and transliterate. The manual morphosyntactic annotation of the digitized historical resources demands a rare expertise and is a slow and painstaking process (Bennett et al., 2010). It is frequently impossible to annotate the amount of data sufficient for training a supervised part-of-speech (POS) tagger. Thus, NLP for historical languages frequently uses distantly supervised methods to compensate for the lack of training data (Piotrowski, 2012).

Traditionally, historians and historical linguists apply manual qualitative methods to the data. Such work usually involves a narrow expertise that focuses on a particular phenomenon or a time period. For example, presently, Hittite texts can only be read and understood by trained cuneiform specialists whose scope of interests is confined to certain texts, diachronic periods or linguistic phenomena. Statistical machine translation (SMT) and information retrieval (IR) methods would make these texts available to a wider public, including historians and sociologists (Daxenberger et al., 2017). The automatic methods are also applicable to whole corpora and have a much wider coverage than qualitative analysis. However, for optimal performance, SMT and IR need basic linguistic annotation such as POS tags and syntactic parses that are currently not available for Hittite. Thus, we propose a distantly supervised tagger and an unsupervised stemmer for Hittite which can be the first milestone in creating more advance NLP tools for cuneiform languages.

Performance of distantly supervised methods such as annotation projection or cross-lingual tool adaptation depends on the diachronic relatedness between the source and the target languages. For example, annotation projection from modern English into middle English gives better results than into old English because middle English grammatically and lexically resembles modern English much more than Old English (Sukhareva and Chiarcos, 2014). Annotation projection is thus typically applied to related languages (Tiedemann

Joint SIGHUM Workshop on Computational Linguistics for Cultural Heritage, Social Sciences, Humanities and Literature.
Proceedings, pages 95–104, Vancouver, BC, August 4, 2017. ©2017 Association for Computational Linguistics

and Agic, 2016).

In this paper we show that our annotation projection method is robust enough to reach decent performance on a highly inflectional language that has been extinct over millennia and does not have any modern relatives. Also, the data sparsity caused by multilingualism and rich Hittite morphology poses additional challenges for statistical NLP methods. On a small parallel corpus of Hittite and German, we use character-based alignment to create an unsupervised stemmer for Hittite and word-based alignment as a basis for annotation projection from POS tagged German translations. The resulting POS projections are used as training data for a POS tagger. Our evaluation shows that stemming Hittite and German texts prior to annotation projection largely improves POS tagging accuracy for Hittite as compared to a POS tagger trained on unstemmed projections.

The paper is structured as follows: Section 2 introduces the data used in this research and outlines linguistic characteristics of Hittite that affect the performance of our method. It also describes the manually annotated evaluation dataset for Hittite that was created for the sake of this study. Our main contributions, the unsupervised Hittite stemmer and annotation projection approach to Hittite POS tagging, are described in Section 3. The evaluation of the presented approach is in Section 4. Section 5 discusses related work and the state-of-the-art of NLP for cuneiform languages. Finally, we discuss the results and outline future work in Section 6.

2   Data

Hittite texts pose such challenges as developed inflectional morphology, non-standardized orthography, diachronic variations and multilingualism. Given a relatively small amount of data available for Hittite, direct application of state-of-the-art NLP approaches leads to sub-optimal results. Also, modern machine learning techniques are not directly applicable because of the limited amount of data. With data sparsity being the main obstacle, we see the solution in understanding the linguistic reasons for data sparsity and based on them to exploit means of data sparsity reduction.

2.1   Hittite language

Hittite is an extinct language spoken between 16 and 12 c.c. BCE in the territories of modern Turkey and Northern Syria. It is an inflectional synthetic Indo-European language. Hittite belongs to a dead Anatolian branch of Indo-European languages along with Luwian and Palaic. Hittite as well as its closely related languages do not have any modern descendants. This poses an additional challenge to the application of distantly supervised methods to our data as their performance depends on diachronic relatedness (Section 1).

There are three chronological periods of the Hittite language: old Hittite (OH, 1650-1500 BCE), middle Hittite (MH, 1500 - 1350 BCE) and new Hittite (NH, 1350 - 1180 BCE). Diachronic orthographic variations are strongly pronounced between the time periods: The shapes of many cuneiform signs differ in these three periods. Also, the so called plene writing occurs when a vowel already present in a cuneiform sign is expressed by a further unnecessary vocal. Plene writing is a typical feature of OH and MH texts, disappearing progressively with NH and is practically absent in late NH.

During all periods Hittite was a highly inflectional language with a wide variety of word forms. For example, the nominal declension included inflectional paradigms determined by two genders, nine cases and two numbers (van den Hout, 2011). Also, adjectives had a rich inflectional paradigm as they agreed with nouns in gender, case and number. As for the verbal inflectional paradigm, it was relatively simple and was determined by only two tenses, two moods and two voices. Though Hittite in all periods did not have any grammatical definiteness marking (e.g. articles), it had determiners that would indicate the class of the nouns (e.g. city, land, woman, bread, etc.) and were expressed in writing by unpronounced Sumerograms (e.g. ^{URU}*ḫatti, "the land of ḫatti"*; ^{GIŠ}*natḫi, "(wooden) bed"*)

To sum up, rich inflectional morphology, spelling variations and diachronic variations in Hittite greatly increase the data sparsity making the automatic statistical processing of Hittite texts extremely challenging. The key to successful automatic annotation of Hittite is the reduction of the data sparsity by normalizing diachronic variations and reducing the word form paradigm to a single stem or lemma. While we leave the problem of normalization open, the paper will further discuss the reduction of word forms and propose a method for data sparsity reduction through stemming.

(1)   Types of transliteration used in the DPHT and multilingualism.

a.	*nu*	*ma-ah-ha-an*	*A-NA*	[GIŠ]*GU.ZA*	*A-BI-IA*	*eš-ha-ha-at*	(Syllabic transliteration)
	nu	*mahhan*	*ANA*	[GIŠ]*GU.ZA*	*ABI=IA*	*ešhahat*	(Bound transcription)
	HIT	HIT	AKK	SUM	AKK	HIT	(Language)
	and	as soon as	on	throne	father-my	sit	

And as soon as I sat down on the throne of my father

2.2   Corpus of Hittite Texts

The Digitale Publikation Hethitischer Texte corpus (DPHT) is available via the Hittitology Portal Mainz (HPM).[1] It covers more than 30,000 mostly fragments of clay tablets that have been archived in Ancient Anatolia, nowadays Turkey, during the later half of the second millennium BCE. Most of the texts were found in Hittite capital Hattusa, only smaller archives came to light in other towns of the Hittite Empire. Therefore, Hittite texts used in this research do not have dialectal variations which contribute to the data sparsity and negatively influence the performance of the NLP pipeline.

The DPHT is relatively small as compared to modern corpora and has only 60,058 tokens. An additional challenge for NLP processing of Hittite texts is posed by their extreme multilingualism. Several languages are found in the texts: Hittite, Luwian and Palaic are Indo-European languages, Hattic, Hurrian and Sumerian are isolated agglutinating languages and Akkadian is a Semitic language. Sumerian and Akkadian words are particularly frequent in Hittite texts (see ex. 1). Some words can be written both with sumerograms and with akkadograms or in syllabic Hittite. For example, *"god"* is often written by the sumerogram DINGIR. Furthermore, the akkadogram *ILU(M)* and the Hittite word *iu(na)* can be found in the corpus.

Texts cover various genres; most of them belong to a religious sphere, like festival descriptions or magic rituals, but also historic documents like treaties, annals, etc. have been found. As every genre is associated with genre-specific vocabulary and syntactic constructions, this genre variety can negatively affect the performance of the POS tagger. Furthermore, diachronic variations in spelling, morphology and syntax can have a negative impact on the tagging accuracy. The texts cover the whole of Hittite history, from OH throughout MH to NH. More than two thirds of all Hittite texts in our data were written in NH.

Hittite texts are transliterated in accordance with the syllabic and logographic structure of their signs. The transliteration conventions are compatible with generally recognized rules of transliteration of cuneiform languages.[2] The DPHT provides syllabic transliteration which is a syllable-wise literal transliteration of the original texts. Furthermore, a bound transcription is given which focuses on word transcription and is closer to the way the words were most likely pronounced (ex. 1). In our experiments, we used bound transcription as it has less diachronic spelling variations.

2.3   POS Annotation of Hittite

In order to evaluate our pipeline, a hittitologist and co-author of this paper annotated selected documents with Universal POS tagset (Petrov et al., 2012). These were only used for the evaluation. As the pipeline was trained on a diachronic corpus containing various genres, we balanced the evaluation set and included texts that represent all the time periods. Table 1 shows the list of the texts included in the evaluation set. It totals 969 tokens and has proportionally balanced texts from NH, MH and OH. The complexity of the annotation process varied based on the period. While MH and NH are well-researched and there are many available texts in MH and NH, OH is very complicated and has words whose translation is not known.

We decided to create a balanced evaluation set rather than creating three evaluation sets for various periods due to practical reasons. First, annotation of this test set was a painstaking task that demanded a rare expertise. It was practically impossible to annotate large enough evaluation sets for all the three periods. Second, we could not split the training data into time periods as there would not be enough data to train a classifier for

[1] https://www.hethport.uni-wuerzburg.de

[2] http://www.hethport.uni-wuerzburg.de/HPM/hpm.php?p=hpmguide

97

Title	Period	Tokens
Purification Ritual for the Royal Couple	OH	113
Instructions for Bodyguard	MH	144
Military Instructions of Tuthaliya I	MH	137
Ten Years Annals of Muršili II	NH	390
Prayer of Muršili II	NH	127
Apology of Hattušili III	NH	58

Table 1: POS annotated evaluation set

each period. Thus, the POS tagger (see Section 3) was both trained and tested on data from various periods.

3 NLP Pipeline for Hittite

Automatic morphosyntactic annotation of Hittite is a non-trivial task. As discussed in Section 2, the Hittite texts are affected by diachronic variations in the lexicon, morphosyntax and orthography. Additionally, Hittite is a highly inflectional language with the immediate consequence of high type-token ratio. All of these factors lead to a data sparsity that is the key obstacle for statistical NLP processing of the data.

We present an approach that builds a NLP pipeline for automatic morphosyntactic annotation of Hittite. The pipeline (Figure 1) consists of four modules: preprocessing, data sparsity reduction, annotation projection and POS tagging. The initial data are just primary texts that are neither tokenized nor linguistically annotated. The transliteration and translation texts are clause-wise aligned which makes it possible to create word-based and character-based alignment. The morphosyntactic annotations are then projected into the Hittite texts from their German translations.

The quality of the annotation projection imminently depends on the quality of the alignment which is strongly affected by the data sparsity. Nevertheless, some of the data sparsity is relatively easy to reduce. For example, German, though by far not as inflectionally rich as Hittite, still has a relatively rich inflectional morphology. Thus, a noticeable improvement on the annotation projections can already be reached by stemming the German texts. Hittite stemming is also beneficial for word alignment quality though it is a more challenging task as there are no off-the-shelf Hittite stemmers or lemmatizers. Thus, this approach also proposes an unsupervised method for stemming of Hittite.

The final element of the pipeline is the POS

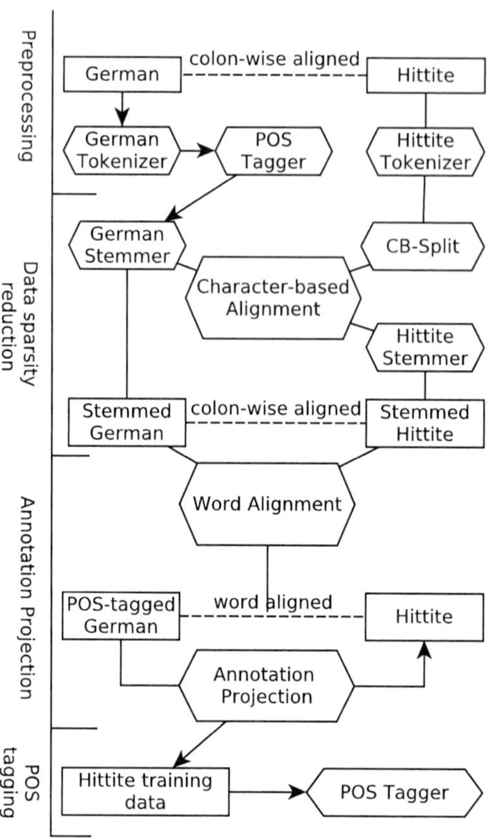

Figure 1: Morphosyntactic NLP pipeline for Hittite

tagging of Hittite texts. The annotation projections are used as training data for a supervised POS tagger. Presently, there are no POS-annotated datasets for Hittite available. We manually annotated several text excerpts to evaluate the output of the Hittite NLP Pipeline (see Section 2.3).

3.1 Data Preprocessing

The input to the pipeline are the initial digitized Hittite transliterations and their German translations provided in a XML format. As modern principles of text segmentation into clauses, sentences and phrases appeared only a few centuries ago, the original Hittite texts do not have any text segmentation nor any punctuation. During transliteration, the texts were split in paragraphs and *colons*. Colons in most cases correspond to clauses which

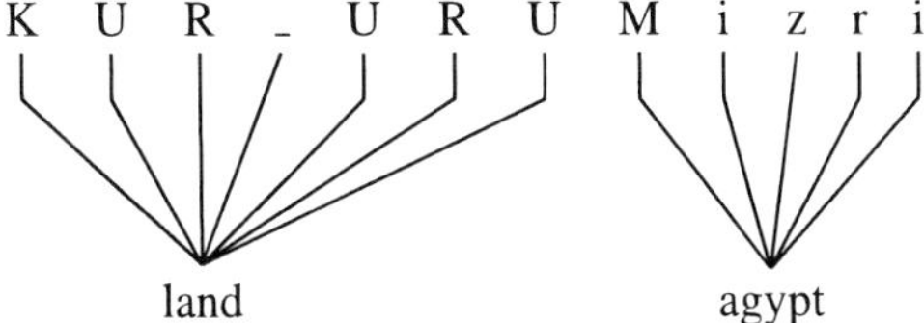

Figure 2: An example of character-based alignment of the Hittite phrase *"the land of Egypt"* with German stems.

start with an introductory particle *nu* or with a conjunctive adverb (e.g. *mahhan* "when"). Each colon (with rare exceptions) has a verb in the final position which is the standard word-order in Hittite. Colons as well as paragraphs are aligned to German translations.

The NLP pipeline for Hittite was built on the basis of the uimaFIT library and, more specifically, DKPro Core libraries (Eckart de Castilho and Gurevych, 2014). In the preprocessing stage, the colon alignments were extracted from the XML files. We used the off-the-shelf OpenNLP tokenizer[3] trained on Tiger corpus (Brants et al., 2004) to tokenize German text. As there is no available tokenization for Hittite, it was decided to use white spaces and equals sign "=" as token separators. It is important to mention that as there is no punctuation in Hittite transliterations, the whitespace tokenization worked quite well but is not sufficient as many function morphemes are bound. The bound function morphemes include, for example, location affixes or possessive pronominal suffixes. Such bound morphemes are usually suffixes marked in the transliteration by the equals sign (e.g. *ABU=IA "father=my"*).

3.2 Reduction of data sparsity

One of the most straight-forward ways to reduce the data sparsity is through lemmatization. Nevertheless, there are no off-the-shelf lemmatizers for Hittite neither is there a machine readable Hittite dictionary with sufficient coverage to create a dictionary-based lemmatizer. An alternative approach is to use stemming. Hittite has developed paradigms of outer flection and does not demonstrate many cases of inner flection, thus, root mor-

phemes do not have a large variance and the separation of inflectional morphemes is likely to suffice. We implemented a character-based stemmer for Hittite that relies on character-based alignment. The purpose of the stemmer is to separate all the affixes from the root morpheme. Affixes are bound morphemes that include both suffixes and prefixes. Affixes can be both derivational and inflectional. The Hittite stemmer splits a word into three parts: prefixes, root and suffixes. As the main purpose of the stemmer is to reduce data sparsity rather provide a morphological analyzer the stemmer does not split prefixes or suffixes e.g. if a word has several suffixes the stemmer treat it as one suffix. Further on, the paper will refer to such complex affixes as "prefix" or "suffix".

First, the parallel German texts were stemmed. For this purpose, we used Snowball stemmer for German.[4] Then, we split all the Hittite words into characters and word boundaries were marked with a special character. To create a character-based (CB) alignment we used Phrasal ITG Aligner (Neubig et al., 2012).

Figure 2 shows a character alignment of Hittite phrase "KUR [URU] *Mizri*" to the German stems *land* and *agypt*.[5] Both the Hittite noun KUR meaning *land* and the Hittite determiner URU are aligned to the German stem *land* while *Mizri* is aligned to the German stem *agypt*. This example shows the basic principals of how the stemmer works: Hittite substring aligned with German stems are likely to be stems themselves. It is particularly effective in Hittite because of the abundance of noun determiners that are frequently translated by a separate German word.

The resulting CB alignment was processed as follows. First, all the character sequences aligned to a single German stem were extracted. The sequences were split by word boundaries. Thus, a German stem could be mapped to several Hittite character sequences. Each character sequence would be assigned with the corresponding frequency of its co-occurrence with the German stem. In order to detect prefixes and suffixes, we would treat each Hittite sequence with co-occurrence frequency over 15 as a potential root. This high threshold for such a small corpus was chosen empirically to ensure that the stemmer is initialized with high quality alignments. Lower thresholds

---

[3] https://opennlp.apache.org

[4] http://snowballstem.org
[5] Full German word form is *Ägypten*.

allowed too many low quality alignments and a higher thresholds did not have enough alignments to initialize the training. The assumption behind this is that more frequently aligned sequences tend to be root morphemes as they co-occur with the German stem more often. In other words, any Hittite character sequence that is aligned to the same German stem more than 15 times is treated as a potential root. We split all the other aligned sequences by this potential root morpheme r and collected the associated counts $c(r, w_a)$, frequency of r aligned to the German word w_a and $c(\cdot|w_a)$, the total of all the alignments to w_a, and end up with two other sequences: prefix(es) pr and suffix(es) suf. We create a map of prefix and suffix co-occurrences with the initial l_{first} and final l_{last} letters of the root and save the corresponding frequencies $c(pr, l_{first})$ and $c(suf, l_{last})$. Thus, we can define five initialization scores S:

$$S(r) = P(r|w_a) = c(r, w_a)/c(\cdot|w_a) \tag{1}$$

$$S(pr) = P(pr|l_{first}) = c(pr, l_{first})/c(\cdot|l_{first}) \tag{2}$$

$$S(suf) = P(suf|l_{last}) = c(suf, l_{last})/c(\cdot|l_{last}) \tag{3}$$

$$P(pr) = c(pr)|c(\cdot) \tag{4}$$

$$P(suf) = c(suf)|c(\cdot) \tag{5}$$

The initial root score $S(r)$ (eq. 1) is the translation probability $P(r|w_a)$ of a Hittite character sequence r and aligned German stem w_a. There are four affix scores: conditional probabilities of a prefix and a suffix occurring with the first and the last letter of a root respectively (eq. 2, 3) and the overall probabilities of observing a certain affix (eq. 4 and 5) in the corpus. Originally, the prefix and suffix probabilities were conditioned on the root rather than on the first and the last letters but due to the data sparsity, it was not possible to collect reliable statistics. Empirical observations showed that conditioning on the first and last letter improves stemming. This can be explained by the fact that there are phonetic assimilations in Hittite such as regressive assimilation of n by $š$ into $šš$.

The initialization scores are calculated based on the CB-alignment and are further updated in the training phase. In the training phase, the stemmer iterates over all the words in the corpus. It considers all possible segmentations of a word under the following conditions: a root cannot be shorter than two letters, a prefix cannot be longer than fives letter and a suffix cannot be longer than five letters. Words are allowed not to have suffixes or prefixes but any word must have a root. This might seem inefficient but as we are dealing with a small amount of data and Hittite words are seldom longer than six letters, the algorithm is not time consuming. If it encounters an unaligned root, $S(r)$ is set to a smoothing value 10^{-4}. $S(pr)$ and $S(suf)$ are also set to 10^{-4} if counts $c(pr, l_{first})$ and $c(suf, l_{last})$ are 0. The affix scores are updated in a straight-forward way by updating the counts with every segmented word. Updating the root scores is more complicated as in case of the unaligned root morphemes there is no $P(r|w_a)$. Nevertheless, the aligned roots provide important clues for segmentation and should not be abandoned. Thus, each time a root is assigned by the stemmer, its score is increased by 10%. We empirically tried various increase values but 10% delivered optimal results for POS tagging. Nevertheless, we recommend future work to look into ways of learning the increase value from the data. Though this method loses its probability-like elegance, it forces the stemmer to choose aligned roots over unaligned roots unless the unaligned roots were assigned frequently enough. Thus, the overall score assigned by the stemmer is:

$$S = S(r) * S(pr) * S(suf) * P(pr) * P(suf) \tag{6}$$

3.3 Annotation Projection

The core element of the annotation projection module is the word alignment. The word alignment is created automatically with GIZA++. As we have a limited amount of data and are only interested in one-to-one word alignments and lexical translation probabilities, we used the IBM Model-2 to produce word alignments.

The parallel German translations were tagged with OpenNLP POS Tagger using the German model that was provided with the tagger.[6] It is worth mentioning that the performance of the POS Tagger was not affected by the fact that the source Hittite texts do not have sentence marking. The

---

[6]`http://opennlp.sourceforge.net/`
`models-1.5/de-pos-maxent.bin`

parallel translation was done for each Hittite colon and followed modern conventions of text segmentation. Thus, though the sentence segmentation is not available in Hittite, they were introduced in the translation for the purpose of readability. Furthermore, despite the fact that the source Hittite texts did not have any punctuation, their German translations follow the modern punctuation rules.

As we were primarily interested in one-to-one word alignment, we had to eliminate all the German words and symbols that cannot be aligned to a Hittite word before applying GIZA++ to the parallel data. First of all, it involved deleting all the punctuation from the German texts. As the Hittite language does not have any articles, we also eliminated all the German words that were assigned a coarse POS tag "DET". The Hittite texts were stemmed as described in Section 3.2. As the approach cannot differentiate between inflectional and derivational morphemes, we kept the Hittite root and eliminated all the affixes.[7]

Training a POS tagger demands unambiguous POS annotation of the training data, therefore, we had to resolve one-to-many alignments. For this purpose, assuming that f is a source German word and e is the aligned Hittite word, the lexical translation probabilities $P(f|e)$ and $P(e|f)$ were consulted and the alignment with the higher overall probability $P(f|e) * P(e|f)$ was preferred.

3.4 POS Tagging

In order to train a POS tagger we used the annotation projections from German into Hittite. Annotation projection creates rather noisy data and can be unreliable in cases when the word alignment quality is low. Some related work suggests to only use projections based on high confidence alignment to train a tagger. Unfortunately, this approach would not be applicable to our data as the Hittite corpus is relatively small and further reducing the amount of training data would have a negative affect on the tagger's performance.

Also, not all the Hittite sentences were fully annotated. This is not surprising as GIZA++ allows null alignments. A null alignment is not necessarily an error as sometimes there is no corresponding word in the translation (e.g. Hittite determiners described in Section 2.1). Therefore, we had to eliminate all the Hittite sentences with partial POS

stemming	POS Accuracy
None (majority class)	25.4%
None (projection)	39.4%
Hittite only	65.7%
German only	65.1%
Hittite+German	**69.1%**

Table 2: Tagging accuracy of POS taggers trained on annotation projection

annotations which are 30% of all the sentences. Alternatively, it was possible to introduce dummy tags but this would introduce additional noise in already noisy projected data. The amount of fully annotated sentences is sufficient for training a POS tagger and, thus, no dummy tags are needed. Finally, we trained OpenNLP POS Tagger on 11,704 Hittite colons.[8]

4 Evaluation

We evaluated the tagger on the data described in Section 2.3. The taggers' performance was measured as tagging accuracy, a conventional measure that counts the percentage of correctly tagged tokens. The evaluation was done in three set-ups which tested the effect of the data sparsity reduction through stemming on the tagging accuracy. The most straightforward baseline was to tag all the words with the majority class NOUN. This baseline reached only 25.4% tagging accuracy. To create a more elaborated baseline, GIZA++ was directly applied to the parallel data and the data sparsity reduction step was fully omitted. The POS tagger trained on the resulting annotation projection managed to reach 39.4% of accuracy. The low tagging accuracy can be easily explained by the low quality of the word alignment. The performance of statistical word alignment applied to a small parallel corpus of two highly inflectional languages will inevitably be harmed by data sparsity. The data sparsity in the corpus of Hittite texts is very high: For instance, only 1% of all the trigrams and 0.02% of 5-grams in the corpus occur more than five times. Thus, the baseline results confirm that data sparsity is the major problem for distantly supervised POS tagging of Hittite.

As it has been previously discussed, the major

---

[7]The usage of affixes as additional features for training a POS tagger is possible and at the moment remains in the scope of future work.

[8]The average "sentence" (colon) is quite short (often less than six words), which explains the relatively high number of colons, compared to the overall number of tokens in DPHT.

source of the data sparsity in Hittite are the rich inflectional paradigms of Hittite words. In Section 3.2, we propose our CB-based method for stemming of Hittite that reduces the variety of Hittite word forms to the associated stem. Currently, there is no evaluation data available to test the quality of the Hittite stemmer so its usefulness can only be evaluated indirectly by examining the results of POS tagging.

Thus, in the second experimental setup, the Hittite texts were stemmed and then aligned to non-stemmed German texts. The POS tagger trained on the resulting projections showed a large 26,3% improvement over the non-stemming baseline (Table 2). The stems were, however, used only for word alignment and the POS tagger was trained and tested on the original word forms. Similarly, when the non-stemmed Hittite texts were aligned to stemmed German texts, the POS tagger showed a slightly minor improvement of 25,7% over the baseline. The fact that the Hittite stemming leads to better results is actually consistent with the fact that Hittite is morphosyntactically richer than German and, thus, has greater impact on the data sparsity. Finally, we stemmed German and Hittite parallel texts and trained the POS tagger on the annotation projections. The improvement over the baseline is almost 30% and almost 4% over the setup with only Hittite stemming.

All in all, the evaluation results show that our stemming approach to data sparsity reduction improves tagging accuracy by a large margin. While both German and Hittite stemming had a positive effect on the performance of the POS tagger, the best results were achieved through stemming of both Hittite and German translations which lead to the 30% improvement of tagging accuracy over the non-stemming baseline.

5   Related Literature

Despite the fact that low resource and historical languages have been steadily attracting attention of NLP researchers, hardly any NLP methods have been applied to the cuneiform languages. So far, most works have focused on resource building. For example, the Cuneiform Digital Library Initiative (CDLI)[9] is a large project that aims to digitize cuneiform resources. CDLI maps images of original clay tablets with transliterated texts and their translations. CDLI also constructs digitized machine-readable dictionaries for cuneiform languages. The majority of CDLI data are in Sumerian or Akkadian.

A related project that builds on the CDLI data is the Open Richly Annotated Cuneiform Corpus (ORACC).[10] ORACC includes corpora building projects that cover a variety of cuneiform resources. ORACC corpora have varying levels of annotation though most of the corpora are comprised of transliterated texts aligned with their translations. The transliterated words are annotated with a normalized form and a POS tag. However, ORACC does not contain annotated Hittite texts that could be used for training a POS tagger.

While Sumerian and Akkadian are the best researched cuneiform languages, there are also several notable resources in Hittite. Various resources and tools are provided by the Hittitology Portal Mainz (HPM), including the data that were used in this research (see Section 2.2). An important lexicographic resource is Chicago Hittite Dictionary.[11] Unfortunately, as the available digital version covers words for only five initials, we could not use it for our purpose. Daxenberger et al. (2017) describe a method to enable semantic search in translations on the DPHT. Giusfredi (2014) gives a comprehensive overview of further digital resources for Hittite. Despite the availability of digitized resources, there is hardly any NLP research on cuneiform languages other than corpus building. A reason is that many state-of-the-art NLP methods use supervised classifiers such as POS taggers, syntactic parsers etc. but the available digital resources for cuneiform do not provide enough annotated data to train a supervised classifier.

This holds for most historical languages. The only exception are the ancestors of modern world languages (e.g. Latin, historical Germanic dialects). For example, several diachronic annotated corpora have been recently released for historical varieties of modern Germanic languages. The Penn Parsed Corpora of Historical English (PPCHE)[12] covers all the historical stages of English and PPCHE's sister projects on PTB-style annotation of other historical Germanic languages, e.g. Icelandic (Rögnvaldsson et al., 2012) or Early

---

[9]http://cdli.ucla.edu

[10]http://oracc.museum.upenn.edu

[11]https://hittitedictionary.uchicago.edu/page/chicago-hittite-dictionary

[12]http://www.ling.upenn.edu/hist-corpora

New High German.[13]

Because of the lack of training data, historical NLP frequently uses unsupervised or distantly supervised methods. For example, annotation projection has been successfully applied to a wide variety of low-resource and historical data. Agić et al. (2016) used multilingual annotation projections to train POS taggers for 30 languages. Sukhareva and Chiarcos (2016) trained a neural network on multilingual annotation projections to create rich POS annotations for Middle Low German. Das and Petrov (2011) presented a graph-based approach where high confidence annotations are projected from the target into the source texts and are further propagated within a bilingual co-occurrence graph. They build vertices of the graph by computing trigram cooccurrence using PMI. The drawback of the approach is that it demands a large amount of parallel data which is not available for Hittite. It is not possible to utilize any of these approaches for the task presented in this study because the data sparsity of Hittite texts does not allow this: Only 1% of all the trigrams in Hittite texts occur more than 5 times. Rogati et al. (2003) uses word-based alignment to train an unsupervised Arabic stemmer. It utilizes a small parallel corpus and guesses root morphemes and and affixes by finding common substrings in Arabic words that are aligned to the same English word. This approach inspired our character-based method for Hittite stemming.

6 Conclusion

This paper describes a distantly supervised POS tagging method for Hittite. The proposed method uses a small parallel corpus of Hittite texts and its German translations as a basis for annotation projection. The annotation projections are used as training data for a POS tagger. The small amount of parallel data and developed inflectional morphology of both Hittite and German inevitably lead to data sparsity that had a drastic impact on the quality of the word alignment and, consequently, on the tagging accuracy. In order to reduce the data sparsity, we proposed an unsupervised method for Hittite stemming. The method is based on character-based alignment from which it learns morphological segmentation of Hittite words. Reduction of data sparsity using stemming had a large impact on the tagging accuracy, im-

proving it by 30%.

To our knowledge, this is the first attempt of statistical morphosyntactic annotation of a cuneiform language. We presented a POS tagger for Hittite trained on annotation projection from German translations. We also created an unsupervised character-based stemmer for Hittite. Additionally, we annotated diachronic Hittite text fragments for evaluation. While this approach can be easily portable to other low-resource languages irrespective of the script, cuneiform Latin transcription has features that are not found in conventional phonetic writing. For example, Sumerograms and Akkadograms are transliterated based on their cuneiform sign but the actual pronunciation can differ, additionally, they are frequently followed by phonetic complements that would remind the reader of the correct Hittite word. For example, Sumerian ŠU *"Hand"* is disambiguated by a phonetic complement -it and is written as ŠU-it but is pronounced as *keššarit*.

Tagger, stemmer and evaluation data are freely available.[14] We are confident that our approach can be transferred to other cuneiform and low-resource languages. Though Hittite is an inflectional language, the method of data sparsity reduction and annotation projection is very likely to yield similar if not better results on agglutinating languages. The method is also portable to other cuneiform languages. Applying this method to the agglutinating Sumerian language is in the scope of the future work.

Acknowledgments

The first and third author were supported by the German Federal Ministry of Education and Research (BMBF) under the promotional reference 01UG1416B (CEDIFOR).

References

Željko Agić, Anders Johannsen, Barbara Plank, Héctor Alonso Martínez, Natalie Schluter, and Anders Søgaard. 2016. Multilingual projection for parsing truly low-resource languages. *Transactions of the Association for Computational Linguistics* 4:301–312.

Paul Bennett, Martin Durrell, Silke Scheible, and Richard J Whitt. 2010. Annotating a historical corpus of German: A case study. In *Proceedings*

---

[13]http://enhgcorpus.wikispaces.com

[14]https://github.com/UKPLab/latech-clfl2017-hittitenlppipeline

of *LREC 2010 Workshop on Language Resource and Language Technology: Standards - state of the art, emerging needs, and future developments*. Paris, France, pages 64–68.

Sabine Brants, Stefanie Dipper, Peter Eisenberg, Silvia Hansen-Schirra, Esther König, Wolfgang Lezius, Christian Rohrer, George Smith, and Hans Uszkoreit. 2004. Tiger: Linguistic interpretation of a German corpus. *Research on Language and Computation* 2(4):597–620.

Dipanjan Das and Slav Petrov. 2011. Unsupervised part-of-speech tagging with bilingual graph-based projections. In *Proceedings of the 49th Annual Meeting of the Association for Computational Linguistics: Human Language Technologies - Volume 1*. Portland, OR, USA, pages 600–609.

Johannes Daxenberger, Susanne Görke, Darjush Siahdohoni, Iryna Gurevych, and Doris Prechel. 2017. Semantische Suche in ausgestorbenen Sprachen: eine Fallstudie für das Hethitische. In *Proceedings of the DHd 2017*. Bern, Switzerland, pages 196–200.

Richard Eckart de Castilho and Iryna Gurevych. 2014. A broad-coverage collection of portable NLP components for building shareable analysis pipelines. In *Proceedings of the Workshop on Open Infrastructures and Analysis Frameworks for HLT*. Dublin, Ireland, pages 1–11.

Federico Giusfredi. 2014. Web resources for hittitology. *BiOr* 71:358–361.

Graham Neubig, Taro Watanabe, Shinsuke Mori, and Tatsuya Kawahara. 2012. Machine translation without words through substring alignment. In *Proceedings of the 50th Annual Meeting of the Association for Computational Linguistics: Long Papers-Volume 1*. Jeju Island, Korea, pages 165–174.

Slav Petrov, Dipanjan Das, and Ryan McDonald. 2012. A universal part-of-speech tagset. In *Proceedings of the Eight International Conference on Language Resources and Evaluation*. Istanbul, Turkey.

Michael Piotrowski. 2012. Natural language processing for historical texts. *Synthesis Lectures on Human Language Technologies* 5(2):1–157.

Monica Rogati, Scott McCarley, and Yiming Yang. 2003. Unsupervised learning of Arabic stemming using a parallel corpus. In *Proceedings of the 41st Annual Meeting on Association for Computational Linguistics-Volume 1*. Sapporo, Japan, pages 391–398.

Eiríkur Rögnvaldsson, Anton Karl Ingason, Einar Freyr Sigurdsson, and Joel Wallenberg. 2012. The Icelandic Parsed Historical Corpus (IcePaHC). In *Proceedings of the Eight International Conference on Language Resources and Evaluation*. Istanbul, Turkey.

Maria Sukhareva and Christian Chiarcos. 2014. Diachronic proximity vs. data sparsity in cross-lingual parser projection. a case study on Germanic. In *Proceedings of the First Workshop on Applying NLP Tools to Similar Languages, Varieties and Dialects*. Dublin, Ireland, pages 11–20.

Maria Sukhareva and Christian Chiarcos. 2016. Combining ontologies and neural networks for analyzing historical language varieties. a case study in middle low German. In *Proceedings of the 10th International Conference on Language Resources and Evaluation*. Portoroz, Slovenia, pages 1471–1480.

Jörg Tiedemann and Zeljko Agic. 2016. Synthetic treebanking for cross-lingual dependency parsing. *J. Artif. Intell. Res.(JAIR)* 55:209–248.

Theo van den Hout. 2011. *The Elements of Hittite*. Cambridge University Press.

A Dataset for Sanskrit Word Segmentation

Amrith Krishna, Pavankumar Saturi[*] and Pawan Goyal
[*]School of Linguistics & Literary Studies, Chinmaya Vishwavidyapeeth CEG Campus;
Dept. of Computer Science & Engineering, Indian Institute of Technology Kharagpur
amrith@iitkgp.ac.in

Abstract

The last decade saw a surge in digitisation efforts for ancient manuscripts in Sanskrit. Due to various linguistic peculiarities inherent to the language, even the preliminary tasks such as word segmentation are non-trivial in Sanskrit. Elegant models for Word Segmentation in Sanskrit are indispensable for further syntactic and semantic processing of the manuscripts. Current works in word segmentation for Sanskrit, though commendable in their novelty, often have variations in their objective and evaluation criteria. In this work, we set the record straight. We formally define the objectives and the requirements for the word segmentation task. In order to encourage research in the field and to alleviate the time and effort required in pre-processing, we release a dataset of 115,000 sentences for word segmentation. For each sentence in the dataset we include the input character sequence, ground truth segmentation, and additionally lexical and morphological information about all the phonetically possible segments for the given sentence. In this work, we also discuss the linguistic considerations made while generating the candidate space of the possible segments.

1 Introduction

Sanskrit was the prevalent medium of knowledge transfer in the demographic of Indian Subcontinent for over four millennia. The culture bearing language of India has about 30 million extant manuscripts that are potent for digitisation (Goyal et al., 2012). The last decade witnessed tremendous excitement in digitisation attempts of ancient manuscripts in Sanskrit. The Digital Corpus of Sanskrit[1], The Sanskrit Library[2] and GRETIL[3] are some such laudable efforts. These attempts aim to preserve the cultural heritage of the subcontinent embedded in the works written in Sanskrit.

The writings in Sanskrit follow a '*scriptio continua*' (Hellwig, 2016), thereby making Word Segmentation in Sanskrit a challenging task. Lack of visible markers in written scripts is a prevalent feature observed in numerous Asian languages. Additionally, the sentence constructs in Sanskrit show a high degree of inflection (Scharf and Hyman, 2011), phonemes at the word boundary undergo phonetic transformations called as '*sandhi*' (Goyal and Huet, 2016), and the sentence constructs in Sanskrit follow a loose word order (Hellwig, 2016; Kulkarni et al., 2015). The combination of the aforementioned properties makes the segmentation in Sanskrit a complex task.

Given an input Sanskrit sentence, the word segmentation task can be defined as identification of the semantically most valid split of the input sentence. There have been commendable efforts to tackle the word segmentation task in Sanskrit. Mittal (2010) designed Finite State Transducers (FST) incorporating the rules of *sandhi* obtained from documented grammatical tradition. With the defined FSTs, Mittal (2010) generates all possible splits followed by a probabilistic scoring procedure to select the ideal split. Natarajan and Charniak (2011) proposed 'S3 - Statistical Sandhi Splitter', a Bayesian word segmentation approach for Sanskrit. The work is an extension of Goldwater et al. (2006) and was adapted to handle *sandhi* formations. Hellwig (2015) proposed a neural model that jointly solves the problem of

---

[1]http://kjc-sv013.kjc.uni-heidelberg.de/dcs/
[2]http://sanskritlibrary.org/
[3]http://gretil.sub.uni-goettingen.de/gretil.htm

Joint SIGHUM Workshop on Computational Linguistics for Cultural Heritage, Social Sciences, Humanities and Literature.
Proceedings, pages 105–114, Vancouver, BC, August 4, 2017. ©2017 Association for Computational Linguistics

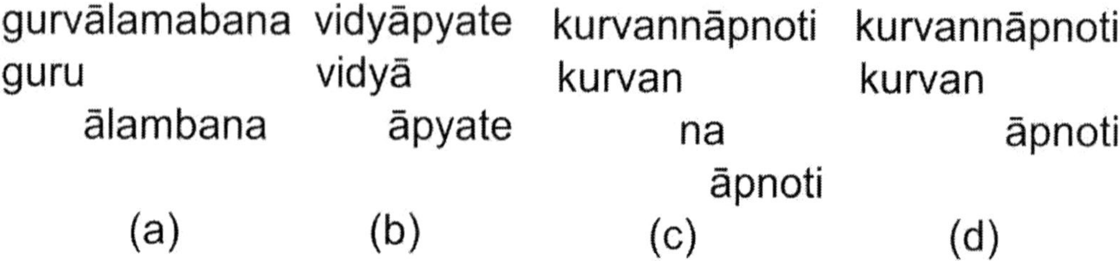

Figure 1: Example instances of sandhi formation in Sanskrit. a) Phonetic transformation of '*u*' and '*ā*' to '*vā*' in the joint form. b) '*ā*' and '*ā*' at the word boundaries of *vidyā* and *āpyate* join together to form a single '*ā*' in the final form. Both the split words have an overlap at the juncture (Goyal and Huet, 2016). c) and d) Two possible analyses for the sandhied chunk '*kurvannāpnoti*' (Krishna et al., 2016a), where c) is the negation of d).

compound splitting and *sandhi* resolution. Krishna et al. (2016a) handled the word segmentation problem as an iterative query expansion task. The authors used Path Constrained Random Walks (PCRW) (Lao and Cohen, 2010) for identifying word segments that are likely to co-occur in the given sentence. This work considers compound splitting as part of the word segmentation task itself.

As the task of Sanskrit word segmentation is gaining traction, it also calls for uniformity and easiness in comparing the competing models. For instance, the aforementioned approaches vary in their defined objectives and are evaluated under different settings, making a direct comparison of the models difficult. For example, Mittal (2010); Natarajan and Charniak (2011) do not discuss the effect of compounds and compound splitting on the dataset. Hellwig (2015) presents the same as a separate task from that of word segmentation, while Krishna et al. (2016a) do not make an explicit difference between both the tasks. Krishna et al. (2016a) report an F-Score of 90.61 % when tested on a curated dataset of 2148 sentences, compared to competing models with an F-Score of 70.07% (Natarajan and Charniak, 2011) and 66.26 % (Mittal, 2010). But, Krishna et al. (2016a) report an F-Score of 77.72 %, when the authors tested their method on a larger dataset of about 10,000 sentences obtained from a digitised corpus. Additionally, The aforementioned systems focus primarily on the correctness of the word-form predicted. Sanskrit is an agglutinative language and the same inflection of a lemma can signify multiple possible morphological classes. Therefore, correctness of the morphological class is also important, when the segmentation is performed. Though Krishna et al. (2016a) report the performance of their system when considering the correctness of lemma and morphological class prediction, they primarily focus on the word-from prediction task.

In perspective of the current scenario of this field, our contributions in this work are two fold:

1. We formally define the objective for word segmentation task in Sanskrit. We see word segmentation not as an end but as a means to facilitate further processing of text in Sanskrit. We define our requirements with an end-goal of making the current digitised content accessible to an end-user when seen from the perspective of an Information Retrieval system. To achieve this, the segmentation task should output the information that is valuable for the subsequent syntactic and semantic tasks such as POS Tagging, dependency parsing, sentence summarisation, etc. The distinction for the correctness of lemma and morphological class, and not just the correctness of the final word-from, is of utmost importance for this.

2. We release[4] a dataset of 115,000 sentences which can be used for further research in word segmentation task in the Sanskrit. With this dataset we aim to alleviate the effort and time that often needs to be spent in prepossessing data. The pre-processing efforts often require the use of multiple sub-systems, and this can lead to inconsistencies with the assumptions made by each of the subsystems involved.

---

[4]`https://zenodo.org/record/803508#.WTuKbSa9UUs`

In Section 2, we discuss in detail about the challenges that need to be tackled in word segmentation in Sanskrit. Section 3 discusses the preliminaries followed by the formal definition of word segmentation task. Section 4 details the structure of the dataset we use. In Section 5, we explain various linguistic considerations that we have made, while preparing the dataset.

2 Challenges in Word Segmentation

Word segmentation is an important prerequisite for further processing of Sanskrit Texts. In addition to having no visible markers in Sanskrit sentence constructs, the linguistic peculiarities inherent in the language make the task a non-trivial one. Sanskrit, primarily being a language used orally, has passed on the euphonic assimilation of phones into the writing as well (Goyal and Huet, 2016). This leads to phonetic transformations at the word boundaries called as 'sandhi'. Figure 1 shows some cases of sandhi. In Figure 1a, the words 'guru' and 'ālambana' join together to form 'gurvālambana', where the 'u' at the boundary of 'guru' gets transformed to 'v'. In case of vidyā + āpyate → vidyāpyate, the 'ā' at the word boundaries of both the words join together to form a 'ā'. Here, the position for 'ā' in the joint form is shared by both the words. Due to *Sandhi*, the word boundaries disappear and the sounds are often replaced or elided. Given two words, the generation of the joint form or what can be called as the '*sandhied*' form is deterministic. The ancient grammar treatise *Aṣṭādhyāyī* mentions the *sandhi* rules by which phonemes at the word boundaries undergo changes, when two words are combined. But analysis of a sentence with *sandhi* in it leads to multiple phonetically valid segments. The analysis for a given sentence may often lead to several semantically valid segments as well. For example, consider the expression *kurvannāpnoti kilbiṣam*. The expression may be split into two possible statements, '*kurvan āpnoti kilbiṣam*' (While doing, you will accumulate sin) and '*kurvan na āpnoti kilbiṣam*' (While doing, you will not accumulate any sin) (Krishna et al., 2016a). The splits shown in Figure 1c and 1d gives a very specific example, where both the possible segmentation analyses differ by a negation term *na*. A more generic example is shown in Figure 2. Figure 2a shows all possible segmentations for the given sentence. Figure 2b the only analysis for the input sentence

which is semantically valid.

Sandhi operation does not modify the sentence constructs at syntactic or semantic levels. It only makes difference at the phonetic level. There is no rationale for two words to undergo 'sandhi', other than the proximity of these words at the time of enunciation. Simply put, successive words tend to form sandhi, and it is the discretion of the composer to choose whether or not to perform *sandhi* between the pair of words. This brings us to the second challenge. Writings in Sanskrit follow free (loose) word order especially in poetry (Kulkarni et al., 2015; Melnad et al., 2015). The free word order in Sanskrit is a convenient tool for poets to arrange the words in accordance with the prescribed meter. By this, the proximity between two words cannot be deemed as an indicator for syntactic or semantic compatibility between them. We need to consider the entire sentence context while processing the text and use the entire co-occurrence context of the words in the sentence.

In addition to the aforementioned linguistic peculiarities, the fact that Sanskrit has a rich morphology, compounds the problem further. Sanskrit expresses high degree of inflection, with 90 and 72 different inflections for verbs and nouns respectively. The inflections for a word generally happen at the boundary of a word. The inflections lead to different final word-forms for a given lemma. To illustrate the problem, let us consider the character sequence '*nagarāṇi*'. Now, '*nagarāṇi*' can be analysed as '*na garāṇi*' which means 'no diseases'. But the character sequence '*nagarāṇi*' can alternatively be analysed as an inflection, specifically the nominative case neuter gender plural, of the lemma '*nagara*' (town). The scenario points to an instance where we have to decide whether there exists a split or not for the character sequence, and the decision changes the number of segments one ends up with.

2.1 Computational Analysis of Sandhi

The rules related to *sandhi* are well documented in the ancient Sanskrit grammar treatise *Aṣṭādhyāyī* by *Pāṇini*. Hyman (2008) observed that the external *sandhi* can be computationally tackled using finite state methods. An efficient Finite State Transducer for segmentation in Sanskrit was later developed by (Huet, 2009). Sanskrit Heritage Reader (Goyal et al., 2012; Goyal and Huet, 2013, 2016), a lexicon driven morphologi-

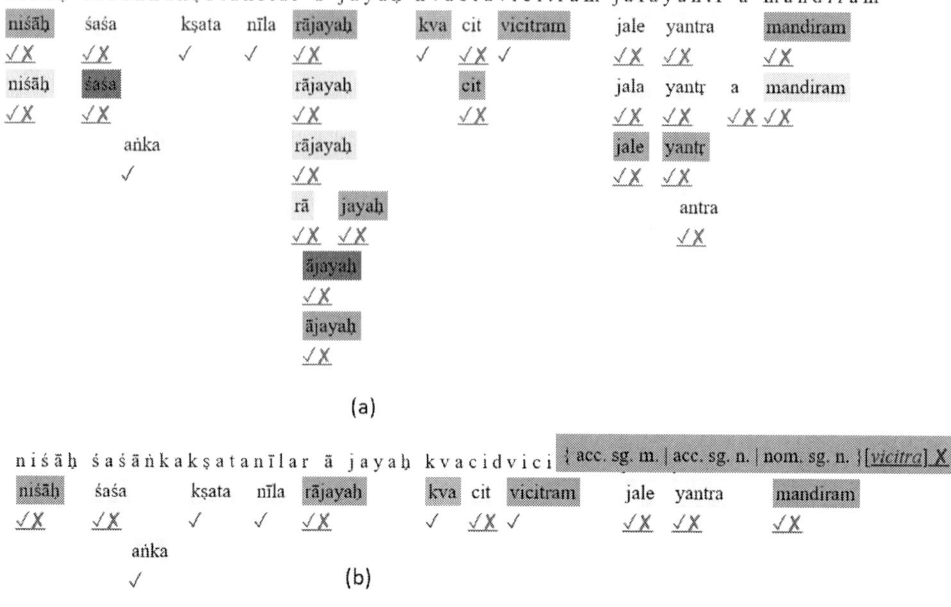

Figure 2: (a): Candidate segments for the sentence '*niśāḥ śaśāṅkakṣhatanīlarājayaḥ kvacidvicitam jalayantramandiram*' as output by the Sanskrit Heritage Reader (b): The correct segmentation for the given sentence. The image also shows the lemma information and possible morphological classes for the word '*vicitram*' (in a blue box) as shown by the morphological analyser

cal analyser for Sanskrit, when input with a sentence, provides all the phonetically valid segmentations for the given sentence. Figure 2a shows the shallow analysis provided by the Sanskrit Heritage Reader for a given sentence. The analyser not only provides the possible word forms, but also gives the morphological analysis for each of the segments. Figure 2b shows the morphological analysis for the word *vicitram*. For the word *vicitram*, it shows that the lemma for the word is '*vicitra*', and the given word-form can belong to three possible morphological classes, namely accusative case singular with masculine or neuter, or it can be nominative case singular neuter class. Similar to the case of *Sandhi*, while the generation of word form for a given morphological class is deterministic, the analysis of given word form is not deterministic and can lead to ambiguities.

3 Sanskrit Word Segmentation Task

Given an input sentence s, represented as a sequence of characters, it is possible to obtain all the possible segmentations for the sentence as output by the Sanskrit Heritage Reader. For the word segmentation task, we assume that the analysis from Sanskrit Heritage Reader is available for an input

sentence, and we reduce our task of word segmentation to finding the proper sequence of segments from the set of all candidate segments as output by the Heritage Reader. We define the word segmentation task formally, with the Heritage Reader being the cornerstone for the entire task. The task is described based on the definitions taken from Goyal and Huet (2016). Sanskrit Heritage Reader is a lexicon driven system and the system is built based on Finite State Methods. The system can be defined as a lexical juncture system.

A *lexical juncture system* on a finite alphabet Σ is composed of a finite set of words $L \subseteq \Sigma^*$ and a finite set R of rewrite rules of the form $u|v \rightarrow f/x\_\_$ (Kaplan and Kay, 1994) , with $x, v, f \in \Sigma^*$ and $u \in \Sigma^+$. In this formalization, Σ is the set of phonemes, R is the set of sandhi rules, and L is the vocabulary as a set of lexical items. We define, $z_i \in L$ as a 3-tuple (l, m, w), where l denotes the lemma of the word, m denotes the morphological class of the word and w denotes the inflected word form for the lemma l with morphological class m. Given a sentence s, a sandhi analysis for s, S_i can be seen as a sequence $\langle z_1, \sigma_1, k_1 \rangle; ... \langle z_p, \sigma_p, k_p \rangle$. Here, $\langle z_j, \sigma_j, k_j \rangle$ is a segment with $z_j \in L$, $k_j \in \mathbb{N}$ denotes the position at which the word w_j begins in the sentence s and $\sigma_j = [x_j]u_j|v_j \rightarrow w_j \in R$ for $(1 \leq j \leq p)$, $v_p = \epsilon$ and $v_j = \epsilon$ for $j < p$ only if $\sigma_j = o$, subject to the matching conditions: $z_j = v_{j-1}y_jx_ju_j$ for some $y_j \in \Sigma^*$ for all $(1 \leq j \leq p)$, where by convention $v_0 = \epsilon$. Finally $s = s_1...s_p$ with $s_j = y_jx_jw_j$ for $(1 \leq j \leq p)$. ϵ denotes the empty word.

But for s, there can be multiple possible segmentation analyses. Let $\mathcal{S}$ be the set of all such possible analyses for s. We find a shared forest representation of all such segmentation analyses

$$D(\mathcal{S}) = \bigcup_{S_i \in \mathcal{S}} S_i$$

.

A segment $\langle z_j, \sigma_j, k_j \rangle \in D(\mathcal{S})$, iff $\langle z_j, \sigma_j, k_j \rangle$ exists in at least one S_i.

We define our word segmentation task formally as follows. For a given sentence s with the set of segmentation analyses $D(\mathcal{S})$, we need to identify a set of segments $\langle z_j, \sigma_j, k_j \rangle \in D(\mathcal{S})$, such that this sequence of segments corresponds to the ground truth analysis (segmentation) S_{GT}. Figure 2b shows the ground truth segments for the sentence 'niśāḥ śaśāṅkakṣhatanīlarājayaḥ kvacidvicitam jalayantramandiram'

4 Dataset

In order to alleviate the time and effort that is often required to spend for preprocessing of Sanskrit data, we release a dataset of 115,000 Sanskrit sentences with all the candidate segments as mentioned in Section 3. Since the sentence constructs in Sanskrit follow a free word order, the proximity between two words cannot be used as an indicator for semantic and syntactic compatibility between both the words. So, we assume that all the words that co-occur in a sentence, are equally prone to influence one another. In order to reflect this in our dataset, we assume our candidate segment representation as a Graph $G(V, E)$. For the graph G, a node $v \in V$ is a unique segment $\langle z_j, \sigma_j, k_j \rangle$. There exists an edge $e \in E$ between every pair of vertices $v_i, v_j \in V$, provided v_i, v_j are not 'conflicting' with each other. Two nodes are 'conflicting' if they have an overlap in the position relative to the sentence and the overlapped portion does not adhere to any of the rules that follow *sandhi*.

Given a sentence in s with n words, the sentence will have t breaks (spaces) between the characters

such that $t < n$. If $t = n-1$, all the words are segmented. Otherwise, there are at least two words which are joined together and will be in the *sandhied* form. We call such fused forms as chunks in our dataset. For example in Figure 2a, there are four chunks. Every node is a possible candidate in the segmentation task. Two nodes are said to be conflicting, if they cannot co-occur in the given sentence, i.e, if two nodes share a character position with respect to the input, and the shared portion does not result in a proper *sandhi* transformation then the nodes are said to be conflicting. In Figure 2a, the words 'ājayaḥ' and 'jayaḥ' share a common portion of the input and hence if one of them exists in the sentence, the other needs to be eliminated. Formally, consider two nodes, represented as (k, z) and (k', z') in a given chunk. Here k and k' are the starting position (offsets) of these nodes relative to the chunk, let $|z|$ and $|z'|$ be the length of the words which nodes represent. We say that (k, z) and (k', z') *conflict* if $k \leq k' < k + |z| - 1$ or $k' \leq k < k' + |z'| - 1$ (Goyal and Huet, 2016). If two nodes are not conflicting, then there is a possibility that the two may co-occur in the sentence and hence one can become the context in resolving the other. Hence we add the edge to all such possible nodes.

4.1 The Corpus

We use the Digital Corpus of Sanskrit (DCS) for obtaining the sentences and the ground truth splits for our segmentation dataset. The DCS consists of about 560,000 sentences tagged with lemma and morphological information for each of the words in the corpus. The corpus essentially consists of partial or fully digitised versions of about 225 manuscripts in Sanskrit. The manuscripts are written as prose, poetry or a mix of both. The manuscripts range from different domains including science, philosophy, religion, literature and poetry. The time period of the various digitised works vary for more than 1000 years. So, in essence, the corpus is a representative sample of various writing styles, time period and domains of writing.

Our dataset is a subset of the mentioned corpus. Our dataset contains all the candidate space segments as output by the Sanskrit Heritage Reader for the 115,000 sentences. Since DCS and the Sanskrit Heritage Reader have differences in the design decisions they have made, it was not en-

109

tirely trivial to match the entries in the DCS with the candidate segments provided by the Sanskrit Heritage Reader. We made sure that the entries in DCS and Heritage reader candidates are matched for 115,000 sentences, taking into consideration the lemma matches, morphological classes and the compound splits.

Since, we require our dataset to be structured for automated processing and also interpretable by humans, we decided to use the XML based graph specification GraphML for representing the candidate space segments.

GraphML - GraphML (Brandes et al., 2001) is an XML based file format, specifically designed for handling Graphs. We considered graphML as the standard for the representation of segments primarily due to the human readability and structured storage of information the format provides, when compared to other space efficient binary formats like pickles or other structured formats like JSON. Additionally, standard libraries across various programming languages exist that can read GraphML structures and if required convert them to other existing formats including the aforementioned ones. By sticking onto a general purpose data representation we make the programming efforts required to process the data easier. Standard graph processing libraries (Schult and Swart, 2008; Leskovec and Sosič, 2016) can be used to apply various network metrics, graph algorithms and use the format for visualisation (Bastian et al., 2009) of the data as well. We represent each sentence in the dataset as a separate GraphML file.

Graph Structure - Each node in the graph stores a set of attributes, which show useful information about the node. The different attributes that are stored in the node and their description are as follows.

1. **Word** - The final inflected form of the segmented word that can be a possible candidate. The word is the generated form of a lemma after the affixation.

2. **Lemma** - The root word of the given form as recognized by the Sanskrit Heritage Reader.

3. **Morphological Information** - The morphological information about a given word as provided by the Sanskrit Heritage Reader.

4. **Morphological Tags by DCS** - The field consists of integer values which is used in

DCS to represent the morphological information. We add the redundant information as the mapping between DCS and the Heritage Reader are not one to one and hence to cross check the correctness, we are keeping the redundant information.

5. **Chunk Number** - Every contiguous stream of sounds in the input sentence is referred to as a chunk. A chunk contains at least one word or *pada*. The position information of each candidate segment is stored relative to the chunk's position.

6. **Word Position** - The field stores integer values which basically refers to the starting position of a given candidate segment relative to the chunk. The first word of every chunk has a position 0.

7. **Word Length** - The length of the generated word form, i.e., the field 'word'.

8. **Pre-verbs** - Certain words might be prefixed with pre-verbs. We store the pre-verbs separately as an additional attribute. But this is also counted when we calculate the 'word length'.

Currently, in the graph we keep the morphological information provided by DCS corpus as well as the Heritage Reader. Though the information is redundant, it acts as a means of validating our mapping scheme. With the aforementioned node attributes we have one edge attribute in the graph. In the graph, we store the information about whether two nodes are conflicting or not by forming edges between them and labeling them with different values. All the edges marked with attribute value '1' are non-conflicting nodes and hence can potentially co-occur. All those node pairs with edges marked with '2' are those nodes which are conflicting with each other, in other words, at most only one among the pair will exist in the final solution. It can be observed that in some files the edge type attribute has a value of '-1'. This implies that the edge is between two nodes where one of the nodes provides supplementary information about the other and hence will not be part of the segmentation. For example, consider the word '*madya*', which is a noun in vocative case with its lemma as '*madya*'. But as an additional information, it can be observed that the word is derived from the root '*mad*' which is in causative periphrastic future tense. Now, '*mad*' is not directly part of the input sentence but is supplementing the node '*madya*'. So the edge between the nodes '*mad*' and '*madya*' will have a label -1. Additionally the position attribute of '*mad*' node will also have the value -1, implying that it is not a node in the candidate space, but is supplementary to one of the candidate nodes.

5 Discussion

In this section, we detail the various linguistic properties that we leverage for mapping the output provided by the Sanskrit Heritage Reader with the information from DCS.

5.1 Compounds and Named Entities

We find that some of the compounds, especially the exo-centric compounds (and few endocentric compounds), are treated as a single word unit in DCS. The component information for the compounds are not provided. This is probably done in order to make the analysis semantically correct, as the resulting compound might be a named entity referring to either the name of a person or the name of a place. For example, the word '*daśaratha*' is a compound word, so is '*rāmalakṣmaṇabharataśatrughnāḥ*' (Krishna et al., 2016a). '*Daśaratha*' literally refers to any person who has ten chariots. But, when used in the sentence '*rāmasya pitā daśarathaḥ asti*' (Daśaratha is the father of rāma), *daśarathaḥ* does not refer to any person who has ten chariots but to a specific person. In such circumstances, it is often desired not to split compounds and represent it in terms of the components, as it is semantically not correct. In DCS, named entities like '*daśaratha*' are not decomposed into their components, but are represented as single nouns. But, '*rāmalakṣmaṇabharataśatrughnāḥ*' is a conjunctive compound containing names of four different people. DCS decomposes the compound into its components. The Heritage Reader, which does not consider the semantic context, gives the component information for all of the compounds.

To provide mapping between both the resources in such cases, we replace the components suggested by the heritage reader with a *sandhied* versions of the compound components. The *sandhied* version is used as the candidate segment, so as to match it with the scheme of the DCS. But multiple component combinations may lead to the same *sandhied* versions. For example, DCS treats the word *nāradam* as a single unit which is desirable, on the other hand Heritage Reader produces different splits for the same word. Figure 3a shows the treatment of the word *nāradam* in DCS, while Figure 3b shows the analysis of the same word by the Heritage Reader. Here, all the possible component combinations that lead to the correct *sandhied* form are added as nodes in the graph but as supplementary nodes with an edge type value of -1. The supplementary information need not be of direct impact for the word segmentation task, and hence can be ignored for the task. But it will be beneficial when it comes to syntactic parsing tasks like dependency parsing or other semantic tasks.

5.2 Secondary Derivative Affixes

The secondary derivative affixes such as '*vat*' and '*tva*' are treated differently in both the systems. While, Sanskrit Heritage Reader remains faithful to the traditional means of analysis, by keeping the morpheme as part of the root word, DCS deviates from this representation. In DCS, the morphemes, i.e., the root word and the secondary derivative affix, are treated as separate words. For example, in the sentence '*śarātisarge śīghratvāt kālāntakayamopamaḥ*', consider the word '*śīghratvāt*'. The word is an ablative case neuter gender singular noun of '*śīghratva*'. Now, this can further be represented as the combination of the morphemes, '*śīghra*' and '*tva*', where the former is a noun and the latter is the secondary derivative affix. In heritage reader, this is represented as '*śīghratva*', implying the traditional analysis of the word into its morphemes. But, in DCS both the morphemes are represented as two individual lemma. Same applies with '*vat*' as well. We take care of this in our dataset.

5.3 Markers in Lemma

The inflections in compounds in Sanskrit are generally added to the final component of the compound (Krishna et al., 2016b). This implies that all the other components are devoid of the inflection and are in pure form. But, certain words in Sanskrit often have additional markers in them when the word is mentioned as its base form. But, when the base form is used as component, the markers are removed. There are entries in DCS where the form of the component is assumed to be the base form. For example, in the compound '*mahādeva*'

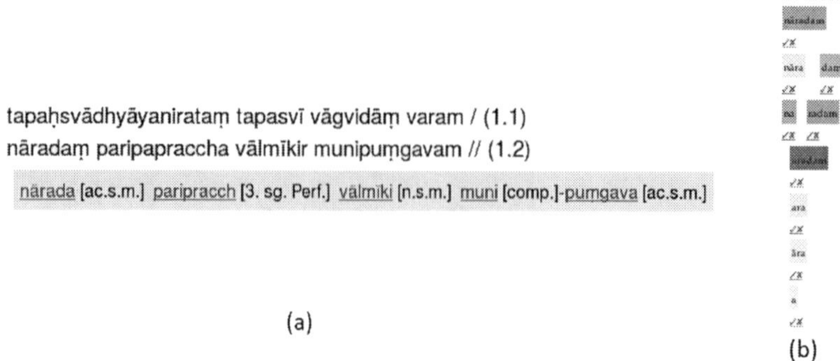

Figure 3: (a) - Morphological analysis of *nāradam* in the DCS. (b) - Morphological analysis of *nāradam* in the Sanskrit Heritage Reader

(The great god or Lord *Śiva*), the compound has the components '*mahān*' (great) and '*deva* '(deity, god). But, the lemma or the base form for '*mahā*' is '*mahat*'. Heritage Reader follows this convention. But in DCS, '*mahān*' is considered as the lemma. We find such cases where similar issues are present and resolve them.

5.4 Phonetic Variations

In Sanskrit, '*ṃ*', known as the *anusvāra*, when followed by one of the predefined set of phonemes from the phoneme list, can optionally undergo a transformation where it is replaced by a nasal (*anunāsika*) variation corresponding to the phone. This can be seen as an internal sandhi. DCS does not consider this internal transformation and the heritage reader does so. In effect there are five such different *anunāsika* variations possible corresponding to various places of articulation. In the case of *Śaṃkara*, the *ṃ* is followed by '*k*'. The *anunāsika* for '*k*' is '*ṅ*'. Thus, *Śaṃkara* becomes *Śaṅkara*. Similarly, for *saṃjaya* where *ṃ* is preceded by '*j*', *saṃjaya* gets transformed to '*sañjaya*'.

Phonetic Variations due to Pre-verbs - Linguistically, preverbs are treated as bound morphemes. But in DCS, there are numerous instances when a verb is prefixed with a preverb, the joint form is treated as a different lemma altogether. This distinction needs to be taken care of, as the Heritage Reader provides the original verbal root. Additionally, internal *sandhi* can take place when the preverb is prefixed to a verb. When obtaining the analysis for each of the morphemes, we need to split the morphemes by undoing the *sandhi* operation as well. But, in DCS whenever the preverb is not separated, the *sandhi* operation also remains embedded in the form. The internal *sandhi* also needs to be taken care of, in order to deal with the analysis from the heritage reader. For example in case of '*praṇam*', the word is an inflection of the verbal root '*nam*' with '*pra*' prefixed as a preverb. Here, due to internal *sandhi*, '*n*' transforms to '*ṇ*'. Similarly, '*s*' changes to '*ṣ*' in case of '*abhiṣic*', which is joint form for the morphemes '*abhi*' and '*sic*'.

6 Conclusion

We release the dataset hoping to catalyse the research in computational processing of Sanskrit. Here, we abstract out language specific details that are often required in handling the data, and makes the data accessible to researchers who otherwise required to rely on linguistic experts in Sanskrit. A considerable amount of time and expertise is often required in pre-processing the data and aligning the ground truth with the output of the morphological analyser. This acts as a barrier to the entry point in the field of Sanskrit Computational Linguistics. We present the pre-processed data by removing all the inconsistencies that are often faced. We expect to eventually roll out the data for all the 560,000 files. Currently we release 115,000 files. Please note that the GraphML files store directly the output of the Heritage Reader for the input sentence in a structured format. The ground truth segmentation is directly taken from DCS, which is manually tagged, and is assumed to be correct. The mapping between the schemes used for defining the morphological classes in both the Sanskrit Heritage Reader and the DCS is not completely unambiguous. Currently, we provide the morpho-

112

logical class information for each word in both the schemes. Hence, the dataset will not be affected by the changes that may occur to the said mapping between the schemes. The current dataset may not be directly usable for dependency parsing, as the current sentences are not properly aligned to sentence boundaries, especially for sentences in poetry formats. Computational means of finding sentence boundaries is a research topic of its own (Hellwig, 2016). Summarily, we bring clarity with regards to the requirements for the word segmentation task and release a dataset for the experiments. We hope to not only increase the collective productivity of the community which would have otherwise been spent on preprocessing, but also believe that this endeavour makes benchmarking of different systems straightforward, as their performance can be tested on the same dataset.

Acknowledgements

The authors are thankful to the anonymous reviewers for their valuable feedback. The authors would like to thank Gérard Huet for providing the Sanskrit Heritage Engine, to be installed on local systems and Oliver Hellwig for contributing the DCS Corpus. We are grateful to Amba Kulkarni, Peter Scharf and again Gérard Huet for their comments and feedback regarding the design and development of this dataset. The authors would also like to acknowledge the efforts put by Bhumi Faldu in programming and maintaining the codebase with which the dataset was created.

Dataset Download

The dataset can be downloaded from `https://zenodo.org/record/803508#.WTuKbSa9UUs`

References

Mathieu Bastian, Sebastien Heymann, Mathieu Jacomy, et al. 2009. Gephi: an open source software for exploring and manipulating networks. *ICWSM* 8:361–362.

Ulrik Brandes, Markus Eiglsperger, Ivan Herman, Michael Himsolt, and M Scott Marshall. 2001. Graphml progress report structural layer proposal. In *International Symposium on Graph Drawing*. Springer, pages 501–512.

Sharon Goldwater, Thomas L Griffiths, and Mark Johnson. 2006. Contextual dependencies in unsupervised word segmentation. In *Proceedings of the 21st International Conference on Computational Linguistics and the 44th annual meeting of the Association for Computational Linguistics*. Association for Computational Linguistics, pages 673–680.

Pawan Goyal and Gérard Huet. 2013. Completeness analysis of a sanskrit reader. In *Proceedings, 5th International Symposium on Sanskrit Computational Linguistics. DK Printworld (P) Ltd.* pages 130–171.

Pawan Goyal and Gérard Huet. 2016. Design and analysis of a lean interface for sanskrit corpus annotation. *Journal of Language Modelling* 4(2):145–182.

Pawan Goyal, Gérard Huet, Amba Kulkarni, Peter Scharf, and Ralph Bunker. 2012. A distributed platform for Sanskrit processing. In *Proceedings of COLING 2012*. The COLING 2012 Organizing Committee, Mumbai, India, pages 1011–1028. http://www.aclweb.org/anthology/C12-1062.

Oliver Hellwig. 2015. Using recurrent neural networks for joint compound splitting and sandhi resolution in sanskrit. In *4th Biennial Workshop on Less-Resourced Languages*.

Oliver Hellwig. 2016. Detecting sentence boundaries in sanskrit texts. In *Proceedings of COLING 2016, the 26th International Conference on Computational Linguistics: Technical Papers*. The COLING 2016 Organizing Committee, Osaka, Japan, pages 288–297. http://aclweb.org/anthology/C16-1028.

Gérard Huet. 2009. Sanskrit Segmentation, South Asian Languages Analysis Roundtable xxviii, Denton, Texas. South Asian Languages Analysis Roundtable XXVIII.

Malcolm D. Hyman. 2008. From Paninian Sandhi to Finite State Calculus. In *Sanskrit Computational Linguistics*. pages 253–265.

Ronald M. Kaplan and Martin Kay. 1994. Regular models of phonological rule systems. *Computational Linguistics* 20,3:331–378.

Amrith Krishna, Bishal Santra, Pavankumar Satuluri, Sasi Prasanth Bandaru, Bhumi Faldu, Yajuvendra Singh, and Pawan Goyal. 2016a. Word segmentation in sanskrit using path constrained random walks. In *Proceedings of COLING 2016, the 26th International Conference on Computational Linguistics: Technical Papers*. The COLING 2016 Organizing Committee, Osaka, Japan, pages 494–504. http://aclweb.org/anthology/C16-1048.

Amrith Krishna, Pavankumar Satuluri, Shubham Sharma, Apurv Kumar, and Pawan Goyal. 2016b. Compound type identification in sanskrit: What roles do the corpus and grammar play? In *Proceedings of the 6th Workshop on South and Southeast Asian Natural Language Processing (WSSANLP2016)*. The COLING 2016 Organizing Committee, Osaka, Japan, pages 1–10. http://aclweb.org/anthology/W16-3701.

Amba Kulkarni, Preethi Shukla, Pavankumar Satuluri, and Devanand Shukl. 2015. How Free is free Word Order in Sanskrit. In *Sanskrit Syntax*. The Sanskrit Library, USA.

Ni Lao and William W Cohen. 2010. Relational retrieval using a combination of path-constrained random walks. *Machine learning* 81(1):53–67.

Jure Leskovec and Rok Sosič. 2016. Snap: A general-purpose network analysis and graph-mining library. *ACM Transactions on Intelligent Systems and Technology (TIST)* 8(1):1.

Keshav S Melnad, Pawan Goyal, and Peter Scharf. 2015. Meter identification of sanskrit verse. In *Sanskrit Syntax*. pages 325–346.

Vipul Mittal. 2010. Automatic sanskrit segmentizer using finite state transducers. In *Proceedings of the ACL 2010 Student Research Workshop*. Association for Computational Linguistics, Uppsala, Sweden, pages 85–90. http://www.aclweb.org/anthology/P10-3015.

Abhiram Natarajan and Eugene Charniak. 2011. s^3 - statistical sandhi splitting. In *Proceedings of 5th International Joint Conference on Natural Language Processing*. Asian Federation of Natural Language Processing, Chiang Mai, Thailand, pages 301–308. http://www.aclweb.org/anthology/I11-1034.

Peter M Scharf and Malcolm D Hyman. 2011. Linguistic issues in encoding sanskrit. *The Sanskrit Library* .

Daniel A Schult and P Swart. 2008. Exploring network structure, dynamics, and function using networkx. In *Proceedings of the 7th Python in Science Conferences (SciPy 2008)*. volume 2008, pages 11–16.

Lexical Correction of Polish Twitter Political Data

Maciej Ogrodniczuk, Mateusz Kopeć

Institute of Computer Science
Polish Academy of Sciences

Jana Kazimierza 5
01-248 Warsaw, Poland

`maciej.ogrodniczuk@ipipan.waw.pl`
`m.kopec@phd.ipipan.waw.pl`

Abstract

Language processing architectures are often evaluated in near-to-perfect conditions with respect to processed content. The tools which perform sufficiently well on electronic press, books and other type of non-interactive content may poorly handle noisy, colloquial and multilingual textual data which make the majority of communication today. This paper aims at investigating how Polish Twitter data (in a slightly controlled 'political' flavour) differs from expectation of linguistic tools and how it could be corrected to be ready for processing by standard language processing chains available for Polish. The setting includes specialised components for spelling correction of tweets as well as hashtag and username decoding.

1 Introduction

The recent massive growth in online media and the rise of user-authored content (e.g. weblogs, Twitter, Facebook) has led to challenges of how to efficiently access and interpret this unique data. Streaming online media pose completely new challenges to linguistic processing due to short message lengths and their noisier and more colloquial character. Moreover, they form a temporal stream strongly grounded in events and context. Consequently, existing language technologies for such languages as Polish, which is by no means an under-resourced language, but still under-researched in streaming media area, fall short on accuracy and scalability.

In this paper we present a component for real-time processing of data retrieved from Twitter — one of the linguistically most demanding large-scale stream medium. We limit our investigation to 'Polish political tweets', i.e. textual data coming from Twitter accounts of actors on the Polish political scene — members of parliament, political parties and government agencies. The motivation for such limitation is practical: tweets coming from official channels tend to be less noisy than the major stream but still reflect the same types of problems which appear in general settings. We investigate lexical characteristics of such content, possibilities of error correction and recognition of unknown words, construct tweet annotation chain with topic and named entity extraction and present a sample environment for visual content aggregation which can be treated as a demonstration of a language analytic environment to be used by Social Studies and Humanities. Each of the above-mentioned steps poses a challenge in its own; topic extraction, for instance, requires application of multi-word unit lemmatization techniques, difficult for inflectional languages, and named entity extraction must be followed by resolution and unification of nicknames of political entities.

Another motivation for using political content is the rising role of social media among opinion-forming channels supplementing the public discourse traditionally represented by official records, paper and electronic media. With the advent of real-time social media, they are becoming the third major channel of political discourse, so tracking propagation of ideas in the public discourse and its growing fragmentation and polarisation seemed a solid motivation for development of linguistic processing chains for social data.

Joint SIGHUM Workshop on Computational Linguistics for Cultural Heritage, Social Sciences, Humanities and Literature.
Proceedings, pages 115–125, Vancouver, BC, August 4, 2017. ©2017 Association for Computational Linguistics

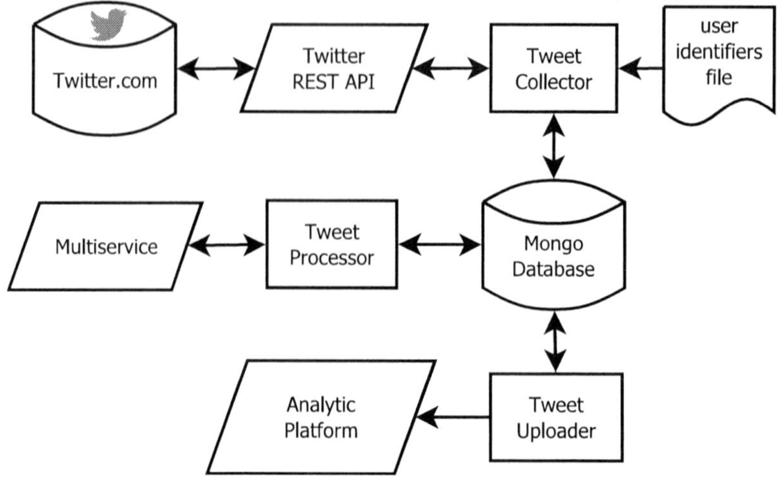

Figure 1: Architecture of the language processing chain

2 Tweet Processing Architecture

2.1 Source Data

Politics-related content was acquired from 766 accounts, the list of which was collated from several existing sources[1] and later supplemented with accounts automatically retrieved from Twitter based on the list of names of politicians and manually verified by experts to exclude fake accounts. This method is the only practical one, also due to Twitter access policy, allowing consumers to access content produced by individual accounts with a publicly available API and at the same time preventing other general access methods such as language- or topic-based filtering.

2.2 Technical Processing

The data was fetched using REST API `statuses/user_timeline` method as it provided the most complete result set (up to 3200 tweets of a given user, usually sufficient to retrieve the whole history of their publication). New activity monitoring was also set and the data was initially filtered based on detected tweet language[2]. Certain cleaning steps were also applied to the content, related to Twitter specificities (words truncated by Twitter as exceeding maximum tweet character size were removed and parts of the message indicating that a post had been retweeted were cleaned).

Twitter data was stored in the database and further processed (see Section 6) with language tools offered as Web services in a common framework called MULTISERVICE (Ogrodniczuk and Lenart, 2012)[3]. The results of the linguistic analysis were saved back to the database. The general view on the architecture of the processing pipeline is presented in Figure 1.

Twitter collection ran every hour. Since user `screen_name`[4] may change, tweets were fetched based on user identifier for users present on the account list. Date boundaries `since_id` and `max_id` were used to retrieve tweets newer than the most recent tweet from last run, and older than the oldest tweet from last request from current run. Tweets with missing identifiers or other vital information such as creation date were discarded. JSON data was stored in MongoDB. Currently the database contains over 1.7M tweets and the volume increases about 100-150K tweets/month.

Due to Twitter rate limiting which restricts free

---

[1]The list by Mateusz Puszczynski (no longer available online), Klub Chwila (`http://www.holdys.pl/polskitwitter/`, top 50 Twitter political accounts by `wirtualnemedia.pl` portal, data offered by ePanstwo Foundation (`http://epf.org.pl/app/webroot/api/dane/`) and manually collected list of alternative names and nicknames.

[2]Language detection was performed using OPEN-IMAJ library (Hare et al., 2011), see `http://www.openimaj.org`; the library reimplements the HTTPS://GITHUB.COM/SAFFSD/LANGID.PY script (Lui and Baldwin, 2012) using the model trained for 97 languages.

[3]See also `http://multiservice.nlp.ipipan.waw.pl/en/`.

[4]Detailed description of the format may be found at `https://dev.twitter.com/docs/platform-objects/tweets`.

of charge requests of each type (e.g. 300 `GET statuses/user_timeline` API calls fetching tweets of a particular user per 15 minutes), the upper bound on tweet downloading speed for the setting is 240,000 tweets per hour which is sufficient for currently available amount of Polish political Twitter content.

3 Twitter Political Language

To be able to verify a meaningful sample of Twitter political data, a 3000 tweet portion was manually inspected to perform categorization of common phenomena which could distinguish 'tweet language' from general Polish. For that purpose, 10,000 tweets were randomly selected from the stream and in the first step one tweet per each user was sampled, starting from the most recent data. Then, the sample was supplemented in a way that maintained the proportion of tweets selected to the overall number of tweets authored by a given person until the dataset reached 3000 entries. The presented method was supposed to maintain high variability in language use by providing content coming from different authors and at the same time keep a higher number of tweets authored by more active users.

The dataset, containing 39,268 words, was manually inspected to detect constructs representing pre-defined language phenomena regarded to pose a challenge for NLP tools, further referred to as 'lexical features' (LFs). The process was carried out by three project participants, each annotating 1000 entries, in one pass, with no additional verification, assuming that the task is straightforward enough to be performed without additional adjudication. For each tweet several categories of LFs were marked, shortly explained below and summarised in Table 1.

The key observation resulting from the manual analysis of political tweets is that language used in that discourse is rather well-formed and close to the quality of news articles (for example, named entities were almost always written correctly in terms of capital letters). This seems to result from rather formal character of Twitter use adopted by Polish political users, keeping this channel in line with other official means of communication. At the same time this finding nurses the hope of reasonable performance of general-purpose NLP tools on this type of data.

However, several differences between tweets

LF category	% of tweets with this LF
Abbreviations	26.23%
Missing diacritical marks	10.93%
Emoticons	12.00%
Trimmed words	6.03%
Spelling errors	3.37%
Foreign language	2.93%
Other	2.77%
Case inconsistencies	1.27%
Any	49.40%

Table 1: Categorization of typical processing problems encountered by reviewing tweet content

and standard written communication were noticed, the most common of which was related to frequency of abbreviations. Over 26% of tweets contained at least one non-standard (out-of general dictionary) abbreviation. Another common issue were spelling errors, 10% of which were related to missing Polish diacritic marks (hardly understandable in smartphone era). Presence of emoticons (in 12% of tweets) and trimmed words (in 6% of tweets, resulting from cutting content due to tweet character limit) were another important findings.

Very interesting result of our manual analysis was that spelling errors other than missing diacritics were quite rare (present in about 3% of tweets) which also seemed specific to the observed group of official accounts expected to use 'correct' language. It also applied to case problems, which were very infrequent. This observation may lead to general conclusion that missing diacritics seem to have a different status than other type of lexical features — our users were rather careful in writing, yet not so strict about using proper diacritic signs. Foreign words occurred in less than 3% of tweets.

Summing up, NLP tools created for general Polish language should be effective for our data type, given that certain preprocessing (fixing diacritics and trimmed words, expanding abbreviations and correctly parsing emoticons) is performed. Still, extensive description of these phenomena covered by the next subsections is intended to present the complexity of the problem.

3.1 Missing Diacritical Marks

A word without diacritics may have a different meaning or no meaning at all, which increases the difficulty of text processing. Missing diacritics are subtypes of general spelling errors, but whenever adding diacritics was sufficient for getting a proper interpretation of a word (e.g. mąz → mąż), the tweet was marked with this category. Whenever both forms (with and without diacritics) were acceptable in the content, the more probable variant was selected, as in 'mblaszczak do JK powiedział chyba "prowokacja"? odczytuje z ruchu warg' (Eng. *it seems mblaszczak said 'provocation' to JK? [unclear, can be 'I am' or 'he is'] lip-reading*), when 3rd person 'odczytuje' (Eng. *he is lip-reading*) is less likely to be used in this context than 1st person 'odczytuję' (Eng. *I am lip-reading*).

Missing foreign diacritics (as in *exposé, Müller*) were not marked: although they are regularly applied by spellcheckers to known word forms (e.g. from *expose* to *exposé*) their English-alphabet variants are much more common since grave accents or umlauts are not easily obtainable with a standard Polish keyboard. In few cases this class also groups related problems, such as excess diacritic marks ('pisałem' → 'pisałem') or puzzling cases foreign diacritics in Polish words ('pomarzyč' → 'pomarzyć').

3.2 Abbreviations and Trimmed Words

Almost all abbreviations were counted, including the following subcategories:

- abbreviations of named entities ('FB' → 'Facebook', 'GW' → 'Gazeta Wyborcza', 'PiS', 'PO')

- initials of people's names ('J.K.' → 'Jarosław Kaczyński', 'JVR' → 'Jan Vincent Rostowski'), also including ad-hoc abbreviations ('PDT' → 'Prime Minister Donald Tusk', 'PEK' → 'Prime Minister Ewa Kopacz')

- foreign abbreviations frequently used in Polish ('CIT', 'NATO', 'OK')

- abbreviations without the obligatory dot at the end ('nt', 'prof')

- ad-hoc abbreviations of common words, resolvable from the context ('dzienn.' → 'dziennikarz', 'dokł' → 'dokładnie')

- certain proper names, initially formed as abbreviations ('TVP', 'TVP2', 'TVN', 'CO2', but not 'ZET' in 'Radio ZET').

Some abbreviations such as Polish slang expressions, not (yet) present in the reference morphological dictionary (Saloni et al., 2015) were excluded from this group and counted as slang words ('other' group). Code or brand names ('F16', 'BMW') were also not treated as abbreviations.

Category of trimmed words resulted from users' attempts to publish longer tweets than the maximum allowed 140 characters. Trimming may occur in the middle of a word, username, hashtag or URL and is marked with triple dots, often leaving only first part of a word.

3.3 Case Problems and Spelling Errors

Category marked as case problems corresponds to entity names started with lowercase (which increases difficulty of finding named entities in the text) or unnecessary capitalization of a whole word. Lowercase letter in the beginning of the sentence was not counted as case problem.

Spelling errors category groups spelling problems other than missing diacritics into one of the following classes:

- misplaced or missing letters ('swrdecznie' → 'serdecznie', 'członkowstwo' → 'członkostwo')

- words stuck together due to missing separating spaces — excluding punctuation problems such as an extra space between a word and a comma ('gospodarkama' → 'gospodarka ma')

- words separated with an excess space ('był by' → 'byłby')

- repetitions of letters or their sequences ('okeeeeeej' → 'okej', 'Hmmmm' → ',Hmm'; not necessarily a spelling error, but not frequent enough to form a separate class).

3.4 Emoticons

Presence of emoticons may be difficult for NLP tools created for traditional written texts, such as books or news articles. Their presence requires special treatment, especially because they make a valuable source of information about the sentiment of a tweet.

3.5 Foreign Language

Most non-Polish expressions in Polish tweets were English ('dream team'), but German and Latin were also observed. Several subcategories of foreign language use can be distinguished:

- single foreign words ('community'), also those functioning as slang expressions ('sorry', 'nerd'), often inflected ('Sammyego', 'iPhone'owi')

- foreign phrases or sentences, both ad hoc interjections ('I like it') and quotations ('Ora et labora')

- titles ('Assassin's Creed Identity')

- polonized foreign words other than named entities ('retlitują' (Eng. *they retweet*, 'hendszejk' (Eng. *handshake*), 'slitfocia' (Eng. *selfie*, from *sweet photo*).

3.6 Other Phenomena

Other interesting observed phenomena included:

- neologisms ('sorkokorki', 'Kopaczinho')

- Polish ('kminię', 'Bolandzie', 'Lemingradu', 'Łomatko', 'pzdr' → 'Pozdrawiam') and foreign slang words and abbreviations ('OMG' → 'My God', 'rl' → 'real life'), sometimes noted in the dictionaries of slang

- new words, still not present in the reference morphosyntactic dictionary, but likely to be included shortly ('smartfon', 'audiobook')

- compound words, with lack of interpretation probably resulting from misconfiguration or missing prefix in the morphosyntactic dictionary ('homopropaganda', 'nadredaktor')

- less frequent forms of common words, evidently missing from the morphosyntactic dictionary ('zmolestowanego')

- non-standard transcription of common words ('nie-by-wa-łe-go')

- inflected forms of named entities, particularly adjectives ('palikotowy')

- forms intentionally distorted for stylistic reasons ('Świętokrzysko', 'szłem', 'pachły', 'wiater', 'jedenu').

4 Spelling Correction

Since our investigation showed that the most frequent lexical features in tweet content are missing diacritic marks or wrong spelling, the obvious first step of the processing was integration of an automatic spellchecker for Polish to introduce the corrections.

Spelling correction issue for Polish is a difficult task due to inflection resulting in high number of distinct word forms. PoliMorf (Woliński et al., 2012)[5], the largest morphological dictionary of Polish, contains over 44,000 lexemes corresponding to 4,000,000 word forms and 6,500,000 morphosyntactic interpretations. Without taking diacritics into consideration they are likely to be homographic. This makes such tasks as adding diacritical marks difficult in general setting. Since there is no evaluation data available, we targeted evaluation of the best available spellchecking tool for Polish — LanguageTool (Miłkowski, 2010). It is a language-independent rule-based open source proofreading software able to detect frequent context-dependent spelling mistakes, as well as grammatical, punctuation, usage, and stylistic errors. It is regarded as the most extensive resource of this type for Polish, features hundreds of thousands of downloads and is available as a standalone tool as well as a plugin for LibreOffice/OpenOffice and Firefox.

The 3000 tweet sample (see Section 3) was used as the test set for our experiment. The sample showed 740 lexical features, corresponding to misspelled words, including abbreviations and named entities ('Polasat' → 'Polsat') and words with missing diacritical marks ('zapytac' → 'zapytać'); other types of extra-lexical errors (punctuation, grammatical, usage, stylistic errors) were not taken into consideration.

The experiment showed that LanguageTool correction rules proved too extensive which resulted in introducing errors for new words ('smartfonów' → 'smart fonów'), named entities ('Baracka Obamy' → 'Baranka Obawy') and non-standard abbreviations ('pracow.' → 'placów.') in the out-of-the-box solution (referred to as version LT0 later in this section). This verification resulted in evaluating two other settings of the tool:

- running only on words which are not entirely capitalized — which corresponds to a setting

---

[5]See also `http://zil.ipipan.waw.pl/PoliMorf`.

	LT0	LT1	LT2	TM
Undetected errors	126	164	268	181
Detected and corrected	614	576	472	559
Wrongly corrected	695	483	178	228

Table 2: Error correction statistics for all investigated settings

	LT0	LT1	LT2	TM
Precision	0.47	0.54	0.73	0.71
Recall	0.83	0.78	0.64	0.76
F1	0.60	0.64	0.68	0.73

Table 3: Evaluation of relevance of all investigated settings

> where all errors except for those in words regarded as abbreviations are corrected (setting LT1)

- running only on words which are not starting with a capital letter — which corresponds to a setting where all errors except for those in words regarded as named entities are corrected (LT2).

Taking into account the greedy behaviour or LanguageTool, another version of the spell-checking solution (later referred to as TM) was created based on the assumption that since the majority of errors are diacritic-related, fixing only this problem could solve many issues without introducing new ones likely to be caused by extensive spelling correction. TM solution implements a simple algorithm using morphosyntactic dictionary PoliMorf to extract all possible strings which by addition of some number of diacritics may represent a valid word (present in the dictionary). This gives a mapping from strings to possibilities for diacritic insertion, which produces a valid word. We also apply a special rule of not adding any diacritics if the string without them is already valid. When a string in our mapping occurs in text, we have two options: leave it unchanged, if there is such option in the mapping, or replace it with some entry from the mapping. To have an efficient way to select valid replacement (or no replacement) we use a unigram frequency count extracted from a 300-million token balanced subcorpus of the National Corpus of Polish (Przepiórkowski et al., 2012). The option which produces the most frequent word in our reference corpus is selected as valid diacritisation variant.

The algorithm works in two different modes depending on presence of diacritic signs in a tweet being corrected. If the tweet does not have any diacritics, we allow to add them if they make valid words (in this way the word 'mowie' may be corrected to 'mówię', even that it is a valid dative form of a noun 'mowa'). Otherwise, we only try to add diacritics to strings, which are not valid words.

Table 2 presents statistics of errors undetected, detected and corrected in the test data by all tools being investigated and Table 3 compares their performance. While TM solution featured more wrong corrections as compared to LT2, at the same time it detected more errors which resulted in better overall F1 score. The possible improvements of the solution might consider using context larger than unigrams or implementing a more sophisticated approach to decide whether tweet author is likely to omit diacritics or not.

5 User Name and Hashtag Normalization

Two interesting Twitter language phenomena are *hashtags* and *user mentions*. Hashtags are sequences of non-whitespace characters (making a keyword or a multi-word 'phraseword') preceded by the 'hash' (#) character, most frequently used to categorize Twitter messages by topic in the general stream of conversations (also those taking place outside writer's immediate connections). Usually composed of natural words and thus able to syntactically interact with other parts of the message, hashtags can also contribute to textual content, making them legitimate subject of natural language processing tasks. But even in case of simple keywords, their decomposition can help categorization task as in *był czechosłowacki chłopiec z plakatu to może być polska #premierzkartki (there was once a czechoslovakian boy from the poster so now we can have polish #primeminister-fromthepieceofpaper)* where decoding reference to the Polish Prime Minister would be impossible without hashtag segmentation.

The second useful referring feature are user mentions: by writing user account name starting with 'at' (@) sign the author can 'link' to a particular Twitter user who gets notified about that in his/her timeline which stimulates interaction. Similarly to hashtags, user names are difficult for direct use (due to their identifying rather than naming character) while at the same time they are frequently used in content not only as reference markers, but also (mostly because of the 140 character limit) as part of communication, cf. *Minister @KosiniakKamysz podaje szczegóły propozycji z expose Ewy Kopacz.* (*Minister @KosiniakKamysz gives details of proposals from Ewa Kopacz's exposé.*)

Normalization of user names is usually a simple process; they can be easily replaced with names indicated in user profiles (although more sophisticated procedures were also put forward, see e.g. (McKelvey et al., 2017)). On the contrary, multiword hashtags are often created ad hoc and are usually not camelCase-encoded so different segmentation methods should be used to process them.

Several normalization procedures have been proposed for hashtag processing, the most frequent of which follow Web domain names segmentation algorithms (Berardi et al., 2011; Wang et al., 2011; Srinivasan et al., 2012, cf. e.g.) treating it as a dictionary-based task and using the frequency distribution for selecting the most probable decomposition variant. Various hashtag harmonization methods were also proposed, e.g. by (Pöschko, 2011), based on co-occurrence of hashtags in a tweet, (Costa et al., 2013), defining meta-hashtags to be used for tweet classification, or (Declerck and Lendvai, 2015) and (Bansal et al., 2015), reducing variation of hashtags to semantically link them to topics and entities.

More recently, the topic has been adopted by a wider scientific audience, resulting in organisation of a series of workshops on tweet normalization (Tweet-Norm 2013, see `http://ceur-ws.org/Vol-1086/`), NLP for Social Media (SocialNLP), started in 2013 (see `https://sites.google.com/site/socialnlp2017/` for its 2017 edition) or Noisy User-generated Text (W-NUT) started in 2015 (see `http://noisy-text.github.io`). Proceedings of these workshops present a broad spectrum of algorithms for general social content normalization, using e.g. maximum entropy models (Arshi Saloot et al., 2015), Conditional Random Fields (Akhtar et al., 2015) or word embeddings (Costa Bertaglia and Volpe Nunes, 2016) as well as their application to languages other than English, e.g. Spanish (Pablo Ruiz, 2013) or Japanese (Ikeda et al., 2016), with numerous system resulting from a shared task on Twitter Lexical Normalization at the 2015 W-NUT.

Our normalization solution uses the PoliMorf dictionary to split hashtags into two or three parts and then select the segmentation using frequency lists from the National Corpus of Polish. Table 4 presents the results of our algorithm on the set of 1048 different hashtags identified in our test data set as unrecognized Polish words.

Result type	Count	%
Proper variant selected	**682**	**65,14%**
2 segments	573	54,73%
3 segments	109	10,41%
Wrong variant selected	**342**	**32,66%**
Foreign word	143	13,66%
New word	132	12,61%
Misspelling	14	1,34%
Unrecognized form	53	5,06%
All variants wrong	**23**	**2,20%**

Table 4: Hashtag segmentation results

Error analysis shows that the most frequent problems result from overuse of foreign words in hashtags, mostly English (*travel, climate* etc.); some of them tend to function as loans and are now commonly used in Polish (*tweet* (!), *startup, hiking, stalking* etc.) Several 'new words' are neologisms or newest lexical acquisitions not yet present in dictionaries (*euromajdan, tuskolenie, kartodrom, pendolino* (here: new Polish intercity train), *monetyzacja, korpo, polisolokaty* etc.); this category also includes frequent proper names not included in lexical database of the morphological tools such as *Obama, Gazprom* or *Uber*. The category of unknown words includes such forms as *indyref, trapani* or *himym* but also designated hashtags (cf. #MasterChefAU).

6 The Linguistic Platform

After spelling errors have been minimized, linguistic services integrated in MULTISERVICE can be used to perform multi-layer analysis of tweet texts. First, text is segmented and part-of-speech tagged by WCRFT (Radziszewski, 2013b)[6], a disambiguating tagger for Polish. Topics (names, locations, events) are detected using MENTION DETECTOR (Kopeć, 2014)[7], integrating data from shallow parser SPEJD (Przepiórkowski and Buczyński, 2007)[8] and named entity recognizer NERF (Savary et al., 2010)[9] Sentiment analysis is performed by Sentipejd (Buczyński and Wawer, 2008)[10]

While results of segmentation and tagging are taken over directly, results of topic detection are further categorized for visualization purposes. Firstly, nested named entities are discarded and the topic phrases are multi-word lemmatized (see details in Section 6.1). Named entities matched against Polish political ontology are additionally marked. Then noun-phrase topics are discovered using dictionary created from all previously detected mentions and their counts. When a certain, arbitrarily set count is exceeded, the phrase is marked as valid emerging topic. Overly frequent mentions such as pronouns are discarded as stopwords.

Locations are processed separately, by attempting to match lemmatized variants of each geographical named entity retrieved from tweet against Geonames ontology entries (Wick, 2015). If a match is found, GPS coordinates of that location are extracted. Twitter-offered `place` field-based location recognition results are discarded due to unclear source of the field value; according to Twitter documentation, it indicates 'a place the tweet is associated with (but not necessarily originating from)'.

Finally, token-based overall sentiment of the tweet is calculated and the bias in the Internet discourse towards negative sentiment is balanced by having a 1.5 weight in favour of the positive senti-

ment with the following formula:

$$S = \frac{1.5 t_{pos} - t_{neg}}{t}$$

where S is the sentiment value, t is the number of tokens in tweet, t_{pos} is the number of tokens in tweet having positive sentiment and t_{neg} is the number of tokens in tweet having negative sentiment.

Visualisation and mining of data delivered by the language processing chain is further performed by a service developed by TrendMiner project (see Section 6.2).

6.1 Corpus-based Lemmatization

While lemmata for single-word expressions are provided by the tagger, lemmatization of multi-word expressions in Polish (i.e. finding the base form of a MWE) is not a trivial task, usually going far beyond word-by-word lemmatization. Citing (Graliński et al., 2010) who also lists several examples of different agreement types, this results from *complex linguistic properties of compounds, including (i) heterogeneous status of separators in the definition of a MWU's component, (ii) morphological agreement between selected components, (iii) morphosyntactic noncompositionality (exocentricity, irregular agreement, defective paradigms, variability, etc.), (iv) large sizes of inflection paradigms (e.g. dozens of forms in Polish).*

The task has been attempted previously in a narrow setting e.g. by (Degórski, 2012) or (Radziszewski, 2013a) but the results were lower than expected. As we are interested only in topic expressions which occur in multiple tweets, our approach to lemmatization of MWEs was corpus-based. The idea was to collect the number of occurrences of all MWEs (in the inflected form they occurred in text) in our Twitter database, alongside with a word-by-word lemmatization and information, whether the inflected form was analysed by NLP tools as having its syntactic head in nominative case and singular number. In such case, it is likely that the inflected form of MWE is a lemmatization of that expression. With such data, we were able to find for a MWE its lemmatized form simply by taking the most frequent inflected form (with the same word-by-word lemma as our query MWE) from the corpus, assuming we looked only at compatible base-form phrases.

This procedure was evaluated by taking 1000 random MWEs, occurring at least 10 times in our

---

[6]See `http://nlp.pwr.wroc.pl/redmine/projects/wcrft/wiki`.

[7]See `http://zil.ipipan.waw.pl/MentionDetector`.

[8]See `http://zil.ipipan.waw.pl/Spejd`.

[9]See `http://zil.ipipan.waw.pl/Nerf`.

[10]See `http://zil.ipipan.waw.pl/Sentipejd` and the Polish sentiment dictionary `http://zil.ipipan.waw.pl/SlownikWydzwieku`.

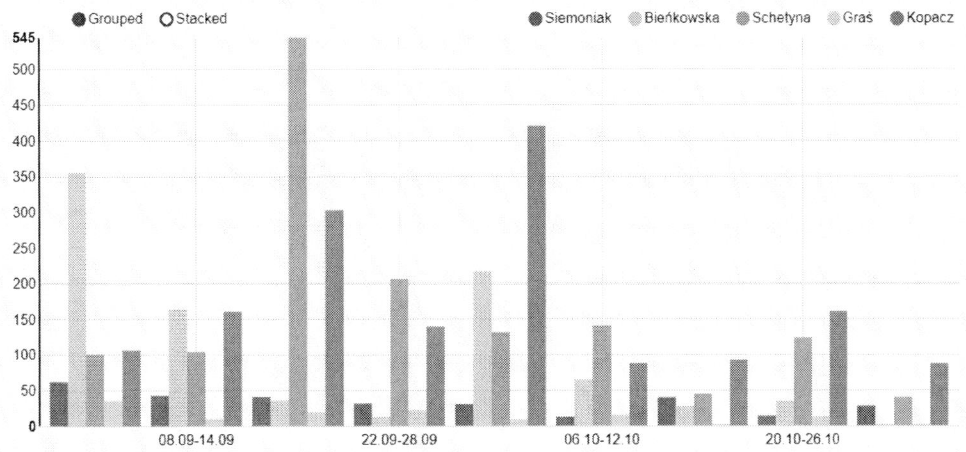

Figure 2: Numbers of mentions of entities for subperiods for five candidates to the position of Polish Prime Minister in September and October 2014

Twitter corpus, and checking validity of lemmata which were proposed for them by our algorithm. The results were encouraging, as all 1000 lemmas (!) were morphologically sound. The only issue was proper capitalization, inaccurate for 332 MWEs. For example, a common noun group may receive first capital letter, if it was most frequently used in nominative case and single number at the beginning of a sentence in our corpus. This issue, however, is less serious than presenting incorrectly inflected lemma to end users.

6.2 Political Use Case in TrendMiner Visualisation Platform

The linguistic platform was made available online in the form of an analytic portal, providing several illustrative scenarios. Figure 2 presents one of them demonstrating how Twitter reacted to the process of electing the new Prime Minister in Poland in September 2014. After it was announced on August 30 that Donald Tusk was designated as the next President of the European Council, several names for replacing him on the position of Polish Prime Minister were mentioned: Tomasz Siemoniak, Elżbieta Bieńkowska, Grzegorz Schetyna, Paweł Graś and Ewa Kopacz, who was eventually elected (on September 22). Bieńkowska, until then the Deputy Prime Minister of Poland, was leading in the first period since most political commentators regarded her as the best candidate before she was nominated as European Commissioner for Internal Market, Industry, Entrepreneurship and SMEs. Schetyna's name hit the headlines when he came back from political exile (he became a big opponent to Tusk once, so Tusk minimized his role in the party to protect his position). We can also see how Kopacz's position was constantly growing until the moment when it was decided. Then Schetyna is coming back since he was designated as the Minister of Foreign Affairs in Kopacz's government.

7 Conclusions and Future Work

The presented setting shows that even the simple methods of correcting social media content can bring improvements to language processing chains. Still, several linguistic engineering extensions of our work can be suggested. Firstly, the new lexical resources could be integrated to provide better interpretation of content, such as abbreviation dictionaries (e.g. `http://www.slownikskrotow.pl`), emoticon dictionaries (e.g. `http://krzywish.republika.pl/emotion.htm`), dictionaries of slang (e.g. `http://www.miejski.pl`) or foreign language lexicons (e.g. English aspell dictionary, see `http://aspell.net`).

More extensive interpretation of non-standard abbreviations could be integrated to handle cases where its proper interpretation is necessary for higher-level processing of content, as in 'Brawa dla PE za rez wzywającą USA do zaprzestania inwigilacji na mas skalę @panoptykon. Szkoda że w spr Snowdena PE nie zabrał głosu', ('rez' → 'rezolucję', 'mas' → 'masową', 'spr' → 'sprawie').

Two problems with this decoding is ambiguity of such abbreviations ('spr' could be equally well interpreted as 'sprawdzian' or 'sprawozdanie') and Polish inflection. Ambiguities could be resolved by context-aware corpus search of forms starting with a given prefix and proper inflected form could be generated using morphosyntactic patterns of the surrounding words.

Due to inflection of words in Polish representations of user account names and hashtags in tweet content may result in either forming grammatically incorrect phrases since hashtags and user names are usually nominative (*'Ważny tekst @ZalewskiPawel o zasadniczym dylemacie obecnej #Ukraina i roli jaka w nim przypada działaniom #Polska'*) or Twitter users inventing own methods of dealing with this problem such as adding inflection suffixes to nominative names (*'Ranking krajów najbardziej przyjaznym #senior.om.'*; it is possible only when suffixes are added and there is no alternation in the word root caused by inflection, so such addition is rather rare). As described earlier, account identifiers are replaced with user names retrieved from Twitter and hashtags decoded by replacing camelCase with spaces. However, this approach is not perfect for cases when no inflection is simulated by the user since the whole phrase must be automatically inflected (the correct version of the sentence from the first example above should read *'Ważny tekst Pawła Zalewskiego o zasadniczym dylemacie obecnej Ukrainy i roli jaka w nim przypada działaniom Polski'*). Possible solution to that problem could identify the correct case of the hashtag/user identifier in the tweet and change the case of the replacement phrase to identified case. Methods borrowed from text-to-speech synthesis systems (Graliński et al., 2007) could also be applied to produce properly inflected forms.

Acknowledgements

The work reported here was carried out within the Polish activities in the *Large-scale, Cross-lingual Trend Mining and Summarisation of Real-time Media Streams (TrendMiner)* project co-financed by the European Commission from the FP7 programme (grant agreement number 287863) and from the Polish Ministry of Science support programme (grant agreement number 3177/7.PR/2014/2).

It was also partially financed as part of the investment in the CLARIN-PL research infrastructure funded by the Polish Ministry of Science and Higher Education.

References

Md Shad Akhtar, Utpal Kumar Sikdar, and Asif Ekbal. 2015. IITP: Hybrid Approach for Text Normalization in Twitter. In *Proceedings of the Workshop on Noisy User-generated Text*, pages 106–110, Beijing. ACL.

Mohammad Arshi Saloot, Norisma Idris, Liyana Shuib, Ram Gopal Raj, and AiTi Aw. 2015. Toward Tweets Normalization Using Maximum Entropy. In *Proceedings of the Workshop on Noisy User-generated Text*, pages 19–27, Beijing. ACL.

Piyush Bansal, Romil Bansal, and Vasudeva Varma. 2015. Towards Deep Semantic Analysis of Hashtags. In Allan Hanbury, Gabriella Kazai, Andreas Rauber, and Norbert Fuhr, editors, *Advances in Information Retrieval — 37th European Conference on IR Research (ECIR 2015)*, volume 9022 of *Lecture Notes in Computer Science*, pages 453–464.

Giacomo Berardi, Andrea Esuli, Diego Marcheggiani, and Fabrizio Sebastiani. 2011. ISTI@TREC Microblog Track: Exploring the Use of Hashtag Segmentation and Text Quality Ranking. In Ellen M. Voorhees and Lori P. Buckland, editors, *Proceedings of the 20th Text REtrieval Conference (TREC 2011)*, volume Special Publication 500-296. National Institute of Standards and Technology (NIST).

Aleksander Buczyński and Aleksander Wawer. 2008. Shallow parsing in sentiment analysis of product reviews. In Sandra Kübler, Jakub Piskorski, and Adam Przepiórkowski, editors, *Proceedings of the LREC 2008 Workshop on Partial Parsing: Between Chunking and Deep Parsing*, pages 14–18, Marrakech. ELRA.

Thales Felipe Costa Bertaglia and Maria das Graças Volpe Nunes. 2016. Exploring word embeddings for unsupervised textual user-generated content normalization. In *Proceedings of the 2nd Workshop on Noisy User-generated Text (WNUT)*, pages 112–120, Osaka. COLING Organizing Committee.

Joana Costa, Catarina Silva, Mário Antunes, and Bernardete Ribeiro, 2013. *Defining Semantic Meta-hashtags for Twitter Classification*, pages 226–235. Springer, Berlin, Heidelberg.

Thierry Declerck and Piroska Lendvai. 2015. Processing and Normalizing Hashtags. In Galia Angelova, Kalina Bontcheva, and Ruslan Mitko, editors, *Proceedings of RANLP 2015*, pages 104–110. INCOMA Ltd.

Lukasz Degórski. 2012. Towards the Lemmatisation of Polish Nominal Syntactic Groups Using a Shallow Grammar. In Pascal Bouvry, Mieczysław A.

Kłopotek, Franck Leprevost, Małgorzata Marciniak, Agnieszka Mykowiecka, and Henryk Rybiński, editors, *Security and Intelligent Information Systems: International Joint Conference (SIIS 2011)*, volume 7053 of *Lecture Notes in Computer Science*. Springer Verlag.

Filip Graliński, Agata Savary, Monika Czerepowicka, and Filip Makowiecki. 2010. Computational Lexicography of Multi-Word Units: How Efficient Can It Be? In *Proceedings of the Workshop on Multiword Expressions: from Theory to Applications (MWE 2010)*, pages 1–9, Beijing, China, August. ACL.

Filip Graliński, Krzysztof Jassem, Agnieszka Wagner, and Mikołaj Wypych. 2007. Linguistic Aspects of Text Normalization in a Polish Text-to-Speech System. *Systems Science*, No. 4 Vol. 32:7–15.

Jonathon S. Hare, Sina Samangooei, and David P. Dupplaw. 2011. OpenIMAJ and ImageTerrier: Java libraries and tools for scalable multimedia analysis and indexing of images. In *Proceedings of the 19th ACM international conference on Multimedia (MM 2011)*, pages 691–694, New York. ACM.

Taishi Ikeda, Hiroyuki Shindo, and Yuji Matsumoto. 2016. Japanese Text Normalization with Encoder-Decoder Model. In *Proceedings of the 2nd Workshop on Noisy User-generated Text (WNUT)*, pages 129–137, Osaka. COLING Organizing Committee.

Mateusz Kopeć. 2014. Zero subject detection for Polish. In *Proceedings of the 14th Conference of the European Chapter of the ACL, volume 2: Short Papers*, pages 221–225, Gothenburg. ACL.

Marco Lui and Timothy Baldwin. 2012. Langid.Py: An Off-the-shelf Language Identification Tool. In *Proceedings of the ACL 2012 System Demonstrations*, pages 25–30, Stroudsburg. ACL.

Kevin McKelvey, Peter Goutzounis, Stephen da Cruz, and Nathanael Chambers. 2017. Aligning Entity Names with Online Aliases on Twitter. In *Proceedings of the 5th International Workshop on Natural Language Processing for Social Media*, pages 25–35, Valencia. ACL.

Marcin Miłkowski. 2010. Developing an open-source, rule-based proofreading tool. *Software: Practice and Experience*, 40(7):543–566.

Maciej Ogrodniczuk and Michał Lenart. 2012. Web Service integration platform for Polish linguistic resources. In *Proceedings of the 8th International Conference on Language Resources and Evaluation (LREC 2012)*, pages 1164–1168, Istanbul. ELRA.

Thierry Etchegoyhen Pablo Ruiz, Montse Cuadros. 2013. Lexical normalization of Spanish tweets with preprocessing rules, domain-specific edit distances, and language models. In Julio Villena Alberto Díaz, Iñaki Alegría, editor, *Proceedings of the Tweet Normalization Workshop at SEPLN 2013*, Madrid.

Jan Pöschko. 2011. Exploring Twitter Hashtags. *CoRR*, abs/1111.6553.

Adam Przepiórkowski, Mirosław Bańko, Rafał L. Górski, and Barbara Lewandowska-Tomaszczyk, editors. 2012. *Narodowy Korpus Języka Polskiego*. Wydawnictwo Naukowe PWN, Warsaw.

Adam Przepiórkowski and Aleksander Buczyński. 2007. Spejd: Shallow Parsing and Disambiguation Engine. In Zygmunt Vetulani, editor, *Proceedings of the 3rd Language & Technology Conference*, pages 340–344, Poznań.

Adam Radziszewski. 2013a. Learning to lemmatise Polish noun phrases. In *Proceedings of the 51st Annual Meeting of the Association for Computational Linguistics (ACL 2013). Volume 1: Long Papers*, pages 701–709. ACL.

Adam Radziszewski. 2013b. A tiered CRF tagger for Polish. In R. Bembenik, Ł. Skonieczny, H. Rybiński, M. Kryszkiewicz, and M. Niezgódka, editors, *Intelligent Tools for Building a Scientific Information Platform: Advanced Architectures and Solutions*. Springer Verlag.

Zygmunt Saloni, Marcin Woliński, Robert Wołosz, Włodzimierz Gruszczyński, and Danuta Skowrońska. 2015. Słownik gramatyczny języka polskiego. Online publication.

Agata Savary, Jakub Waszczuk, and Adam Przepiórkowski. 2010. Towards the Annotation of Named Entities in the National Corpus of Polish. In Nicoletta Calzolari, Khalid Choukri, Bente Maegaard, Joseph Mariani, Jan Odijk, Stelios Piperidis, Mike Rosner, and Daniel Tapias, editors, *Proceedings of the 7th International Conference on Language Resources and Evaluation (LREC 2010)*, Valletta. ELRA.

Sriram Srinivasan, Sourangshu Bhattacharya, and Rudrasis Chakraborty. 2012. Segmenting Web-domains and Hashtags Using Length Specific Models. In *Proceedings of the 21st ACM International Conference on Information and Knowledge Management (CIKM 2012)*, pages 1113–1122, New York. ACM.

Kuansan Wang, Christopher Thrasher, and Bo-June Paul Hsu. 2011. Web Scale NLP: A Case Study on URL Word Breaking. In *Proceedings of the 20th International Conference on World Wide Web (WWW 2011)*, pages 357–366, New York. ACM.

Marc Wick. 2015. Geonames ontology.

Marcin Woliński, Marcin Miłkowski, Maciej Ogrodniczuk, Adam Przepiórkowski, and Łukasz Szałkiewicz. 2012. PoliMorf: a (not so) new open morphological dictionary for Polish. Istanbul. ELRA.

Author Index

Association for Computational Linguistics
209 N. Eighth Street
Stroudsburg, Pennsylvania 18360

ISBN 978-1-5108-4572-5